LETTERS

ON THE

STUDY and USE

OF

HISTORY.

By the late RIGHT HONOURABLE

HENRY ST. JOHN,

LORD VISCOUNT BOLINGBROKE.

A NEW EDITION, Corrected.

LONDON:

PRINTED FOR T. CADELL, IN THE STRAND.

M,DCC,LXXIX.

Printing Statement:

Due to the very old age and scarcity of this book, many of the pages may be hard to read due to the blurring of the original text, possible missing pages, missing text, dark backgrounds and other issues beyond our control.

Because this is such an important and rare work, we believe it is best to reproduce this book regardless of its original condition.

Thank you for your understanding.

THE CONTENTS.

Letter I.

Of the study of history. Page 3

Letter II.

Concerning the true use and advantages of it. p. 11

Letter III.

1. An objection against the utility of history removed. 2. The false and true aims of those who study it. 3. Of the history of the first ages, with reflections on the state of ancient history, profane and sacred p. 43

Letter IV.

1. That there is in history sufficient authenticity to render it useful, notwithstanding all objections to the contrary. 2. Of the method and due restrictions to be observed in the study of it. p. 95

Letter V.

1. The great use of history, properly so called, as distinguished from the writings of mere annalists and antiquaries. 2. Greek and Roman historians. 3. Some idea of a complete history. 4. Further cautions to be observed in this study, and the regulation of it according to the different professions,

and

CONTENTS.

and situations of men: above all, the use to be made of it (1) *by divines, and* (2) *by those who are called to the service of their country.* p. 119

LETTER VI.

From what period modern history is peculiarly useful to the service of our country, viz. From the end of the fifteenth century to the present. The division of this into three particular periods; in order to a sketch of the history and state of Europe from that time. p. 159

LETTER VII.

A sketch of the state and history of Europe from the Pyrenean treaty, in one thousand six hundred and fifty nine, to the year one thousand six hundred and eighty-eight. p. 197

LETTER VIII.

The same subject continued from the year one thousand six hundred and eighty eight. p. 255

LETTER I.

A plan for a general history of Europe. p. 391

LETTER II.

Of the true use of retirement and study. p. 401

Reflections upon Exile. p. 433

OF THE

Study of History.

LETTER I.

Chantelou in Touraine, Nov. 6, 1735.

My Lord,

I Have confidered formerly, with a good deal of attention, the fubject on which you command me to communicate my thoughts to you: and I practifed in thofe days, as much as bufinefs and pleafure allowed me time to do, the rules that feemed to me neceffary to be obferved in the ftudy of hiftory. They were very different from thofe which writers on the fame fubject have recommended, and which are commonly practifed. But I confefs to your lordfhip, that this neither gave me then, nor has given me fince, any diftruft of them. I do not affect fingularity. On the contrary, I think that a due deference is to be paid to received opinions, and that a due com-

LETTER I.

compliance with received customs is to be held; though both the one and the other should be, what they often are, absurd or ridiculous. But this servitude is outward only, and abridges in no sort the liberty of private judgment. The obligations of submitting to it likewise, even, outwardly, extend no further, than to those opinions and customs which cannot be opposed; or from which we cannot deviate without doing hurt, or giving offence, to society. In all these cases, our speculations ought to be free: in all other cases, our practice may be so. Without any regard therefore to the opinion and practice even of the learned world, I am very willing to tell you mine. But, as it is hard to recover a thread of thought long ago laid aside, and impossible to prove some things, and explain others, without the assistance of many books which I have not here; your lordship must be content with such an imperfect sketch, as I am able to send you at present in this letter.

THE motives that carry men to the study of history are different. Some intend, if such as they may be said to study, nothing more than amusement, and read the life of ARISTIDES or PHOCION, of EPAMINONDAS or SCIPIO, ALEXANDER or CÆSAR, just as they

they play a game at cards, or as they would read the ſtory of the ſeven champions.

OTHERS there are, whoſe motive to this ſtudy is nothing better, and who have the further diſadvantage of becoming a nuiſance very often to ſociety, in proportion to the progreſs they make. The former do not improve their reading to any good purpoſe: the latter pervert it to a very bad one, and grow in impertinence as they encreaſe in learning. I think I have known moſt of the firſt kind in England, and moſt of the laſt in France. The perſons I mean are thoſe who read to talk, to ſhine in converſation, and to impoſe in company; who having few ideas to vend of their own growth, ſtore their minds with crude unruminated facts and ſentences; and hope to ſupply, by bare memory, the want of imagination and judgment.

BUT theſe are in the two loweſt forms. The next I ſhall mention, are in one a little higher; in the form of thoſe who grow neither wiſer nor better by ſtudy themſelves, but who enable others to ſtudy with greater eaſe, and to purpoſes more uſeful; who make fair copies of foul manuſcripts, give the ſignification of hard words, and take a great deal of other grammatical pains. The obligation to thefe men would be great indeed, if they were in general able to do any thing better, and fubmitted to this drudgery for the fake of the public; as fome of them, it muſt be owned with gratitude, have done, but not later, I think, than about the time of the refurrection of letters. When works of importance are preffing, generals themfelves may take up the pick-axe and the fpade; but in the ordinary courfe of things, when that preffing neceffity is over, fuch tools are left in the hands deftined to ufe them, the hands of common foldiers and peafants. I approve therefore very much the devotion of a ftudious man at Chrift-Church, who was over-heard in his oratory entering into a detail with GOD, as devout perfons are apt to do, and, amongft other particular thankfgivings, acknowledging the divine goodnefs in furnifhing the world with makers of Dictionaries! thefe men court fame, as well as their betters, by fuch means as GOD has given them to acquire it: and LITTLETON exerted all the genius he had, when he made a dictionary, though STEPHENS did not. They deferve encouragement, however, whilft they continue to compile, and neither affect wit, nor prefume to reafon.

THERE is a fourth clafs, of much lefs ufe than thefe, but of much greater name. Men of the firft rank in learning, and to whom the whole tribe of fcholars bow with reverence. A man muft be as indifferent as I am to common cenfure or approbation, to avow a thorough contempt for the whole bufinefs of thefe learned lives; for all the refearches into antiquity, for all the fyftems of chronology and hiftory, that we owe to the immenfe labours of a SCALIGER, a BOCHART, a PETAVIUS, an USHER, and even a MARSHAM. The fame materials are common to them all; but thefe materials are few, and there is a moral impoffibility that they fhould ever have more. They have combined thefe into every form that can be given to them: they have fuppofed, they have gueffed, they have joined disjointed paffages of different authors, and broken traditions of uncertain originals, of various people, and of centuries remote from one another as well as from ours. In fhort, that they might leave no liberty untaken, even a wild fantaftical fimilitude of founds has ferved to prop up a fyftem. As the materials they have are few, fo are the very beft, and fuch as pafs for authentic, extremely precarious: as fome of thefe learned perfons themfelves confefs.

JULIUS AFRICANUS, EUSEBIUS, and GEORGE the monk opened the principal sources of all this science; but they corrupted the waters. Their point of view was to make prophane history and chronology agree with sacred; though the latter chronology is very far from being established, with the clearness and certainty necessary to make it a rule. For this purpose, the ancient monuments that these writers conveyed to posterity, were digested by them according to the system they were to maintain: and none of these monuments were delivered down in their original form, and genuine purity. The Dynasties of MANETHO, for instance, are broken to pieces by EUSEBIUS, and such fragments of them as suited his design, are struck into his work. We have, we know, no more of them. The Codex Alexandrinus we owe to GEORGE the monk. We have no other authority for it: and one cannot see without amazement such a man as Sir JOHN MARSHAM undervaluing this authority in one page, and building his system upon it in the next. He seems even by the lightness of his expressions, if I remember well, for it is long since I looked into his canon, not to be much concerned what foundation his system had, so he shewed

his

his skill in forming one, and in reducing the immense antiquity of the Ægyptians within the limits of the Hebraic calculation. In short, my lord, all these systems are so many enchanted castles; they appear to be something, they are nothing but appearances: like them too, dissolve the charm, and they vanish from the sight. To dissolve the charm, we must begin at the beginning of them: the expression may be odd, but it is significant. We must examine scrupulously and indifferently the foundations on which they lean: and when we find these either faintly probable, or grosly improbable, it would be foolish to expect any thing better in the superstructure. This science is one of those that are " a limine salutandæ." To do thus much may be necessary, that grave authority may not impose on our ignorance: to do more would be to assist this very authority in imposing false science upon us. I had rather take the Darius whom Alexander conquered, for the son of Hystaspes, and make as many anachronisms as a Jewish chronologer, than sacrifice half my life to collect all the learned lumber that fills the head of an antiquary.

OF THE

Study of History.

LETTER II.

Concerning the true use and advantages of it.

LET me say something of history in general, before I descend into the consideration of particular parts of it, or of the various methods of study, or of the different views of those that apply themselves to it, as I had begun to do in my former letter.

THE love of history seems inseparable from human nature because it seems inseparable from self-love. The same principle in this instance carries us forward and backward, to future and to past ages. We imagine that the things, which affect us, must affect posterity: this sentiment runs through mankind, from Cæsar down to
the

the parish clerk in Pope's miscellany. We are fond of preserving, as far as it is in our frail power, the memory of our own adventures, of those of our own time, and of those that preceded it. Rude heaps of stones have been raised, and ruder hymns have been composed, for this purpose, by nations who had not yet the use of arts and letters. To go no further back, the triumphs of ODIN were celebrated in runic songs, and the feats of our British ancestors were recorded in those of their bards. The savages of America have the same custom at this day: and long historical ballads of their huntings and their wars are sung at all their festivals. There is no need of saying how this passion grows, among civilized nations, in proportion to the means of gratifying it: but let us observe that the same principle of nature directs us as strongly, and more generally as well as more early, to indulge our own curiosity, instead of preparing to gratify that of others. The child hearkens with delight to the tales of his nurse: he learns to read, and he devours with eagerness fabulous legends and novels: in riper years he applies himself to history, or to that which he takes for history, to authorized romance: and, even in age, the desire

fire of knowing what has happened to other men, yields to the defire alone of relating what has happened to ourfelves. Thus hiftory, true or falfe, fpeaks to our paffions always. What pity is it, my lord, that even the beft fhould fpeak to our underftandings fo feldom? That it does fo, we have none to blame but ourfelves. Nature has done her part. She has opened this ftudy to every man who can read and think: and what fhe has made the moft agreeable, reafon can make the moft ufeful, application of our minds. But if we confult our reafon, we fhall be far from following the examples of our fellow-creatures, in this as in moft other cafes, who are fo proud of being rational. We fhall neither read to foothe our indolence, nor to gratify our vanity: as little fhall we content ourfelves to drudge like grammarians and critics, that others may be able to ftudy with greater eafe and profit, like philofophers and ftatefmen: as little fhall we affect the flender merit of becoming great fcholars at the expence of groping all our lives in the dark mazes of antiquity. All thefe miftake the true drift of ftudy, and the true ufe of hiftory. Nature gave us curiofity to excite the induftry of our minds; but fhe never intended it fhould be
made

made the principal, much lefs the fole object of their application. The true and proper object of this application is a conftant improvement in private and in public virtue. An application to any ftudy, that tends neither directly nor indirectly to make us better men and better citizens, is at beft but a fpecious and ingenious fort of idlenefs, to ufe an expreffion of TILLOTSON: and the knowledge we acquire by it is a creditable kind of ignorance, nothing more. This creditable kind of ignorance is, in my opinion, the whole benefit which the generality of men, even of the moft learned, reap from the ftudy of hiftory: and yet the ftudy of hiftory feems to me, of all other, the moft proper to train us up to private and public virtue.

YOUR lordfhip may very well be ready by this time, and after fo much bold cenfure on my part, to afk me, what then is the true ufe of hiftory? in what refpects it may ferve to make us better and wifer? and what method is to be purfued in the ftudy of it, for attaining thefe great ends? I will anfwer you by quoting what I have read fomewhere or other, in DIONYSIUS HALICARN, I think, that hiftory is philofophy teaching by examples. We need but
to

to cast our eyes on the world, and we shall see the daily force of example: we need but to turn them inward, and we shall soon discover why example has this force. "Pauci prudentia, says Tacitus, "ho-"nesta ab deterioribus, utilia ab noxiis "discernunt: plures aliorum eventis do-centur." Such is the imperfection of human understanding, such the frail temper of our minds, that abstract or general propositions, though ever so true, appear obscure or doubtful to us very often, till they are explained by examples, and that the wisest lessons in favour of virtue go but a little way to convince the judgment, and determine the will, unless they are enforced by the same means; and we are obliged to apply to ourselves what we see happen to other men. Instructions by precept have the further disadvantage of coming on the authority of others, and frequently require a long deduction of reasoning. "Homines amplius "oculis, quam auribus, credunt: longum "iter est per præcepta, breve et efficax "per exempla." The reason of this judgment, which I quote from one of Seneca's epistles in confirmation of my own opinion, rests, I think, on this; that when examples are pointed out to us, there is a kind of appeal, with which we are flattered, made to

our

our senses, as well as to our understandings. The instruction comes then upon our own authority; we frame the precept after our own experience, and yield to fact when we resist speculation. But this is not the only advantage of instruction by example; for example appeals not to our understanding alone, but to our passions likewise. Example assuages these, or animates them; sets passion on the side of judgment, and makes the whole man of a piece; which is more than the strongest reasoning, and the clearest demonstration can do: and thus forming habits by repetition, example secures the observance of those precepts which example insinuated. Is it not PLINY, my lord, who says, that the gentlest, he should have added, the most effectual way of commanding, is by example? "Mitius jubetur ex-"emplo." The harshest orders are softened by example, and tyranny itself becomes persuasive. What pity it is that so few princes have learned this way of commanding? But again: the force of examples is not confined to those alone, that pass immediately under our sight: the examples, that memory suggests, have the same effect in their degree, and an habit of recalling them will soon produce the habit of imitating them. In the same

epistle

epiftle, from whence I cited a paffage juft now, SENECA fays that CLEANTHES had never become fo perfect a copy of ZENO, if he had not paffed his Life with him; that PLATO, ARISTOTLE, and the other philofophers of that fchool, profited more by the example, than by the difcourfe of SOCRATES. [But here, by the way, SENECA miftook; for SOCRATES died two years, according to fome, and four years, according to others, before the birth of ARISTOTLE: and his miftake might come from the inaccuracy of thofe who collected for him; as ERASMUS obferves, after QUINTILIAN, in his judgment on SENECA.] But be this, which was fcarce worth a parenthefis, as it will; he adds that METRODORUS, HERMACHUS and POLYAENUS, men of great note, were formed by living under the fame roof with EPICURUS, not by frequenting his fchool. Thefe are inftances of the force of immediate example. But your lordfhip knows that the citizens of Rome placed the images of their anceftors in the veftibules of their houfes; fo that, whenever they went in or out, thefe venerable buftos met their eyes, and recalled the glorious actions of the dead, to fire the living, to excite them to imitate, and even to emulate their great forefathers. The fuc-

B   cefs

cefs anfwered the defign. The virtue of one generation was transfufed, by the magic of example, into feveral: and a fpirit of heroifm was maintained through many ages of that common-wealth. Now thefe are fo many inftances of the force of remote example; and from all thefe inftances we may conclude, that examples of both kinds are neceffary.

The fchool of example, my lord, is the world: and the mafters of this fchool are hiftory and experience. I am far from contending that the former is preferable to the latter. I think upon the whole otherwife: but this I fay, that the former is abfolutely neceffary to prepare us for the latter, and to accompany us whilft we are under the difcipline of the latter, that is, through the whole courfe of our lives. No doubt fome few men may be quoted, to whom nature gave what art and induftry can give to no man. But fuch examples will prove nothing againft me, becaufe I admit that the ftudy of hiftory, without experience, is infufficient; but affert, that experience itfelf is fo without genius. Genius is preferable to the other two; but I would wifh to find the three together: for how great foever a genius may be, and how much foever he
may

may acquire new light and heat, as he proceeds in his rapid course, certain it is that he will never shine with the full lustre, nor shed the full influence he is capable of, unless to his own experience he adds the experience of other men and other ages. Genius, without the improvement, at least, of experience, is what comets once were thought to be, a blazing meteor, irregular in his course, and dangerous in his approach; of no use to any system, and able to destroy any. Mere sons of earth, if they have experience without any knowledge of the history of the world, are but half scholars in the science of mankind. And if they are conversant in history without experience, they are worse than ignorant; they are pedants, always incapable, sometimes meddling and presuming. The man, who has all three, is an honour to his country, and a public blessing: and such, I trust, your lordship will be in this century, as your great-grand-father* was in the last.

I have insisted a little the longer on this head, and have made these distinctions the rather, because tho' I attribute a great deal more, than many will be ready to al-

* Earl of CLARENDON.

low, to the study of history; yet I would not willingly even seem to fall into the ridicule of ascribing to it such extravagant effects, as several have done, from TULLY down to CASAUBON, LA MOTHE LE VAYER, and other modern pedants. When TULLY informs us, in the second book of his Tusculan disputations, that the first SCIPIO AFRICANUS had always in his hands the works of XENOPHON, he advances nothing but what is probable and reasonable. To say nothing of the retreat of the ten thousand, nor of other parts of XENOPHON's writings; the images of virtue, represented in that admirable picture the Cyropaedia, were proper to entertain a soul that was fraught with virtue, and CYRUS was worthy to be imitated by SCIPIO. So SELIM emulated CÆSAR, whose Commentaries were translated for his use against the customs of the Turks: so CÆSAR emulated ALEXANDER; and ALEXANDER, ACHILLES. There is nothing ridiculous here, except the use that is made of this passage by those who quote it. But what the same TULLY says, in the fourth book of his academical disputations, concerning LUCULLUS, seems to me very extraordinary. " In Asiam fac-
" tus imperator venit; cum esset Roma
" profectus rei militaris rudis;" [one would
be

be ready to afcribe fo fudden a change, and fo vaft an improvement, to nothing lefs than knowledge infufed by infpiration, if we were not affured in the fame place that they were effected by very natural means, by fuch as it is in every man's power to employ] " partim percontando a peritis par- " tim in rebus geftis legendis." Lucullus, according to this account, verified the reproach on the Roman nobility, which Sallust puts into the mouth of Marius. But as I difcover the paffion of Marius, and his prejudices to the patricians, in one cafe; fo I difcover, methinks, the cunning of Tully, and his partiality to himfelf, in the other. Lucullus, after he had been chofen conful, obtained by intrigue the government of Cilicia, and fo put himfelf into a fituation of commanding the Roman army againft Mithridates: Tully had the fame government afterwards, and tho' he had no Mithridates, nor any other enemy of confequence, oppofed to him; tho' all his military feats confifted in furprizing and pillaging a parcel of Highlanders and wild Cilicians; yet he affumed the airs of a conqueror, and defcribed his actions in fo pompous a ftile, that the account becomes burlefque. He laughs, indeed, in one of his letters to Atticus, at his generalfhip:

but if we turn to those he writ to COELIUS RUFUS, and to CATO, upon this occasion, or to those wherein he expresses to ATTICUS his resentment against CATO, for not proposing in his favour the honours usually decreed to conquerors, we may see how vanity turned his head, and how impudently he insisted on obtaining a triumph. Is it any strain now to suppose, that he meant to insinuate, in the passage I have quoted about LUCULLUS, that the difference between him and the former governor of CILICIA, even in military merit, arose from the different conjuncture alone; and that LUCULLUS could not have done in Cilicia, at that time, more than he himself did? CICERO had read, and questioned at least as much as LUCULLUS, and would therefore have appeared as great a captain, if he had had as great a prince as MITHRIDATES to encounter. But the truth is, that LUCULLUS was made a great captain by theory, or the study of history alone, no more than FERDINAND of Spain and ALPHONSUS of Naples were cured of desperate distempers by reading LIVY and QUINTUS CURTIUS: a silly tale, which BODIN, AMYOT, and others have picked up and propagated. LUCULLUS had served in his youth against the Marsi, probably in other wars, and SYLLA

took

took early notice of him; he went into the east with this general, and had a great share in his confidence. He commanded in several expeditions. It was he who restored the Colophonians to their liberty, and who punished the revolt of the people of Mytelene. Thus we see that Lucullus was formed by experience, as well as study, and by an experience gained in those very countries, where he gathered so many laurels afterwards, in fighting against the same enemy. The late duke of Marlborough never read Xenophon, most certainly, nor the relation perhaps of any modern wars; but he served in his youth under Monsieur de Turenne, and I have heard that he was taken notice of in those early days, by that great man. He afterwards commanded in an expedition to Ireland, served a campaign or two, if I mistake not, under king William in Flanders: and, besides these occasions, had none of gaining experience in war, till he came to the head of our armies in one thousand seven hundred and two, and triumphed not over Asiatic troops, but over the veteran armies of France. The Roman had on his side genius and experience cultivated by study: The Briton had genius improved by experience, and no more. The first therefore is not an example of what study can do alone; but the latter is an example of what genius and experience can do without study. They can do much, to be sure, when the first is given in a superior degree. But such examples are very rare: and when they happen, it will be still true, that they would have had fewer blemishes, and would have come nearer to the perfection of private and public virtue, in all the arts of peace and atchievements of war, if the views of such men had been enlarged, and their sentiments ennobled, by acquiring that cast of thought, and that temper of mind, which will grow up and become habitual in every man who applies himself early to the study of history, as to the study of philosophy, with the intention of being wiser and better, without the affectation of being more learned.

The temper of the mind is formed, and a certain turn given to our ways of thinking; in a word, the seeds of that moral character which cannot wholly alter the natural character, but may correct the evil and improve the good that is in it, or do the very contrary, are sown betimes, and much sooner than is commonly supposed.

It

It is equally certain, that we shall gather or not gather experience, be the better or the worse for this experience when we come into the world and mingle amongst mankind, according to the temper of mind, and the turn of thought, that we have acquired beforehand, and bring along with us. They will tincture all our future acquisitions; so that the very same experience, which secures the judgment of one man, or excites him to virtue, shall lead another into error, or plunge him into vice. From hence it follows, that the study of history has in this respect a double advantage. If experience alone can make us perfect in our parts, experience cannot begin to teach them till we are actually on the stage: whereas, by a previous application to this study, we conn them over at least, before we appear there: we are not quite unprepared, we learn our parts sooner, and we learn them better.

Let me explain what I mean by an example. There is scarce any folly or vice more epidemical among the sons of men than that ridiculous and hurtful vanity by which the people of each country are apt to prefer themselves to those of every other; and to make their own customs, and manners,

ners, and opinions, the ſtandards of right and wrong, of true and falſe. The Chineſe mandarins were ſtrangely ſurpriſed, and almoſt incredulous, when the Jeſuits ſhewed them how ſmall a figure their empire made in the general map of the world. The Samojedes wondered much at the Czar of Muſcovy for not living among them: and the Hottentot, who returned from Europe, ſtripped himſelf naked as ſoon as he came home, put on his bracelets of guts and garbage, and grew ſtinking and lowſy as faſt as he could. Now nothing can contribute more to prevent us from being tainted with this vanity, than to accuſtom ourſelves early to contemplate the different nations of the earth, in that vaſt map which hiſtory ſpreads before us, in their riſe and their fall, in their barbarous and civilized ſtates, in the likeneſs and unlikeneſs of them all to one another, and of each to itſelf. By frequently renewing this proſpect to the mind, the Mexican with his cap and coat of feathers, ſacrificing a human victim to his god, will not appear more ſavage to our eyes, than the Spaniard with an hat on his head, and a gonilla round his neck, ſacrificing whole nations to his ambition, his avarice, and even the wantonneſs of his cruelty. I might

might shew, by a multitude of other examples, how history prepares us for experience, and guides us in it: and many of these would be both curious and important. I might likewise bring several other instances, wherein history serves to purge the mind of those national partialities and prejudices that we are apt to contract in our education, and that experience for the most part rather confirms than removes: because it is for the most part confined, like our education. But I apprehend growing too prolix, and shall therefore conclude this head by observing, that tho' an early and proper application, to the study of history will contribute extremely to keep our minds free from a ridiculous partiality in favour of our own country, and a vicious prejudice against others; yet the same study will create in us a preference of affection to our own country. There is a story told of ABGARUS. He brought several beasts taken in different places to Rome, they say, and let them loose before AUGUSTUS: every beast ran immediately to that part of the Circus, where a parcel of earth taken from his native soil had been laid. "Crédat Judæus Apella." This tale might pass on JOSEPHUS; for in him, I believe I read it: but surely the love of our country is a lesson of reason, not an inſtitution of nature. Education and habit, obligation and intereſt, attach us to it, not inſtinct. It is however ſo neceſſary to be cultivated, and the proſperity of all ſocieties, as well as the grandeur of ſome, depends upon it ſo much, that orators by their eloquence, and poets by their enthuſiaſm, have endeavoured to work up this precept of morality into a principle of paſſion. But the examples which we find in hiſtory, improved by the lively deſcriptions, and the juſt applauſes or cenſures of hiſtorians, will have a much better and more permanent effect, than declamation, or ſong, or the dry ethics of mere philoſophy. In fine, to converſe with hiſtorians is to keep good company: many of them were excellent men, and thoſe who were not ſuch, have taken care however to appear ſuch in their writings. It muſt be therefore of great uſe to prepare ourſelves by this converſation for that of the world; and to receive our firſt impreſſions, and to acquire our firſt habits, in a ſcene where images of virtue and vice are continually repreſented to us in the colours that belong properly to them, before we enter on another ſcene, where virtue and vice are too often confounded, and what belongs to one is aſcribed to the other.

Be-

Of the Study of History.

BESIDES the advantage of beginning our acquaintance with mankind fooner, and of bringing with us into the world, and the bufinefs of it, fuch a caft of thought and fuch a temper of mind, as will enable us to make a better ufe of our experience; there is this further advantage in the ftudy of hiftory, that the improvement we make by it extends to more objects, and is made at the expence of other men: whereas that improvement which is the effect of our own experience, is confined to fewer objects, and is made at our own expence. To ftate the account fairly therefore between thefe two improvements, tho' the latter be the more valuable, yet allowance being made on one fide for the much greater number of examples that hiftory prefents to us, and deduction being made on the other of the price we often pay for our experience, the value of the former will rife in proportion. " I have recorded thefe
" things," fays POLYBIUS, after giving an account of the defeat of REGULUS, " that
" they who read thefe commentaries may
" be rendered better by them; for all men
" have two ways of improvement, one arif-
" ing from their own experience, and one
" from the experience of others. Evi-
" dentior quidem illa eft, quæ per propria
" ducit

LETTER II.

"ducit infortunia; at tutior illa, quæ per
"aliena." I ufe CASAUBON's tranflation.
POLYBIUS goes on, and concludes, " that
" fince the firft of thefe ways expofes us to
" great labour and peril, whilft the fecond
" works the fame good effect, and is at-
" tended by no evil circumftance, every
" one ought to take for granted, that the
" ftudy of hiftory is the beft fchool where
" he can learn how to conduct himfelf in
" all the fituations of life." REGULUS had
feen at Rome many examples of magnanimity, of frugality, of the contempt of riches
and of other virtues; and thefe virtues he
practifed. But he had not learned, nor had
opportunity of learning another leffon, which
the examples recorded in hiftory inculcate
frequently, the leffon of moderation. An
infatiable thirft of military fame, an uncon-
fined ambition of extending their empire,
an extravagant confidence in their own courage and force, an infolent contempt of their
enemies, and an impetuous over-bearing
fpirit with which they purfued all their enterprizes, compofed in his days the diftin-
guifhing character of a Roman. Whatever
the fenate and people refolved to the members of that common-wealth, appeared both
practicable and juft. Neither difficulties
nor dangers could check them; and their
fages

sages had not yet difcovered, that virtues in excefs degenerate into vices. Notwithftanding the beautiful rant which HORACE puts into his mouth, I make no doubt that REGULUS learned at Carthage thofe leffons of moderation which he had not learned at Rome; but he learned them by experience, and the fruits of this experience came too late, and coft too dear; for they coft the total defeat of the Roman army, the prolongation of a calamitous war which might have been finifhed by a glorious peace, the lofs of liberty to thoufands of Roman citizens, and to REGULUS himfelf the lofs of life in the midft of torments, if we are entirely to credit what is perhaps exaggeration in the Roman authors.

THERE is another advantage, worthy our obfervation, that belongs to the ftudy of hiftory; and that I fhall mention here, not only becaufe of the importance of it, but becaufe it leads me immediately to fpeak of the nature of the improvement we ought to have in our view, and of the method in which it feems to me that this improvement ought to be purfued: two particulars from which your lordfhip may think perhaps that I digrefs too long. The advantage I mean confifts in this, that the examples which hiftory prefents to us, both of men and

and of events, are generally complete: the whole example is before us, and consequently the whole lesson, or sometimes the various lessons, which philosophy proposes to teach us by this example. For first, as to men; we see them at their whole length in history, and we see them generally there through a medium less partial at least than that of experience; for I imagine, that a whig or a tory, whilst those parties subsisted, would have condemned in Saturninus the spirit of faction which he applauded in his own tribunes, and would have applauded in Drusus the spirit of moderation which he despised in those of the contrary party, and which he suspected and hated in those of his own party. The villain who has imposed on mankind by his power or cunning, and whom experience could not unmask for a time, is unmasked at length: and the honest man, who has been misunderstood or defamed, is justified before his story ends. Or if this does not happen, if the villain dies with his mask on, in the midst of applause, and honour, and wealth, and power, and if the honest man dies under the same load of calumny and disgrace under which he lived, driven perhaps into exile, and exposed to want; yet we see historical justice executed, the name of one

branded

branded with infamy, and that of the other celebrated with panegyric to succeeding ages. "Præcipuum munus annalium reor, ne "virtutes sileantur; utque pravis dictis, "factisque ex posteritate et infamia metus "sit." Thus, according to Tacitus, and according to truth, from which his judgments seldom deviate, the principal duty of history is to erect a tribunal, like that among the Egyptians, mentioned by Diodorus Siculus, where men and princes themselves were tried, and condemned or acquitted, after their deaths; where those who had not been punished for their crimes, and those who had not been honoured for their virtues, received a just retribution. The sentence is pronounced in one case, as it was in the other, too late to correct or recompense; but it is pronounced in time to render these examples of general instruction to mankind. Thus Cicero, that I may quote one instance out of thousands, and that I may do justice to the general character of that great man, whose particular failing I have censured so freely, Cicero, I say, was abandoned by Octavius, and massacred by Anthony. But let any man read this fragment of Arellius Fuscus, and chuse which he would wish to have been, the orator, or the triumvir? "Quoad humanum genus

"in-

" incolume manserit, quamdiu usus literis,
" honor summæ eloquentiæ pretium erit,
" quamdiu rerum natura aut fortuna ste-
" terit, aut memoria duraverit, admirabile
" posteris vigebis ingenium, et uno pro-
" scriptus seculo, proscribes Antonium om-
" nibus."

THUS again, as to events that stand recorded in history; we see them all, we see them as they followed one another, or as they produced one another, causes or effects, immediate or remote. We are cast back, as it were, into former ages: we live with the men who lived before us, and we inhabit countries that we never saw. Place is enlarged, and time prolonged, in this manner; so that the man who applies himself early to the study of history, may acquire in a few years, and before he sets his foot abroad in the world, not only a more extended knowledge of mankind, but the experience of more centuries than any of the patriarchs saw. The events we are witnesses of, in the course of the longest life, appear to us very often original, unprepared, single, and un-relative, if I may use such an expression for want of a better in English; in French I would say isolés: they appear such very often, are called accidents, and looked
on

Of the Study of History.

on as the effects of chance; a word, by the way, which is in constant use, and has frequently no determinate meaning. We get over the present difficulty, we improve the momentary advantage, as well as we can, and we look no farther. Experience can carry us no farther; for experience can go a very little way back in discovering causes: and effects are not the objects of experience till they happen. From hence many errors in judgment, and by consequence in conduct, necessarily arise. And here too lies the difference we are speaking of between history and experience. The advantage on the side of the former is double. In antient history, as we have said already, the examples are complete, which are incomplete in the course of experience. The beginning, the progression, and the end appear, not of particular reigns, much less of particular enterprizes, or systems of policy alone, but of governments, of nations, of empires, and of all the various systems that have succeeded one another in the course of their duration. In modern history, the examples may be, and sometimes are, incomplete; but they have this advantage when they are so, that they serve to render complete the examples of our own time. Experience is doubly defective; we are born too late to see the beginning, and we die too soon to see the end

end of many things. History supplies both these defects. Modern history shews the causes, when experience presents the effects alone: and ancient history enables us to guess at the effects, when experience presents the causes alone. Let me explain my meaning by two examples of these kinds; one past, the other actually present.

WHEN the revolution of one thousand six hundred and eighty-eight happened, few men then alive, I suppose, went farther in their search after the causes of it, than the extravagant attempt of king JAMES against the religion and liberty of his people. His former conduct, and the passages of king CHARLES the second's reign might rankle still at the hearts of some men, but could not be set to account among the causes of his deposition; since he had succeeded, notwithstanding them, peaceably to the throne: and the nation in general, even many of those who would have excluded him from it, were desirous, or at least, willing, that he should continue in it. Now this example, thus stated, affords, no doubt, much good instruction to the kings, and people of Britain. But this instruction is not entire, because the example thus stated, and confined to the experience of that age, is imperfect. King JAMES's mal-administra-
·tion

tion rendered a revolution neceſſary and practicable; but his mal-adminiſtration, as well as all his preceding conduct, was cauſed by his bigot-attachment to popery, and to the principles of arbitrary government, from which no warning could divert him. His bigot-attachment to theſe was cauſed, by the exile of the royal family; this exile was cauſed by the uſurpation of CROMWEL: and CROMWEL's uſurpation was the effect of a former rebellion, begun not without reaſon on account of liberty, but without any valid pretence on account of religion. During this exile, our princes caught the taint of popery and foreign politics. We made them unfit to govern us, and after that were forced to recal them, that they might reſcue us out of anarchy. It was neceſſary therefore, your lordſhip ſees, at the revolution, and it is more ſo now, to go back in hiſtory, at leaſt as far as I have mentioned, and perhaps farther, even to the beginning of King JAMES the firſt's reign, to render this event a complete example, and to develope all the wiſe, honeſt, and ſalutary precepts, with which it is pregnant, both to king and ſubject.

THE other example ſhall be taken from what has ſucceeded the revolution. Few men

men at that time looked forward enough, to foresee the necessary consequences of the new constitution of the revenue, that was soon afterwards formed; nor of the method of funding that immediately took place; which, absurd as they are, have continued ever since, till it is become scarce possible to alter them. Few people, I say, foresaw how the creation of funds, and the multiplication of taxes, would encrease yearly the power of the crown, and bring our liberties, by a natural and necessary progression, into more real, though less apparent danger, than they were in before the revolution. The excessive ill husbandry practised from the very beginning of king WILLIAM's reign; and which laid the foundations of all we feel and all we fear, was not the effect of ignorance, mistake, or what we call chance, but of design and scheme in those who had the sway at that time. I am not so uncharitable, however, as to believe that they intended to bring upon their country all the mischiefs that we, who came after them, experience, and apprehend. No, they saw the measures they took singly, and unrelatively, or relatively alone to some immediate object. The notion of attaching men to the new government, by tempting them to embark

bark their fortunes on the same bottom, was a reason of state to some: the notion of creating a new, that is, a moneyed interest, in opposition to the landed interest, or as a balance to it; and of acquiring a superior influence in the city of London, at least by the establishment of great corporations, was a reason of party to others: and I make no doubt that the opportunity of amassing immense estates by the management of funds, by trafficking in paper, and by all the arts of jobbing, was a reason of private interest to those who supported and improved this scheme of iniquity, if not to those who devised it. They looked no farther. Nay, we who came after them, and have long tasted the bitter fruits of the corruption they planted, were far from taking such an alarm at our distress, and our danger, as they deserved; till the most remote and fatal effect of causes, laid by the last generation, was very near becoming an object of experience in this. Your lordship, I am sure, sees at once how much a due reflection on the passages of former times, as they stand recorded in the history of our own, and of other countries, would have deterred a free people from trusting the sole management of so great a revenue, and the sole nomination of those legions of officers employed

employed in it, to their chief magiftrate. There remained indeed no pretence for doing fo, when once a falary was fettled on the prince, and the public revenue was no longer in any fenfe his revenue, nor the public expence his expence. Give me leave to add, that it would have been, and would be ftill, more decent with regard to the prince, and lefs repugnant if not more conformable to the principles and practice too of our government, to take this power and influence from the prince, or to fhare it with him; than to exclude men from the privilege of reprefenting their fellow-fubjects who would chufe them in parliament, purely becaufe they are employed and trufted by the prince.

Your lordfhip fees not only, how much a due reflection upon the experience of other ages and countries would have pointed out national corruption, as the natural and neceffary confequence of invefting the crown with the management of fo great a revenue; but alfo the lofs of liberty, as the natural and neceffary confequence of national corruption.

THESE

THESE two examples explain sufficiently what they are intended to explain. It only remains therefore upon this head, to observe the difference between the two manners in which history supplies the defects of our own experience. It shews us causes as in fact they were laid, with their immediate effects: and it enables us to guess at future events. It can do no more, in the nature of things. My lord BACON, in his second book of the Advancement of learning, having in his mind, I suppose, what PHILO and JOSEPHUS asserted of MOSES, affirms divine history to have this prerogative, that the narration may be before the fact as well as after. But since the ages of prophecy, as well as miracles, are past, we must content ourselves to guess at what will be, by what has been: we have no other means in our power, and history furnishes us with these. How we are to improve, and apply these means, as well as how we are to acquire them, shall be deduced more particularly in another letter.

OF

OF THE

STUDY OF HISTORY.

LETTER III.

1. An objection againſt the utility of hiſtory removed. 2. The falſe and true aims of thoſe who ſtudy it. 3. Of the hiſtory of the firſt ages, with reflections on the ſtate of ancient hiſtory prophane and ſacred.

WERE theſe letters to fall into the hands of ſome ingenious perſons who adorn the age we live in, your lordſhip's correſpondent would be joked upon for his project of improving men in virtue and wiſdom by the ſtudy of hiſtory. The general characters of men it would be ſaid, are determined by their natural conſtitutions, as their particular actions are by immediate objects. Many very converſant in hiſtory would be cited, who have proved ill men, or bad politicians; and a long roll would be produced of others, who

who have arrived at a great pitch of private, and public virtue, without any affiftance of this kind. Something has been faid already to anticipate this objection; but, fince I have heard feveral perfons affirm fuch propofitions with great confidence, a loud laugh, or a filent fneer at the pedants who prefumed to think otherwife; I will fpend a few paragraphs, with your lordfhip's leave, to fhew that fuch affirmations, for to affirm amongft thefe fine men is to reafon, either prove too much, or prove nothing.

If our general characters were determined abfolutely, as they are certainly influenced, by our conftitutions, and if our particular actions were fo by immediate objects; all inftruction by precept, as well as example, and all endeavours to form the moral character by education, would be unneceffary. Even the little care that is taken, and furely it is impoffible to take lefs, in the training up our youth, would be too much. But the truth is widely different from this reprefentation of it; for, what is vice, and what is virtue? I fpeak of them in a large and philofophical fenfe. The former, is, I think no more than the excefs, abufe, and mifapplication of

appetites,

appetites, defires, and paffions, natural and innocent, nay ufeful and neceffary. The latter confifts in the moderation and government, in the ufe and application of thefe appetites, defires, and paffions, according to the rules of reafon, and therefore, often in oppofition to their own blind impulfe.

WHAT now is education? that part, that principal and moft neglected part of it, I mean, which tends to form the moral character? It is, I think, an inftitution defigned to lead men from their tender years, by precept and example, by argument and authority, to the practice, and to the habit of practifing thefe rules. The ftronger our appetites, defires, and paffions are, the harder indeed is the tafk of education: but when the efforts of education are proportioned to this ftrength, although our keeneft appetites and defires, and our ruling paffions cannot be reduced to a quiet and uniform fubmiffion, yet, are not their exceffes affwaged? are not their abufes and mifapplicarions, in fome degree, diverted or checked? Tho' the pilot cannot lay the ftorm, cannot he carry the fhip, by his art, better through it, and often prevent the wreck that would always happen, without him?

If

If ALEXANDER, who loved wine, and was naturally choleric, had been bred under the severity of Roman discipline, it is probable he would neither have made a bonfire of Persepolis for his whore, nor have killed his friend. If SCIPIO, who was naturally given to women, for which anecdote we have, if I mistake not, the authority of POLYBIUS, as well as some verses of NAEVIUS preserved by A. GELLIUS, had been educated by OLYMPIAS at the court of PHILIP, it is improbable that he would have restored the beautiful Spaniard. In short, if the renowned SOCRATES had not corrected nature by art, this first apostle of the gentiles had been a very profligate fellow, by his own confession; for he was inclined to all the vices ZOPYRUS imputed to him, as they say, on the observation of his physiognomy.

WITH him therefore, who denies the effects of education, it would be in vain to dispute; and with him who admits them, there can be no dispute, concerning that share which I ascribe to the study of history, in forming our moral characters, and making us better men. The very persons who pretend that inclinations cannot be restrained, nor habits corrected, against our natural

Of the STUDY of HISTORY.

natural bent, would be the firſt perhaps to prove, in certain caſes, the contrary. A fortune at court, or the favours of a lady, have prevailed on many to conceal, and they could not conceal without reſtraining, which is one ſtep towards correcting, the vices they were by nature addicted to the moſt. Shall we imagine now, that the beauty of virtue and the deformity of vice, the charms of a bright and laſting reputation, the terror of being delivered over as criminals to all poſterity, the real benefit ariſing from a conſcientious diſcharge of the duty we owe to others, which benefit, fortune can neither hinder nor take away, and the reaſonableneſs of conforming ourſelves to the deſigns of GOD manifeſted in the conſtitution of the human nature; ſhall we imagine, I ſay, that all theſe are not able to acquire the ſame power over thoſe who are continually called upon to a contemplation of them, and they who apply themſelves to the ſtudy of hiſtory, are ſo called upon, as other motives, mean and ſordid in compariſon of theſe, can uſurp on other men?

2. That the ſtudy of hiſtory, far from making us wiſer, and more uſeful citizens, as well as better men, may be of no advantage

vantage whatsoever; that it may serve to render us mere antiquaries and scholars; or that it may help to make us forward coxcombs, and prating pedants, I have already allowed. But this is not the fault of history; and to convince us that it is not, we need only contrast the true use of history, with the use that is made of it by such men as these. We ought always to keep in mind, that history is philosophy teaching by examples how to conduct ourselves in all the situations of private and public life; that therefore we must apply ourselves to it in a philosophical spirit and manner; that we must rise from particular to general knowledge, and that we must fit ourselves for the society and business of mankind by accustoming our minds to reflect and meditate on the characters we find described, and the course of events we find related there. Particular examples may be of use sometimes in particular cases; but the application of them is dangerous. It must be done with the utmost circumspection, or it will be seldom done with success. And yet one would think that this was the principal use of the study of history, by what has been written on the subject. I know not whether MACHIAVEL himself is quite free from defect on this account:

account: he seems to carry the use and application of particular examples sometimes too far. Marius and Catulus passed the Alps, met and defeated the Cimbri beyond the frontiers of Italy. Is it safe to conclude from hence, that whenever one people is invaded by another, the invaded ought to meet and fight the invaders at a distance from their frontiers? Machiavel's countryman, Guicciardin, was aware of the danger that might arise from such an application of examples. Peter of Medicis had involved himself in great difficulties, when those wars and calamities began which Lewis Sforza first drew and entailed on Italy, by flattering the ambition of Charles the eighth, in order to gratify his own, and calling the French into that country. Peter owed his distress to his folly, in departing from the general tenor of conduct his father Laurence had held, and hoped to relieve himself by imitating his father's example in one particular instance. At a time when the wars with the pope and king of Naples had reduced Laurence to circumstances of great danger, he took the resolution of going to Ferdinand, and of treating in person with that prince. The resolution appears in history imprudent and almost desperate:

were we informed of the secret reasons on which this great man acted, it would appear very possibly a wise and safe measure. It succeeded, and LAURENCE brought back with him public peace, and private security. As soon as the French troops entered the dominions of Florence, PETER was struck with a panic terror, went to CHARLES the eighth, put the port of Leghorn, the fortresses of Pisa, and all the keys of the country, into this prince's hands; whereby he disarmed the Florentine commonwealth, and ruined himself. He was deprived of his authority, and driven out of the city, by the just indignation of the magistrates and people: and in the treaty which they made afterwards with the king of France, it was stipulated, that PETER should not remain within an hundred miles of the state, nor his brothers within the same distance of the city of Florence. On this occasion GUICCIARDIN observes how dangerous it is to govern ourselves by particular examples; since, to have the same success, we must have the same prudence, and the same fortune; and since the example must not only answer the case before us in general, but in every minute circumstance. This is the sense of that admirable historian, and these are his words—" è senza dubio molto
"peri-

Of the STUDY of HISTORY. 51

" pericolofo il governarfi con gl' efempi,
" fe non concorrono, non folo in generale,
" ma in tutti i particulari, le medifime
" ragioni; fe le cofe non fono regolate con
" la medefima prudenza, & fe oltre a tutti
" li altri fondamenti, non, v'ha la parte
" fua la medifima fortuna." An obfervation that BOILEAU makes, and a rule he
lays down in fpeaking of tranflations, will
properly find their place here, and ferve to
explain ftill better what I would eftablifh.
" To tranflate fervilely into modern lan-
" guage an ancient author phrafe by phrafe,
" and word by word, is prepofterous: no-
" thing can be more unlike the original
" than fuch a copy. It is not to fhew, it
" is to difguife the author: and he who
" has known him only in this drefs, would
" not know him in his own. A good
" writer, inftead of taking this inglorious
" and unprofitable tafk upon him, will
" joufter contre l'original, rather imitate
" than tranflate, and rather emulate than
" imitate: he will transfufe the fenfe and
" fpirit of the original into his own work,
" and will endeavour to write as the ancient
" author would have wrote, had he writ in
" the fame language." Now, to improve by
examples is to improve by imitation. We
muft catch the fpirit if we can, and conform

LETTER II.

form ourselves to the reason of them; but we must not affect to translate servilely into our conduct, if your lordship will allow me the expression, the particular conduct of those good and great men, whose images history sets before us. CODRUS and the DECII devoted themselves to death: one, because an oracle had foretold that the army whose general was killed, would be victorious; the others in compliance with a superstition that bore great analogy to a ceremony practised in the old Egyptian church, and added afterwards, as many others of the same origin were, to the ritual of the Israelites. These are examples of great magnanimity, to be sure, and of magnanimity employed in the most worthy cause. In the early days of the Athenian and Roman government, when the credit of oracles and all kinds of superstition prevailed, when heaven was piously thought to delight in blood, and even human blood was shed under wild notions of atonement, propitiation, purgation, expiation, and satisfaction; they who set such examples as these, acted an heroical and a rational part too. But if a general should act the same part now, and in order to secure his victory, get killed as fast as he could; he might pass for an hero, but, I am sure, he would pass
for

for a madman. Even thefe examples, however, are of ufe: they excite us at leaft to venture our lives freely in the fervice of our country, by propofing to our imitation, men who devoted themfelves to certain death in the fervice of theirs. They fhew us what a turn of imagination can operate, and how the greateft trifle, nay the greateft abfurdity, dreffed up in the folemn arts of religion, can carry ardour and confidence, or the contrary fentiments, into the breafts of thoufands.

THERE are certain general principles, and rules of life and conduct, which always muft be true, becaufe they are conformable to the invariable nature of things. He who ftudies hiftory as he would ftudy philofophy, will foon diftinguifh and collect them, and by doing fo will foon form to himfelf a general fyftem of ethics and politics on the fureft foundations, on the trial of thefe principles and rules in all ages, and on the confirmation of them by univerfal experience. I faid, he will diftinguifh them; for once more I muft fay, that as to particular modes of actions, and meafures of conduct, which the cuftoms of different countries, the manners of different ages, and the circumftances of different conjunctures, have appropriated, as it were;

were; it is always ridiculous, or imprudent and dangerous to employ them. But this is not all. By contemplating the vast variety of particular characters and events; by examining the strange combinations of causes, different, remote, and seemingly opposite, that often concur in producing one effect; and the surprising fertility of one single and uniform cause in the producing of a multitude of effects as different, as remote, and seemingly as opposite; by tracing carefully, as carefully as if the subject he considers were of personal and immediate concern to him, all the minute, and sometimes scarce perceivable circumstances, either in the characters of actors, or in the course of actions, that history enables him to trace, and according to which the success of affairs, even the greatest, is mostly determined; by these, and such methods as these, for I might descend into a much greater detail, a man of parts may improve the study of history to it's proper and principal use; he may sharpen the penetration, fix the attention of his mind, and strengthen his judgment; he may acquire the faculty and the habit of discerning quicker, and looking farther; and of exerting that flexibility, and steadiness, which are necessary to be joined in the conduct of all affairs, that
depend

depend on the concurrence or oppofition of other men.

Mr. LOCKE, I think, recommends the ftudy of geometry even to thofe who have no defign of being geometricians: and he gives a reafon for it, that may be applied to the prefent cafe. Such perfons may forget every problem that has been propofed, and every folution that they or others have given; but the habit of purfuing long trains of ideas will remain with them, and they will appear through the mazes of fophifm, and difcover a latent truth, where perfons who have not this habit will never find it.

IN this manner, the ftudy of hiftory will prepare us for action and obfervation. Hiftory is the antient author: experience is the modern language. We form our tafte on the firft; we tranflate the fenfe and reafon, we transfufe the fpirit and force; but we imitate only the particular graces of the original: we imitate them according to the idiom of our own tongue, that is, we fubftitute often equivalents in the lieu of them, and are far from affecting to copy them fervilely. To conclude, as experience is converfant about the prefent, and the prefent enables

enables us to guefs at the future; fo hiftory is converfant about the paft, and by knowing the things that have been, we become better able to judge of the things that are.

THIS ufe, my lord, which I make the proper and principal ufe of the ftudy of hiftory, is not infifted on by thofe who have wrote concerning the method to be followed in this ftudy: and fince we propofe different ends, we muft of courfe take different ways. Few of their treatifes have fallen into my hands: one, the method of BODIN, a man famous in his time, I remember to have read. I took it up with much expectation many years ago; I went through it, and remained extremely difappointed. He might have given almoft any other title to his book, as properly as that which ftands before it. There are not many pages in it that relate any more to his fubject than a tedious fifth chapter, wherein he accounts for the characters of nations according to their pofitions on the globe, and according to the influence of the ftars; and affures his reader, that nothing can be more neceffary than fuch a difquifition, " ad univer-" fam hiftoriarum cognitionem, et incor-" ruptum earum judicium." In his method, we we are to take firſt a general view of univerſal hiſtory, and chronology, in ſhort abſtracts, and then to ſtudy all particular hiſtories and ſyſtems. SENECA ſpeaks of men who ſpend their whole lives in learning how to act in life, " dum vitæ inſtrumenta " conquirunt." I doubt that this method of BODIN would conduct us in the ſame, or as bad a way; would leave us no time for action, or would make us unfit for it. A huge common-place book, wherein all the remarkable ſayings and facts that we find in hiſtory are to be regiſtered, may enable a man to talk or write like BODIN, but will never make him a better man, nor enable him to promote, like an uſeful citizen, the ſecurity, the peace, the welfare, or the grandeur of the community to which he belongs. I ſhall proceed therefore to ſpeak of a method that leads to ſuch purpoſes as theſe directly and certainly, without any regard to the methods that have been preſcribed by others.

I THINK, then, we muſt be on our guard againſt this very affectation of learning, and this very wantonneſs of curioſity, which the examples and precepts we commonly meet with are calculated to flatter and indulge.

dulge. We muſt neither dwell too long in the dark, nor wander about till we loſe our way in the light. We are too apt to carry ſyſtems of philoſophy beyond all our ideas, and ſyſtems of hiſtory beyond all our memorials. The philoſopher begins with reaſon, and ends with imagination. The hiſtorian inverts this order: he begins without memorials, and he ſometimes ends with them. This ſilly cuſtom is ſo prevalent among men of letters who apply themſelves to the ſtudy of hiſtory, and has ſo much prejudice and ſo much authority on the ſide of it, that your lordſhip muſt give me leave to ſpeak a little more particularly and plainly than I have done, in favour of common ſenſe, againſt an abſurdity which is almoſt ſanctified.

REFLECTIONS

REFLECTIONS
On the ſtate of ancient History.

THE nature of man, and the conſtant courſe of human affairs, render it impoſſible that the firſt ages of any new nation which forms itſelf, ſhould afford authentic materials for hiſtory. We have none ſuch concerning the originals of any of thoſe nations that actually ſubſiſt. Shall we expect to find them concerning the originals of nations diſperſed, or extinguiſhed, two or three thouſand years ago? If a thread of dark and uncertain traditions, therefore, is made, as it commonly is, the introduction to hiſtory, we ſhould touch it lightly, and run ſwiftly over it, far from inſiſting on it, either as authors or readers. Such introductions are at beſt no more than fanciful preludes, that try the inſtruments, and precede the concert. He muſt be void of judgment and taſte, one would think, who can take the firſt for true hiſtory, or the laſt for true harmony. And yet ſo it has been, and ſo it is, not in Germany and Holland alone; but in Italy, in France, and in England, where genius has abounded, and taſte has been long refined. Our great ſcholars have dealt and deal in fables, at leaſt

as much as our poets, with this difference to the difadvantage of the former, to whom I may apply the remark as juftly as Seneca applied it to the dialecticians——" triftius " inepti funt. Illi ex profeffo lafciviunt; hi " agere feipfos aliquid exiftimant." Learned men, in learned and inquifitive ages, who poffeffed many advantages that we have not, and among others that of being placed fo many centuries nearer the original truths that are the objects of fo much laborious fearch, defpaired of finding them, and gave fair warning to pofterity, if pofterity would have taken it. The ancient geographers, as Plutarch fays in the life of Theseus, when they laid down in their maps the little extent of fea and land that was known to them, left great fpaces void. In fome of thefe fpaces they wrote, Here are fandy defarts, in others, Here are impaffable marfhes, Here is a chain of inhofpitable mountains, or Here is a frozen ocean. Juft fo, both he and other hiftorians, when they related fabulous originals, were not wanting to fet out the bounds beyond which there was neither hiftory nor chronology. Censorinus has preferved the diftinction of three æras eftablifhed by Varro. This learned Roman antiquary did not determine whether the firft period
had

had any beginning, but fixed the end of it at the first, that is, according to him, the Ogygian, deluge; which he placed, I think, some centuries backwarder than Julius Africanus thought fit to place it afterwards. To this æra of absolute darkness he supposed that a kind of twilight succeeded, from the Ogygian deluge to the Olympic æra, and this he called the fabulous age. From this vulgar æra, when Coraebus was crowned victor, and long after the true æra when these games were instituted by Iphitus, the Greeks pretend to be able to digest their history with some order, clearness, and certainty: Varro therefore looked on it as the break of day, or the beginning of the historical age. He might do so the rather, perhaps, because he included by it the date he likewise fixed, or, upon recollection, that the elder Cato had fixed, of the foundation of Rome within the period from which he supposed that historical truth was to be found. But yet most certain it is, that the history and chronology of the ages that follow, are as confused and uncertain, as the history and chronology of those which immediately precede this æra.

1. The

LETTER III.

1. The state of ancient profane history.

THE Greeks did not begin to write in prose till PHERECIDES of SYROS introduced the custom: and CADMUS MILESIUS was their first historian. Now these men flourished long after the true, or even the vulgar Olympic æra; for JOSEPHUS affirms, and in this he has great probability on his side, that CADMUS MILESIUS, and ACUSILAUS ARGIVUS, in a word, the oldest historians in Greece, were very little more ancient than the expedition of the Persians against the Greeks. As several centuries passed between the Olympic æra and these first historians, there passed likewise several more between these and the first Greek chronologers. TIMOEUS about the time of PTOLOMY PHILADELPHUS, and ERATOSTHENES about that of PTOLOMY EVERGETES, seem first to have digested the events recorded by them, according to the olympiads. Precedent writers mentioned sometimes the olympiads; but this rule of reckoning was not brought into established use sooner. The rule could not serve to render history more clear and certain till it was followed; it was not followed till about five hundred years

after

Of the STUDY of HISTORY.   63

after the Olympic æra. There remains therefore no pretence to place the beginning of the hiſtorical age ſo high as VARRO placed it, by five hundred years.

HELLANICUS indeed and others pretended to give the originals of cities and governments, and to deduce their narrations from great antiquity. Their works are loſt, but we can judge how inconſiderable the loſs is, by the writings of that age which remain, and by the report of thoſe who had ſeen the others. For inſtance, HERODOTUS was cotemporary with HELLANICUS. HERODOTUS was inquiſitive enough in all conſcience, and propoſed to publiſh all he could learn of the antiquities of the Ionians, Lydians, Phrygians, Egyptians, Babylonians, Medes, and Perſians; that is, of almoſt all the nations who were known in his time to exiſt. If he wrote Aſſyriacs, we have them not; but we are ſure that this word was uſed proverbially to ſignify fabulous legends, ſoon after his time, and when the mode of publiſhing ſuch relations and hiſtories prevailed among the Greeks.

IN the nine books we have, he goes back indeed almoſt to the Olympic æra,
without

LETTER III.

out taking notice of it, however; but he goes back only to tell an old woman's tale, of a king who loft his crown for fhewing his wife naked to his favourite; and from CANDAULES and GYGES he haftens, or rather he takes a great leap, down to CYRUS.

SOMETHING like a thread of hiftory of the Medes and then of the Perfians, to the flight of XERXES, which happened in his own time, is carried on. The events of his own time are related with an air of hiftory. But all accounts of the Greeks as well as the Perfians, which precede thefe, and all the accounts which he gives occafionally of other nations,, were drawn up moft manifeftly on broken, perplexed, and doubtful fcraps of tradition. He had neither original records, nor any authentic memorials to guide him, and yet thefe are the fole foundations of true hiftory. HERODOTUS flourifhed, I think, little more than half a century, and XENOPHON little more than a whole century, after the death of CYRUS: and yet how various and repugnant are the relations made by thefe two hiftorians, of the birth, life and death of this prince! If moft hiftories had come down from thefe ages to ours, the uncertainty and inutility

of

Of the STUDY of HISTORY. 65
of them all would be but the more manifeft. We fhould find that ACUSILAUS rejected the traditions of HESIOD, that HELLANICUS contradicted ACUSILAUS, that EPHORUS accufed HELLANICUS, that TIMAEUS accufed EPHORUS, and all pofterior writers TIMAEUS. This is the report of JOSEPHUS. But, in order to fhew the ignorance and falfhood of all thofe writers through whom the traditions of profane antiquity came to the Greeks, I will quote to your lordfhip a much better authority than that of JOSEPHUS; the authority of one who had no prejudice to bias him, no particular caufe to defend, nor fyftem of ancient hiftory to eftablifh, and all the helps as well as talents, neceffary to make him a competent judge. The man I mean is STRABO.

SPEAKING of the Maffagetae in his eleventh book, he writes to this effect: that no author had given a true account of them, though feveral had wrote of the war that CYRUS waged againft them; and that hiftorians had found as little credit in what they had related concerning the affairs of the Perfians, Medes, and Syrians; that this was due to their folly; for obferving that thofe who wrote fables profeffedly, were held in efteem, thefe men imagined they fhould ren-

E der

der their writings more agreeable, if under the appearance and pretence of true history, they related what they had neither seen nor heard from persons able to give them true information; and that accordingly their only aim had been to dress up pleasing and marvellous relations: that one may better give credit to Hesiod and Homer, when they talk of their heroes, nay even to dramatic poets, than to Ctesias, Herodotus, Hellanicus, and their followers: that it is not safe to give credit even to the greatest part of the historians who wrote concerning Alexander; since they too, encouraged by the greater reputation of this conqueror, by the distance to which he carried his arms; and by the difficulty of disproving what they said of actions performed in regions so remote, were apt to deceive: that indeed when the Roman empire on one side, and the Parthian on the other, came to extend themselves, the truth of things grew to be better known.

You see, my lord, not only how late profane history began to be wrote by the Greeks, but how much later it began to be wrote with any regard to truth; and consequently what wretched materials the learned men, who arose after the age of

Alex-

ALEXANDER, had to employ, when they attempted to form syftems of ancient hiftory and chronology. We have fome remains of that laborious compiler DIODORUS SICULUS, but do we find in him any thread of ancient hiftory, I mean, that which paffed for ancient in his time? What complaints, on the contrary, does he not make of former hiftorians? how frankly does he confefs the little and uncertain light he had to follow in his refearches? Yet DIODORUS, as well as PLUTARCH, and others, had not only the older Greek hiftorians, but the more modern antiquaries, who pretended to have fearched into the records and regifters of nations; even at that time renowned for their antiquity. BEROSUS, for inftance, and MANETHO, one a Babylonian, and the other an Egyptian prieft, had publifhed the antiquities of their countries in the time of the PTOLEMYS. BEROSUS pretended to give the hiftory of four hundred and eighty years. PLINY, if I remember right, for I fay this on memory, fpeaks to this effect in the fixth book of his Natural Hiftory: and if it was fo, thefe years were probably years of NABONASSAR. MANETHO began his hiftory, God knows when, from the progrefs of ISIS, or fome other as well afcertained period. He followed the Egyptian traditions of dynasties of Gods and Demi-Gods; and derived his anecdotes from the first MERCURY, who had inscribed them in sacred characters, on antediluvian pillars, antediluvian at least, according to our received chronology, from which the second MERCURY had transcribed them, and inserted them into his works. We have not these antiquities; for the monk of VITERBO was soon detected: and if we had them, they would either add to our uncertainty, and encrease the chaos of learning, or tell us nothing worth our knowlege. For thus I reason. Had they given particular and historical accounts conformable to the scriptures of the Jews, JOSEPHUS, JULIUS AFRICANUS, and EUSEBIUS would have made quite other extracts from their writings, and would have altered and contradicted them less. The accounts they gave, therefore, were repugnant to sacred writ, or they were defective: they would have established pyrrhonism, or have baulked our curiosity.

2. Of Sacred History:

What memorials therefore remain to give us light into the originals of ancient nations, and the hiſtory of thoſe ages, we commonly call the firſt ages? The Bible, it will be ſaid; that is, the hiſtorical part of it in the Old Teſtament. But, my lord, even theſe divine books muſt be reputed inſufficient to the purpoſe, by every candid and impartial man who conſiders either their authority as hiſtories, or the matter they contain. For what are they? and how came they to us? At the time when ALEXANDER carried his arms into Aſia, a people of Syria, till then unknown, became known to the Greeks: this people had been ſlaves to the Egyptians, Aſſyrians, Medes, and Perſians, as theſe ſeveral empires prevailed: ten parts in twelve of them had been tranſplanted by ancient conquerors, and melted down and loſt in the eaſt, ſeveral ages before the eſtabliſhment of the empire that ALEXANDER deſtroyed: the other two parts had been carried captive to Babylon, a little before the ſame æra. This captivity was not indeed perpetual, like the other; but it laſted ſo long, and ſuch circumſtances, whatever they

LETTER III.

they were, accompanied it; that the captives forgot their country, and even their language, the Hebrew dialect at leaft, and character: and a few of them only could be wrought upon, by the zeal of fome particular men, to return home, when the indulgence of the Perfian monarchs gave them leave to rebuild their city, and to re-people their ancient patrimony. Even this remnant of the nation did not continue long entire. Another great tranfmigration followed; and the Jews, that fettled under the protection of the PTOLEMYS, forgot their language in Egypt, as the forefathers of thefe Jews had forgot theirs in Chaldea. More attached however to their religion in Egypt, for reafons eafy to be deduced from the new inftitutions that prevailed after the captivity among them than their anceftors had been in Chaldea, a verfion of their facred writings was made into Greek at Alexandria, not long after the canon of thefe fcriptures had been finifhed at Jerufalem; for many years could not intervene between the death of SIMON the juft, by whom this canon was finifhed, if he died during the reign of PTOLEMY SOTER, and the beginning of this famous tranflation under PTOLEMY PHILADELPHUS. The Hellenift Jews reported as many marvellous things to

authorize,

Of the STUDY of HISTORY.　71

authorize, and even to sanctify this tranflation, as the other Jews had reported about ESDRAS who began, and SIMON the juft who finifhed, the canon of their fcriptures. Thefe holy romances flid into tradition, and tradition became hiftory: the fathers of our chriftian church did not difdain to employ them. St. JEROME, for inftance, laughed at the ftory of the feventy-two elders, whofe tranflations were found to be, upon comparifon, word for word the fame, though made feparately, and by men who had no communication with one another. But the fame St. JEROME, in the fame place, quotes ARISTEAS, one of the guard of PTOLEMY PHILADELPHUS, as a real perfonage.

THE account pretended to be wrote by this ARISTEAS, of all that paffed relating to the tranflation, was enough for his purpofe. This he retained, and he rejected only the more improbable circumftances, which had been added to the tale, and which laid it open to moft fufpicion. In this he fhewed great prudence, and better judgment, than that zealous, but weak apologift JUSTIN, who believed the whole ftory himfelf, and endeavoured to impofe it on mankind.

LETTER III.

THUS you see, my lord, that when we consider these books barely as histories, delivered to us on the faith of a superstititious people, among whom the custom and art of pious lying prevailed remarkably, we may be allowed to doubt whether greater credit is to be given to what they tell us concerning the original, compiled in their own country, and as it were out of the sight of the rest of the world; than we know, with such a certainty as no scholar presumes to deny, that we ought to give to what they tell us concerning the copy?

THE Hellenist Jews were extremely pleased, no doubt, to have their scriptures in a language they understood, and that might spread the fame of their antiquity, and do honour to their nation, among their masters the Greeks. But yet we do not find that the authority of these books prevailed, or that even they were much known among the Pagan world. The reason of this cannot be, that the Greeks admired nothing that was not of their own growth, " sua tantum mirantur:" for, on the contrary, they were inquisitive and credulous in the highest degree, and they collected and published at least as many idle traditions of other nations, as they propagated

gated of their own. Josephus pretended that Theopompus, a difciple of Isocrates, being about to infert in his hiftory fome things he had taken out of holy writ, the poor man became troubled in mind for feveral days; and that having prayed to God, during an intermiffion of his illnefs, to reveal to him the caufe of it, he learned in his fleep that this attempt was the caufe; upon which he quitted the defign and was cured. If Josephus had been a little more confiftent than he is very often, fuch a ftory as this would not have been told by one, who was fond, as Jews and Chriftians in general have been, to create an opinion that the Gentiles took not their hiftory alone, but their philofophy and all their valuable knowledge, from the Jews. Notwithftanding this ftory therefore, which is told in the fifteenth book of the Jewifh Antiquities, and means nothing, or means to fhew that the divine Providence would not fuffer anecdotes of facred, to be mingled with profane hiftory; the practice of Josephus himfelf, and of all thofe who have had the fame defign in view, has been to confirm the former by the latter, and at any rate to fuppofe an appearance at leaft of conformity between them. We are told Hecatæus Abderita, for there were

two

two of that name, wrote a history favourable to the Jews: and, not to multiply instances, though I might easily do it, even ALEXANDER POLYHISTOR is called in. He is quoted by JOSEPHUS, and praised by EUSEBIUS as a man of parts and great variety of learning. His testimony, about the deluge and tower of Babel, is produced by St. CYRIL in his first book against JULIAN: and JUSTIN the apologist and martyr, in his exhortation to the Greeks, makes use of the same authority, among those that mention MOSES as a leader and prince of the Jews. Though this POLYHISTOR, if I remember right, what I think I have met with in SUIDAS, spoke only of a woman he called Moso, " cujus scriptum est lex he-" bræorum*." Had the Greek historians been conformable to the sacred, I cannot see that their authority, which was not cotemporary, would have been of any weight. They might have copied MOSES, and so they did CTESIAS. But even this was not

---

* Μωσὰ, γυνὴ Ἑβραια· ἧς ἐςι σύγγραμμα ὁ παρ᾽ Ἑβρα´οις νομ☉ ἁς φησιν Ἀλέξανδρ☉ ὁ Μιλήσι☉ ὁ Πολυίςωρ. Sui. Lex. tom. ii. p. 583.

Ἀλέξανδρ☉ .... ἐς Πολυίςωρ ... συνέγραψε βιβλ´α ἀριθμῆς κρείτω. κ᾽ περὶ Ῥώμης βιβλία πέντε. ἐν τούτοις λ. γιι, ὡς γυνὴ γέγονεν Ἑβρα´α Μωσὰ, ἧς ἐςι σύγραμμα ὁ παρ᾽ Ἑβρα οις νομος. Id. tom. i. p. 105. Edit. Cantab. 1725.

the

the case: whatever use a particular writer here and there might make occasionally of the scriptures, certain it is that the Jews continued to be as much despised, and their history to be as generally neglected, nay almost as generally unknown, for a long time at least after the version was made at Alexandria, as they had been before. APION, an Egyptian, a man of much erudition, appeared in the world some centuries afterwards. He wrote, among other antiquities, those of his own country: and as he was obliged to speak very often of the Jews, he spoke of them in a manner neither much to their honour, nor to that of their histories. He wrote purposely against them: and JOSEPHUS attempted afterwards, but APION was then dead, to refute him. APION passed, I know, for a vain and noisy pedant; but he passed likewise for a curious, a laborious, and a learned antiquary. If he was cabalistical or superstitious, JOSEPHUS was at least as much so as he: and if he flattered CALIGULA, JOSEPHUS introduced himself to the court of NERO and the favour of POPPÆA, by no very honourable means, under the protection of ALITURUS, a player, and a Jew; to say nothing of his applying to VESPASIAN the prophecies concerning the Messiah,

nor

nor of his accompanying Titus to the siege of Jerusalem.

In short, my lord, the Jewish history never obtained any credit in the world, till christianity was established. The foundations of this system being laid partly in these histories, and in the prophecies joined to them or inserted in them, christianity has reflected back upon them an authority which they had not before, and this authority has prevailed wherever christianity has spread. Both Jews and Christians hold the same books in great veneration, whilst each condemns the other for not understanding, or for abusing them. But I apprehend that the zeal of both has done much hurt, by endeavouring to extend their authority much farther than is necessary for the support perhaps of Judaism, but to be sure of christianity. I explain myself that I may offend no pious ear.

Simon, in the preface to his Critical history of the Old Testament, cites a divine of the faculty of Paris, who held that the inspirations of the authors of those books, which the church receives as the word of God, should be extended no farther than to matters purely of doctrine, or to such as as have a near and neceffary relation to thefe; and that whenever thefe authors write on other fubjects, fuch as Egyptian, Affyrian, or other hiftory, they had no more of the divine affiftance than any other perfons of piety. This notion of infpirations that came occcafionally, that illuminated the minds and guided the hands of the facred penmen while they were writing one page, and reftrained their influence, while the fame authors were writing another, may be cavilled againft: and what is there that may not? But furely it deferves to be treated with refpect, fince it tends to eftablifh a diftinction between the legal, doctrinal, or prophetical parts of the Bible, and the hiftorical: without which diftinction it is impoffible to eftablifh the firft, as evidently and as folidly as the interefts of religion require; at leaft it appears impoffible to me, after having examined and confidered, as well as I am able, all the trials of this kind that have been made by fubtle as well as learned men. The Old is faid to be the foundation of the New, and fo it is in one fenfe: the fyftem of religion contained in the latter, refers to the fyftem of religion contained in the former, and fuppofes the truth of it. But the authority on which we receive the books of the New teftament testament, is so far from being founded on the authority of the Old testament, that it is quite independent on it; the New being proved, gives authority to the Old, but borrows none from it; and gives this authority to the particular parts only. CHRIST came to fulfill the prophecies; but not to consecrate all the written, any more than the oral, traditions of the Jews. We must believe these traditions as far as they relate to christianity, as far as christianity refers to them, or supposes them necessary; but we can be under no obligation to believe them any farther, since without christianity we should be under no obligation to believe them at all.

It has been said by ABBADIE, and others, "That the accidents which have "happened to alter the texts of the Bible, "and to disfigure, if I may say so, the "scriptures in many respects, could not "have been prevented without a perpetual "standing miracle, and that a perpetual "standing miracle is not in the order of "providence." Now I can by no means subscribe to this opinion. It seems evident to my reason, that the very contrary must be true; if we suppose that GOD acts towards men according to the moral fitness
of

of things: and if we suppose that he acts arbitrarily, we can form no opinion at all. I think that these accidents would not have happened, or that the scriptures would have been preserved entirely in their genuine purity notwithstanding these accidents, if they had been entirely dictated by the HOLY GHOST; and the proof of this probable proposition, according to our clearest and most distinct ideas of wisdom and moral fitness, is obvious and easy. But these scriptures are not so come down to us: they are come down broken and confused, full of additions, interpolations, and transpositions, made we neither know when, nor by whom; and such, in short, as never appeared on the face of any other book, on whose authority men have agreed to rely.

THIS being so, my lord, what hypothesis shall we follow? Shall we adhere to some such distinction as I have mentioned? Shall we say, for instance, that the scriptures were written originally by the authors to whom they are vulgarly ascribed, but that these authors wrote nothing by inspiration, except the legal, the doctrinal, and the prophetical parts, and that in every other respect, their authority is purely human, and therefore fallible? Or shall we say that these

these histories are nothing more than compilations of old traditions, and abridgements of old records, made in later times, as they appear to every one who reads them without prepossession, and with attention? Shall we add, that which ever of these probabilities be true, we may believe, consistently with either, notwithstanding the decision of any divines, who know no more than you or I, or any other man, of the order of Providence, that all those parts and passages of the Old testament, which contain prophecies, or matters of law or doctrine, and which were from the first of such importance in the designs of providence to all future generations, and even to the whole race of mankind, have been from the first the peculiar care of providence? Shall we insist that such particular parts and passages, which are plainly marked out, and sufficiently confirmed by the system of the Christian revelation, and by the completion of the prophecies, have been preserved from corruption by ways impenetrable to us, amidst all the changes and chances to which the books wherein they are recorded have been exposed; and that neither original writers, nor later compilers, have been suffered to make any essential alterations, such 'as would have falsified the law of GOD and

the

the principles of the Jewish and Christian religions, in any of those divine fundamental truths? Upon such hypotheses, we may assert without scruple, that the genealogies and histories of the Old testament are in no respect sufficient foundations for a chronology from the beginning of time, nor for universal history. But then the same hypotheses will secure the infallibility of scripture authority, as far as religion is concerned. Faith and reason may be reconciled a little better than they commonly are. I may deny that the Old testament is transmitted to us under all the conditions of an authentic history, and yet be at liberty to maintain, that the passages in it which establish original sin, which seem favourable to the doctrine of the Trinity, which foretell the coming of the Messiah, and all others of similar kind, are come down to us as they were originally dictated by the HOLY GHOST.

IN attributing the whole credibility of the Old testament to the authority of the New, and in limiting the authenticity of the Jewish scriptures, to those parts alone that concern law, doctrine, and prophecy, by which their chronology and the far greatest part of their history are excluded, I will venture to assure your lordship that I do not assume

LETTER III.

so much, as is assumed in every hypothesis that affixes the divine seal of inspiration to the whole canon; that rests the whole proof on Jewish veracity; and that pretends to account particularly and positively for the descent of these ancient writings in their present state.

ANOTHER reason, for which I have insisted the rather on the distinction so often mentioned, is this. I think we may find very good foundation for it even in the Bible: and though this be a point very little attended to, and much disguised, it would not be hard to shew, upon great inducements of probability, that the law and the history were far from being blended together as they now stand in the Pentateuch, even from the time of MOSES down to that of ESDRAS. But the principal and decisive reason for separating in such manner the legal, doctrinal, and prophetical parts, from the historical, is the necessity of having some rule to go by: and, I protest, I know of none that is yet agreed upon. I content myself therefore to fix my opinion concerning the authority of the Old testament in this manner, and carry it thus far only. We must do so, or we must enter into that labyrinth of dispute and contradiction, wherein even the most orthodox Jews and
Christians

Christians have wandered so many ages, and still wander. It is strange, but it is true; not only the Jews differ from the Christians, but Jews and Christians both differ among themselves, concerning almost every point that is necessary to be certainly known and agreed upon, in order to establish the authority of books which both have received already as authentic and sacred. So that whoever takes the pains to read what learned men have wrote on this subject, will find that they leave the matter as doubtful as they took it up. Who were the authors of these scriptures, when they were published, how they were composed and preserved, or renewed, to use a remarkable expression of the famous Huet in his Demonstration; in fine, how they were lost during the captivity, and how they were retrieved after it, are all matters of controversy to this day.

It would be easy for me to descend into a greater detail, and to convince your lordship of what I have been saying in general by an induction of particulars, even without any other help than that of a few notes which I took when I applied myself to this examination, and which now lye before me. But such a digression would carry me too far: and I fear that you will think I have said already more than enough upon this part of my subject. I go on therefore to obferve to your lordfhip, that if the hiftory of the Old teftament was as exact and authentic, as the ignorance and impudence of fome Rabbies have made them affert that it is: if we could believe with them that Moses wrote every fyllable in the Pentateuch as it now ftands, or that all the pfalms were written by David: nay, if we could believe, with Philo and Josephus, that Moses wrote the account of his own death and fepulture, and made a fort of a funeral panegyric on himfelf, as we find them in the laft chaper of Deuteronomy; yet ftill would I venture to affert, that he who expects to find a fyftem of chronology, or a thread of hiftory, or fufficient materials for either, in the books of the Old teftament, expects to find what the authors of thefe books, whoever they were, never intended. They are extracts of genealogies, not genealogies; extracts of hiftories, not hiftories. The Jews themfelves allow their genealogies to be very imperfect, and produce examples of omiffions and errors in them, which denote fufficiently that thefe genealogies are extracts, wherein every generation in the courfe of defcent is not mentioned. I have read fomewhere, perhaps in the works of St. Jerome, that

that this farther juſtifies the opinion of thoſe who think it impoſſible to fix any certain chronology on that of the Bible: and this opinion will be juſtified ſtill better, to the underſtanding of every man that confiders how groſly the Jews blunder whenever they meddle with chronology; for this plain reaſon, becauſe their ſcriptures are imperfect in this reſpect, and becauſe they rely on their oral, to rectify and ſupply their written, traditions: that is, they rely on traditions compiled long after the canon of their ſcriptures, but deemed by them of equal antiquity and authority. Thus, for inſtance, DANIEL and SIMON the juſt, according to them, were members at the ſame time of the great ſynagogue which began and finiſhed the canon of the Old teſtament, under the preſidency of ESDRAS. This ESDRAS was the prophet MALACHI. DARIUS the ſon of HYSTASPES was ARTAXERXES LONGIMANUS; he was A ASUERUS, and he was the ſame DARIUS whom ALEXANDER conquered. This may ſerve as a ſample of Jewiſh chronology, formed on their ſcriptures which afford inſufficient lights, and on their traditions which afford falſe lights. We are indeed more correct, and come nearer to the truth in theſe inſtances, perhaps in ſome others, becauſe we make uſe of prophane chronology to help us. But

profane chronology is itself so modern, so precarious, that this help does not reach to the greatest part of that time to which sacred chronology extends; that when it begins to help, it begins to perplex us too; and finally, that even with this help we should not have had so much as the appearance of a complete chronological system, and the same may be said of universal history, if learned men had not proceeded very wisely, on one uniform maxim, from the first ages of christianity, when a custom of sanctifying profane learning, as well as prophane rites, which the Jews had imprudently laid aside, was taken up by the Christians. The maxim I mean is this, that prophane authority be admitted without scruple or doubt, whenever it says, or whenever it can be made to say, if not " totidem verbis, yet " totidem syl- " labis," or " totidem literis" at least, or whenever it can be made by any interpretation to mean, what confirms or supplies in a consistent manner, the holy writ; and that the same authority be rejected, when nothing of this kind can be done, but the contradiction or inconsistency remains irreconcileable. Such a liberty as this would not be allowed in any other case; because it supposes the very thing that is to be proved. But we see it taken, very properly to be sure, in favour of
sacred

sacred and infallible writings, when they are compared with others.

In order to perceive with the utmost evidence, that the scope and design of the author or authors of the Pentateuch, and of the other books of the Old testament, answer as little the purpose of antiquaries, in history, as in chronology, it will be sufficient briefly to call to mind the sum of what they relate, from the creation of the world, to the establishment of the Persian empire. If the antediluvian world continued one thousand six hundred and fifty-six years, and if the vocation of ABRAHAM is to be placed four hundred and twenty-six years below the deluge, these twenty centuries make almost two thirds of the period mentioned: and the whole history of them is comprized in eleven short chapters of Genesis; which is certainly the most compendious extract that ever was made. If we examine the contents of these chapters, do we find any thing like an universal history, or so much as an abridgement of it? ADAM and EVE were created, they broke the commandment of GOD, they were driven out of the garden of Eden, one of their sons killed his brother, but their race soon multiplied and peopled the earth. What geography now have we, what history of this antediluvian world?

world? Why, none. The fons of God, it is faid, lay with the daughters of men, and begot giants, and God drowned all the inhabitants of the earth, except one family. After this we read, that the earth was repeopled; but thefe children of one family were divided into feveral languages, even whilft they lived together, fpoke the fame language, and were employed in the fame work. Out of one of the countries into which they difperfed themfelves, in Chaldea, God called ABRAHAM fome time afterwards, with magnificent promifes, and conducted him to a country called Canaan. Did this author, my lord, intend an univerfal hiftory? Certainly not. The tenth chapter of Genefis names indeed fome of the generations defcending from the fons of NOAH, fome of the cities founded, and fome of the countries planted by them. But what are bare names, naked of circumftances, without defcriptions of countries, or relations of events? they furnifh matter only for guefs and difpute; and even the fimilitude of them, which is often ufed as a clue to lead us to the difcovery of hiftorical truth, has notoriously contributed to propagate error, and to encreafe the perplexity of ancient tradition. Thefe imperfect and dark accounts have not furnifhed matter for guefs and difpute alone; but a much worfe ufe has been

made

made of them by Jewish Rabbies, Christian fathers, and Mahometan doctors, in their prophane extensions of this part of the Mosaic history. The creation of the first man is described by some, as if, Preadamites, they had assisted at it. They talk of his beauty as if they had seen him, of his gigantic size as if they had measured him, and of his prodigious knowledge as if they had conversed with him. They point out the very spot where Eve laid her head the first time he enjoyed her. They have minutes of the whole conversation between this mother of mankind, who damned her children before she bore them, and the serpent. Some are positive that Cain quarrelled with Abel about a point of doctrine, and others affirm that the dispute arose about a girl. A great deal of such stuff may be easily collected about Enoch, about Noah, and about the sons of Noah; but I wave any farther mention of such impertinencies as Bonzes or Talapoins would almost blush to relate. Upon the whole matter, if we may guess at the design of an author, by the contents of his book, the design of Moses, or of the author of the history ascribed to him, in this part of it, was to inform the people of Israel of their descent from Noah by Shem, and of Noah's from Adam by Seth; to illustrate their original;

to eſtabliſh their claim to the land of Canaan, and to juſtify all the cruelties committed by Joshua in the conqueſt of the Canaanites, in whom, ſays Bochart, " the prophecy " of Noah was completed, when they were " ſubdued by the Iſraelites, who had been ſo " long ſlaves to the Egyptians."

Allow me to make, as I go along, a ſhort reflection or two on this prophecy, and the completion of it, as they ſtand recorded in the Pentateuch, out of many that might be made. The terms of the prophecy then are not very clear: and the curſe pronounced in it contradicts all our notions of order and of juſtice. One is tempted to think, that the patriarch was ſtill drunk; and that no man in his ſenſes could hold ſuch language, or paſs ſuch a ſentence. Certain it is, that no writer but a Jew could impute to the œconomy of divine providence the accompliſhment of ſuch a prediction, nor make the Supreme Being the executor of ſuch a curſe.

Ham alone offended, Canaan was innocent; for the Hebrew and other doctors, who would make the ſon an accomplice with his father, affirm not only without, but againſt, the expreſs authority of the text. Canaan was however alone curſed:

curfed: and he became, according to his grandfather's prophecy, "a fervant of fer-vants," that is, the vileft and worft of flaves (for I take thefe words in a fenfe, if not the moft natural, the moft favourable to the prophecy, and the leaft abfurd) to SHEM, though not to JAPHET, when the If-raelites conquered Paleftine; to one of his uncles, not to his brethren. Will it be faid— it has been faid—that where we read CANA-AN, we are to underftand HAM, whofe brethren SHEM and JAPHET were? At this rate, we fhall never know what we read: as thefe critics never care what they fay. Will it be faid—this has been faid too---that HAM was punifhed in his pofterity, when CANAAN was curfed, and his defcendants were exter-mined? But who does not fee that the curfe, and the punifhment, in this cafe, fell on CANAAN and his pofterity, exclu-fively of the reft of the pofterity of HAM; and were therefore the curfe and punifh-ment of the fon, not of the father, properly? The defcendants of MESRAIM, another of his fons, were the Egyptians: and they were fo far from being fervants of fervants to their coufins the SEMITES, that thefe were fervants of fervants to them, during more than fourfcore years. Why the pofterity of CANAAN was to be deemed an accurfed race, it is eafy to account; and I have

men-

mentioned it juft now. But it is not fo eafy to account, why the pofterity of the righteous SHEM, that great example of filial reverence, became flaves to another branch of the family of HAM.

IT would not be worth while to lengthen this tedious letter, by fetting down any more of the contents of the hiftory of the bible. Your lordfhip may pleafe to call the fubftance of it to your mind; and your native candour and love of truth will oblige you then to confefs, that thefe facred books do not aim, in any part of them, at any thing like univerfal chronology and hiftory. They contain a very imperfect account of the Ifraelites themfelves; of their fettlement in the land of promife, of which, by the way, they never had entire, and fcarce ever peaceable poffeffion; of their divifions, apoftacies, repentances, relapfes, triumphs, and defeats under the occafional government of their judges, and under that of their kings; of the Galilean and Samaritan captivites, into which they were carried by the kings of Affyria, and of that which was brought on the remnant of this people when the kingdom of Judah was deftroyed by thofe princes who governed the empire, founded on the union of Nineveh and Babylon. Thefe things are all related, your lord-

lordship knows, in a very summary and confused manner: and we learn so little of other nations by these accounts, that if we did not borrow some light from the traditions of other nations, we should scarce understand them. One particular observation, and but one, I will make, to shew what knowledge in the history of mankind, and in the computation of time, may be expected from these books. The Assyrians were their neighbours, powerful neighbours, with whom they had much and long to do. Of this empire therefore, if of any thing, we might hope to find some satisfactory account. What do we find? The scripture takes no notice of any Assyrian kingdom, till just before the time when prophane history makes that empire to end. Then we hear of PHUL, of TEGLATH-PHALASSER, who was perhaps the same person, and of SALMANASER, who took Samaria in the twelfth of the æra of NABONASSER, that is, twelve years after the Assyrian empire was no more. SENACHERIB succeeds to him, and ASSERHADDON to SENACHERIB. What shall we say to this apparent contrariety? If the silence of the bible creates a strong presumption against the first, may not the silence of prophane authority create some against the second Assyrian Monarchs? The pains that are taken to persuade, that
there

there is room enough between Sardanapa-
lus and Cyrus for the second, will not
resolve the difficulty. Something much
more plausible may be said, but even this
will be hypothetical, and liable to great
contradiction. So that upon the whole
matter, the scriptures are so far from giving
us light into general history, that they encrease the obscurity even of those parts to
which they have the nearest relation. We
have therefore neither in prophane nor in
sacred authors such authentic, clear, distinct,
and full accounts of the originals of ancient
nations, and of the great events of those
ages that are commonly called the first ages,
as deserve to go by the name of history, or as
afford sufficient materials for chronology and
history.

I might now proceed to observe to your
lordship how this has happened, not only by the
necessary consequences of human nature, and
the ordinary course of human affairs, but by
the policy, artifice, corruption, and folly of
mankind. But this would be to heap digression upon digression, and to presume too much
on your patience. I shall therefore content
myself to apply these reflections on the state of
ancient history to the study of history, and to
the method to be observed in it: as soon as
your lordship has rested yourself a little after
reading, and I after writing so long a letter.

OF

OF THE

STUDY OF HISTORY.

LETTER IV.

I. That there is in history sufficient authenticity to render it useful, notwithstanding all objections to the contrary.
II. Of the method and due restrictions to be observed in the study of it.

WHETHER the letter I now begin to write will be long or short, I know not: but I find my memory is refreshed, my imagination warmed, and matter flows in so fast upon me, that I have not time to press it close. Since therefore you have provoked me to write, you must be content to take what follows.

I have observed already, that we are apt naturally to apply to ourselves what has happened to other men, and that examples take their force from hence; as well those which history, as those which experience, offers to our reflection. What we do not believe to have happened therefore, we shall not

not thus apply: and for want of the same application, such examples will not have the same effect. Antient history, such ancient history as I have described, is quite unfit therefore in this respect to answer the ends that every reasonable man should propose to himself in this study; because such ancient history will never gain sufficient credit with any reasonable man. A tale well told, or a comedy or a tragedy well wrought up, may have a momentary effect upon the mind, by heating the imagination, surprizing the judgment, and affecting strongly the passions. The Athenians are said to be transported into a kind of martial phrenzy by the representation of a tragedy of Æschylus, and to have marched under this influence from the theatre to the plains of Marathon. These momentary impressions might be managed, for aught I know, in such manner as to contribute a little, by frequent repetitions of them, towards maintaining a kind of habitual contempt of folly, detestation of vice, and admiration of virtue in well-policed common-wealths. But then these impressions cannot be made, nor this little effect be wrought, unless the fables bear an appearance of truth. When they bear this appearance, reason connives at the innocent fraud of imagination; reason dispenses,

in

in favour of probability, with thofe ſtrict rules of criticiſm that ſhe has eſtabliſhed to try the truth of fact: but, after all, ſhe receives theſe fables as fables; and as ſuch only ſhe permits imagination to make the moſt of them. If they pretended to be hiſtory, they would be ſoon ſubjected to another and more ſevere examination. What may have happened, is the matter of an ingenious fable: what has happened, is that of an authentic hiſtory: the impreſſions which one or the other makes are in proportion. When imagination grows lawleſs and wild, rambles out of the precincts of nature, and tells of heroes and giants, fairies and enchanters, of events and of phænomena repugnant to univerſal experience, to our cleareſt and moſt diſtinct ideas, and to all the known laws of nature, reaſon does not connive a moment; but, far from receiving ſuch narrations as hiſtorical, ſhe rejects them as unworthy to be placed even among the fabulous. Such narrations therefore cannot make the ſlighteſt momentary impreſſions on a mind fraught with knowledge, and void of ſuperſtition. Impoſed by authority, and aſſiſted by artifice, the deluſion hardly prevails over common ſenſe; blind ignorance almoſt ſees, and raſh ſuperſtition heſitates: nothing leſs than enthuſiaſm thufiafm and phrenfy can give credit to fuch hiftories, or apply fuch examples. Don Quixote believed; but even Sancho doubted.

What I have faid will not be much controverted by any man who has read Amadis of Gaul, or has examined our ancient traditions without prepoffeffion. The truth is, the principal difference between them feems to be this. In Amadis of Gaul, we have a thread of abfurdities that are invented without any regard to probability, and that lay no claim to belief: ancient traditions are an heap of fables, under which fome particular truths, infcrutable, and therefore ufelefs to mankind, may lie concealed; which have a juft pretence to nothing more, and yet impofe themfelves upon us, and become, under the venerable name of ancient hiftory, the foundations of modern fables, the materials with which fo many fyftems of fancy have been erected.

But now, as men are apt to carry their judgments into extremes, there are fome that will be ready to infift that all hiftory is fabulous, and that the very beft is nothing better than a probable tale, artfully contrived, and plaufibly told, wherein truth and

and falshood are indistinguishably blended together. All the instances, and all the common-place argument, that Bayle and others have employed to establish this sort of Pyrrhonism, will be quoted: and from thence it will be concluded, that if the pretended histories of the first ages, and of the originals of nations, be too improbable and too ill-vouched to procure any degree of belief, those histories that have been wrote later, that carry a greater air of probability, and that boast even cotemporary authority, are at least insufficient to gain that degree of firm belief, which is necessary to render the study of them useful to mankind. But here that happens which often happens: the premises are true, and the conclusion is false; because a general axiom is established precariously on a certain number of partial observations. This matter is of consequence; for it tends to ascertain the degrees of assent that we may give to history.

I agree then, that history has been purposely and systematically falsified in all ages, and that partiality and prejudice have occasioned both voluntary and involuntary errors even in the best. Let me say without offence, my lord, since I may say it with truth, and am able to prove it, that ecclesiastical authority has led the way to this corruption in all ages, and all religions. How monstrous were the absurdities that the priesthood imposed on the ignorance and superstition of mankind, in the Pagan world, concerning the originals of religions and governments, their institutions and rites, their laws and customs? What opportunities had they for such impositions, whilst the keeping the records and collecting the traditions was in so many nations the peculiar office of this order of men? A custom highly extolled by Josephus, but plainly liable to the grossest frauds, and even a temptation to them. If the foundations of Judaism and Christianity have been laid in truth, yet what numberless fables have been invented to raise, to embellish, and to support these structures, according to the interest and taste of the several architects? That the Jews have been guilty of this will be allowed: and, to the shame of Christians, if not of Christianity, the fathers of one church have no right to throw the first stone at the fathers of the other. Deliberate systematical lying has been practised and encouraged from age to age; and among all the pious frauds that have been employed to maintain a reverence and zeal

for

for their religion in the minds of men, this abuse of history has been one of the principal and most successful: an evident and experimental proof by the way, of what I have insisted upon so much, the aptitude and natural tendency of history to form our opinions, and to settle our habits. This righteous expedient was in so much use and repute in the Greek church, that one METAPHRASTUS wrote a treatise on the art of composing holy romances: the fact, if I remember right, is cited by BAILLET in his book of the lives of the saints. He and other learned men of the Roman church have thought it of service to their cause, since the resurrection of letters, to detect some impostors, and to depose, or to unniche, (according to the French expression,) now and then a reputed saint; but they seem in doing this, to mean no more than a sort of composition: they give up some fables that they may defend others with greater advantage, and they make truth serve as a stalking-horse to error. The same spirit, that prevailed in the Eastern church, prevailed in the Western, and prevails still. A strong proof of it appeared lately in the country where I am. A sudden fury of devotion seized the people of Paris for a

little

little priest*, undistinguished during his life and dubbed a saint by the Jansenists after his death. Had the first minister been a Jansenist, the saint had been a saint still. All France had kept his festival: and, since there are thousands of eye-witnesses ready to attest the truth of all the miracles supposed to have been wrought at his tomb, notwithstanding the discouragement which these zealots have met with from the government; we may assure ourselves, that these silly impostors would have been transmitted in all the solemn pomp of history, from the knaves of this age to the fools of the next.

This lying spirit has gone forth from ecclesiastical to other historians: and I might fill many pages with instances of extravagant fables that have been invented in several nations, to celebrate their antiquity, to ennoble their originals, and to make them appear illustrious in the arts of peace and the triumphs of war. When the brain is well heated, and devotion or vanity, the semblance of virtue or real vice, and, above all, disputes and contests, have inspired that complication of passions we term zeal,

* The abbé Paris.

the

the effects are much the same, and history becomes very often a lying panegyric or a lying satire; for different nations, or different parties in the same nation, belie one another without any respect for truth, as they murder one another without any regard to right or sense of humanity. Religious zeal may boast this horrid advantage over civil zeal, that the effects of it have been more sanguinary, and the malice more unrelenting. In another respect they are more alike, and keep a nearer proportion: different religions have not been quite so barbarous to one another, as sects of the same religion; and, in like manner, nation has had better quarter from nation, than party from party. But, in all these controversies, men have pushed their rage beyond their own and their adversaries lives: they have endeavoured to interest posterity in their quarrels, and by rendering history subservient to this wicked purpose, they have done their utmost to perpetuate scandal, and to immortalize their animosity. The Heathen taxed the Jews even with idolatry; the Jews joined with the Heathen to render Christianity odious: but the church, who beat them at their own weapons during these contests, has had this further triumph over them, as well as over the several sects that have arisen within

LETTER IV.

her own pale: the works of those who have wrote against her have been destroyed; and whatever she advanced, to justify herself, and to defame her adversaries, is preserved in her annals, and the writings of her doctors.

THE charge of corrupting history, in the cause of religion, has been always committed to the most famous champions, and greatest saints of each church; and, if I was not more afraid of tiring, than of scandalizing your lordship, I could quote to you examples of modern churchmen, who have endeavoured to justify foul language by the New testament, and cruelty by the Old: nay, what is execrable beyond imagination, and what strikes horror into every mind that entertains due sentiments of the supreme Being, GOD himself has been cited for rallying and insulting ADAM after his fall. In other cases, this charge belongs to the pedants of every nation, and the tools of every party. What accusations of idolatry and superstition have not been brought, and aggravated against the Mahometans? Those wretched Christians who returned from those wars, so improperly called the holy wars, rumoured these stories about the West: and you may find, in
some

some of the old chroniclers and romance-writers, as well as poets, the Saracens called Paynims; though surely they were much further off from any suspicion of Polytheism, than those who called them by that name. When MAHOMET the second took Constantinople in the fifteenth century, the Mahometans began to be a little better, and but a little better known, than they had been before, to these parts of the world. But their religion, as well as their customs and manners, was strangely misrepresented by the Greek refugees that fled from the Turks: and the terror and hatred which this people had inspired by the rapidity of their conquests, and by their ferocity, made all these misrepresentations universally pass for truths. Many such instances may be collected from MARACCIO's refutation of the Koran, and RELANDUS has published a very valuable treatise on purpose to refute these calumnies, and to justify the Mahometans. Does not this example incline your lordship to think, that the Heathens, and the Arians, and other heretics, would not appear quite so absurd in their opinions, nor so abominable in their practice, as the orthodox Christians have represented them; if some RELANDUS could arise, with the materials necessary to their justification in his hands? He who reflects on the circumstances that attended letters, from the time when CONSTANTINE, instead of uniting the characters of emperor and sovereign pontiff in himself, when he became Christian, as they were united in him and all the other emperors in the Pagan system of government, gave so much independent wealth and power to the clergy, and the means of acquiring so much more: he who carries these reflections on through all the latter empire, and through those ages of ignorance and superstition, wherein it was hard to say which was greatest, the tyranny of the clergy, or the servility of the laity: he who considers the extreme severity, for instance, of the laws made by THEODOSIUS in order to stifle every writing that the orthodox clergy, that is, the clergy then in fashion, disliked; or the character and influence of such a priest as GREGORY called the great, who proclaimed war to all heathen learning in order to promote Christian verity; and flattered BRUNEHAULT, and abetted PHOCAS: he who considers all these things, I say, will not be at a loss to find the reasons, why history, both that which was wrote before, and a great part of that which has been wrote since the Christian æra, is come to us so imperfect and so corrupt.

WHEN

When the imperfection is due to a total want of memorials, either becaufe none were originally written, or becaufe they have been loft by devaftations of countries, extirpations of people, and other accidents in a long courfe of time; or becaufe zeal, malice, and policy have joined their endeavours to deftroy them purpofely; we muft be content to remain in our ignorance, and there is no great harm in that. Secure from being deceived, I can fubmit to be uninformed. But when there is not a total want of memorials, when fome have been loft or deftroyed, and others have been preferved and propagated, then we are in danger of being deceived: and therefore he muft be very implicit indeed, who receives for true, the hiftory of any religion or nation, and much more that of any fect or party, without having the means of confronting it with fome other hiftory. A reafonable man will not be thus implicit. He will not eftablifh the truth of hiftory on fingle, but on concurrent teftimony. If there be none fuch, he will doubt abfolutely: if there be a little fuch, he will proportion his affent or diffent accordingly. A fmall gleam of light, borrowed from foreign anecdotes, ferves often to difcover a whole fyftem of falfhood: and even they who

who corrupt hiſtory, frequently betray themſelves by their ignorance or inadvertency. Examples whereof I could eaſily produce. Upon the whole matter, in all theſe caſes we cannot be deceived eſſentially, unleſs we pleaſe: and therefore there is no reaſon to eſtabliſh Pyrrhoniſm, that we may avoid the ridicule of credulity.

IN all other caſes, there is leſs reaſon ſtill to do ſo; for when hiſtories and hiſtorical memorials abound, even thoſe that are falſe, ſerve to the diſcovery of the truth. Inſpired by different paſſions, and contrived for oppoſite purpoſes, they contradict; and, contradicting, they convict one another. Criticiſm ſeparates the ore from the droſs, and extracts from various authors a ſeries of true hiſtory, which could not have been found entire in any one of them, and will command our aſſent, when it is formed with judgment, and repreſented with candour. If this may be done, as it has been done ſometimes, with the help of authors who wrote on purpoſe to deceive; how much more eaſily, and more effectually may it be done, with the help of thoſe who paid a greater regard to truth? In a multitude of writers there will be always ſome, either incapable of groſs prevarication

tion from the fear of being discovered, and of acquiring infamy whilst they seek for fame; or else attached to truth upon a nobler and surer principle. It is certain that these, even the last of them, are fallible. Bribed by some passion or other, the former may venture now and then to propagate a falshood, or to disguise a truth; like the painter that drew in profile, as LUCIAN says, the picture of a prince that had but one eye. MONTAGNE objects to the memorials of DU BELLAY, that though the gross of the facts be truly related, yet these authors turned every thing they mentioned to the advantage of their master, and mentioned nothing which could not be so turned. The old fellow's words are worth quoting.---" De contourner le jugement, " des evenemens souvene contre raison à " notre avantage, & d'obmettire tout ce " qui'il y a de chatouilleux en la vie de " leur maistre, ils en font mestier." These, and such as these, deviate occasionally and voluntarily from truth; but even they who are attached to it the most religiously may slide sometimes into involuntary error. In matters of history we prefer very justly cotemporary authority; and yet cotemporary authors are the most liable to be warped from the straight rule of truth, in

writing

writing on subjects which have affected them strongly, "et quorum pars magna fuerunt." I am so persuaded of this from what I have felt in myself, and observed in others, that if life and health enough fall to my share, and I am able to finish what I meditate, a kind of history from the late queen's accession to the throne, to the peace of Utrecht, there will be no materials that I shall examine more scrupulously and severely, than those of the time when the events to be spoken of were in transaction. But though the writers of these two sorts, both of whom pay as much regard to truth as the various infirmities of our nature admit, are fallible; yet this fallibility will not be sufficient to give colour to Pyrrhonism. Where their sincerity as to fact is doubtful, we strike out truth by the confrontation of different accounts: as we strike out sparks of fire by the collision of flints and steel. Where their judgments are suspicious of partiality, we may judge for ourselves; or adopt their judgments, after weighing them with certain grains of allowance. A little natural sagacity will proportion these grains according to the particular circumstances of the authors, or their general characters; for even these influence. Thus MONTAGNE pretends, but he exaggerates a little, that
Guic-

Guicciardin no where ascribes any one action to a virtuous, but every one to a vicious principle. Something like this has been reproached to Tacitus: and, notwithstanding all the sprightly loose observations of Montagne in one of his essays, where he labours to prove the contrary, read Plutarch's comparisons in what language you please: I am of Bodin's mind, you will perceive that they were made by a Greek. In short, my lord, the favourable opportunites of corrupting history have been often interrupted, and are now over in so many countries, that truth penetrates even into those where lying continues still to be part of the policy ecclesiastical and civil; or where, to say the best we can say, truth is never suffered to appear, till she has passed through hands, out of which she seldom returns entire and undefiled.

But it is time I should conclude this head, under which I have touched some of those reasons that shew the folly of endeavouring to establish universal Pyrrhonism in matters of history, because there are few histories without some lies, and none without some mistakes; and that prove the body of history which we possess, since ancient

cient memorials have been so critically examined, and modern memorials have been so multiplied, to contain in it such a probable series of events easily distinguishable from the improbable, as force the assent of every man who is in his senses, and are therefore sufficient to answer all the purposes of the study of history. I might have appealed perhaps without entering into the argument at all, to any man of candour whether his doubts concerning the truth of history have hindered him from applying the examples he has met with in it, and from judging of the present, and sometimes of the future, by the past? whether he has not been touched with reverence and admiration, at the virtue and wisdom of some men, and of some ages; and whether he has not felt indignation and contempt for others? whether EPAMINONDAS, or PHOCION, for instance, the DECII, or the SCIPIOS, have not raised in his mind a flame of public spirit, and private virtue? and whether he has not shuddered with horror at the prescriptions of MARIUS and SYLLA, at the treachery of THEODOTUS and ACHILLAS, and at the consummate cruelty of an infant king? Quis non con-
" tra Marii arma, et contra Syllæ pro-
" scrip-

"scriptionem concitatur? Quis non Theo-
"doto, et Achillæ, et ipsi puero, non
"puerile auso facinus, infestus est?" If
all this be a digression therefore, your lordship will be so good as to excuse it.

II. What has been said concerning the multiplicity of histories, and of historical memorials wherewith our libraries abound since the resurrection of letters happened, and the art of printing began, puts me in mind of another general rule, that ought to be observed by every man who intends to make a real improvement, and to become wiser as well as better, by the study of history. I hinted at this rule in a former letter, where I said that we should neither grope in the dark, nor wander in the light. History must have a certain degree of probability, and authenticity, or the examples we find in it will not carry a force sufficient to make due impressions on our minds, nor to illustrate nor to strengthen the precepts of philosophy and the rules of good policy. But besides, when histories have this necessary authenticity and probability, there is much discernment to be employed in the choice and the use we make of them. Some are to be read, some are to be studied; and some may be neglected entirely,

entirely, not only without detriment, but with advantage. Some are the proper objects of one man's curiosity, some of another's, and some of all men's, but all history is not an object of curiosity for any man. He who improperly, wantonly, and absurdly makes it so, indulges a sort of canine appetite: the curiosity of one, like the hunger of the other, devours ravenously and without distinction whatever falls in it's way, but neither of them digests. They heap crudity upon crudity, and nourish and improve nothing but their distemper. Some such characters I have known, though it is not the most common extreme into which men are apt to fall. One of them I knew in this country. He joined, to a more than athletic strength of body, a prodigious memory; and to both a prodigious industry. He had read almost constantly twelve or fourteen hours a day, for five and twenty or thirty years; and had heaped together as much learning as could be crowded into an head. In the course of my acquaintance with him, I consulted him once or twice, not oftener; for I found this mass of learning of as little use to me as to the owner. The man was communicative enough; but nothing was distinct in his mind. How could it be otherwise? he had never spared
time

time to think, all was employed in reading. His reason had not the merit of common mechanism. When you press a watch or pull a clock, they answer your question with precision; for they repeat exactly the hour of the day, and tell you neither more nor less than you desire to know. But when you asked this man a question, he overwhelmed you by pouring forth all that the several terms or words of your question recalled to his memory: and if he omitted any thing, it was that very thing to which the sense of the whole question, should have led him and confined him. To ask him a question, was to wind up a spring in his memory, that rattled on with vast rapidity, and confused noise, till the force of it was spent: and you went away with all the noise in your ears, stunned and un-informed. I never left him that I was not ready to say to him, " Dieu " vous fasse la grace de devenir moins sa- " vant!" a wish that La Mothe le Vayer mentions upon some occasion or other, and that he would have done well to have applied to himself upon many.

He who reads with discernment and choice, will acquire less learning, but more knowledge: and as this kowledge is collected with design, and cultivated with art

LETTER IV.

and method, it will be at all times of immediate and ready use to himself and others

Thus useful arms in magazines we place,
All rang'd in order; and dispos'd with grace:
Nor thus alone the curious eye to please;
But to be found, when need requires, with ease:

You remember the verses, my lord, in our friend's Essay on criticism, which was the work of his childhood almost; but is such a monument of good sense and poetry as no other, that I know, has raised in his riper years.

HE who reads without this discernment and choice, and, like BODIN's pupil, resolves to read all, will not have time, no nor capacity neither, to do any thing else. He will not be able to think, without which it is impertinent to read; nor to act, without which it is impertinent to think. He will assemble materials with much pains, and purchase them at much expence, and have neither leisure nor skill to frame them into proper scantlings, or to prepare them for use. To what purpose should he husband his time, or learn architecture? he has no design to build. But then to what purpose all these quarries of stone, all these mountains of sand and lime, all these forests of oak and

deal?

deal? "Magno impendio temporum, mag-
"na alienarum aurium moleftia, laudatio
"hæc conftat, O hominem literatum!
"Simus hoc titulo rufticiore contenti, O
"virum bonum!" We may add, and SE-
NECA might have added in his own ftile,
and according to the manners and characters of his own age, another title as ruftic,
and as little in fafhion, " O virum fapientia
"fua fimplicem, et fimplicitate fua fapien-
"tem! O virum utilem fibi, fuis, reipub-
"licæ, et humano generi!" I have faid
perhaps already, but no matter, it cannot
be repeated too often, that the drift of all
philofophy, and of all political fpeculations,
ought to be the making us better men, and
better citizens. Thofe ftudies which have
no intention towards improving our moral
characters, have no pretence to be ftiled
philofophical. "Quis eft enim." fays TULLY
in his Offices, " qui nullis officii præceptis
" tradendis, philofphum fe audeat dicere?"
Whatever political fpeculations, inftead of
preparing us to be ufeful to fociety, and to
promote the happinefs of mankind, are
only fyftems for gratifying private ambition,
and promoting private interefts at the public expence; all fuch, I fay, deferve to be
burnt, and the authors of them to ftarve,
like MACHIAVEL, in a jail.

OF THE

STUDY OF HISTORY.

LETTER V.

I. The great use of history, properly so called, as distinguished from the writings of mere annalists and antiquaries.

II. Greek and Roman historians.

III. Some idea of a complete history.

IV. Further cautions to be observed in this study, and the regulation of it according to the different professions, and situations of men: above all, the use to be made of it (1) by divines, and (2) by those who are called to the service of their country.

I REMEMBER my last letter ended abruptly, and a long interval has since passed: so that the thread I had then spun has slipt from me. I will try to recover it, and to pursue the task your lordship has obliged me to continue. Besides the pleasure of obeying your orders, it is likewise of some advantage to myself, to re-collect

collect my thoughts, and refume a ftudy in which I was converfant formerly. For nothing can be more true than that faying of SOLON reported by PLATO, though cenfured by him, impertinently enough in one of his wild books of laws—" Affidue addifcens, ad " fenium venio." The truth is, the moft knowing man in the courfe of the longeft life, will have always much to learn, and the wifeft and beft much to improve. This rule will hold in the knowledge and improvement to be acquired by the ftudy of hiftory: and therefore even he who has gone to this fchool in his youth, fhould not neglect it in his age. " I read in LIVY, fays MONTAGNE, " what another man does not: and PLU-" TARCH read there what I do not." Juft fo the fame man may read at fifty what he did not read in the fame book at five-and-twenty: at leaft I have found it fo, by my own experience, on many occafions.

By comparing, in this ftudy, the experience of other men and other ages with our own, we improve both: we analyfe, as it were, philofophy. We reduce all the abftract fpeculations of ethics, and all the general rules of human policy, to their firft principles. With thefe advantages, every man may, though few men do, advance daily towards thofe ideas, thofe increated effences

ces a Platonist would say, which no human creature can reach in practice, but in the nearest approaches to which the pefection of our nature consists; because every approach of this kind renders a man better, and wiser for himself, for his family, for the little community of his own country, and for the great community of the world. Be not surprised, my lord, at the order in which I place these objects. Whatever order divines and moralists, who contemplate the duties belonging to these objects, may place them in, this is the order they hold in nature: and I have always thought that we might lead ourselves and others to private virtue, more effectually by a due observation of this order, than by any of those sublime refinements that pervert it.

> Self-Love but serves the virtuous mind to wake;
> As the small pebble stirs the peaceful lake.
> The centre mov'd, a circle strait succeeds;
> Another still, and still another spreads:
> Friend, parent, neighbour, first it will embrace,
> His country next, and next all human race.

So sings our friend Pope, my lord, and so I believe. So I shall prove too, if I mistake not, in an epistle I am about to write to him, in order to complete a sett that were wrote some years ago,

A MAN

A MAN of my age, who returns to the study of history, has no time to lose, because he has little to live: a man of your lordship's age has no time to lose, because he has much to do. For different reasons therefore the same rules will suit us. Neither of us must grope in the dark, neither of us must wander in the light. I have done the first formerly a good deal; " ne verba mihi daren-
" tur; ne aliquid esse, in hac recondita an-
" tiquitatis scientia, magni ac secreti boni
" judicaremus." If you take my word, you will throw none of your time away in the same manner: and I shall have the less regret for that which I have misspent, if I persuade you to hasten down from the broken traditions of antiquity, to the more entire, as well as more authentic histories of ages more modern. In the study of these we shall find many a complete series of events, preceded by a deduction of their immediate and remote causes, related in their full extent, and accompanied with such a detail of circumstances, and characters, as may transport the attentive reader back to the very time, make him a party to the councils, and an actor in the whole scene of affairs. Such draughts as these, either found in history, or extracted by our own application
from

from it, and such alone, are truly useful. Thus history becomes what she ought to be, and what she has been sometimes called, "magistræ vitæ." the mistress, like philosophy of human life. If she is not this, she is at best " nuntia vetustatis," the gazette of antiquity, or a dry register of useless anecdotes. SUETONIUS says that TIBERIUS used to enquire of the grammarians, "quæ mater " Hecubæ? quod Achillis nomen inter vir- " gines fuisset? quid Syrenes cantare sint so- litæ?" SENECA mentions certain Greek authors, who examined very accurately, whether ANACREON loved wine or women best, whether SAPPHO was a common whore, with other points of equal importance: and I make no doubt but that a man, better acquainted than I have the honour to be with the learned persons of our own country, might find some who have discovered several anecdotes concerning the giant ALBION, concerning SAMOTHES the son of BRITO the grand-son of JAPHET, and concerning BRUTUS who led a colony into our island after the siege of Troy, as the others repeopled it after the deluge. But ten millions of such anecdotes as these, though they were true; and complete authentic volumes of Egyptian or Chaldean, of Greek or Latin, of Gallic or British, of French or Saxon records, would be of no

value

value in my sense, because of no use towards our improvement in wisdom and virtue; if they contained nothing more than dynasties and gnealogies, and a bare mention of remarkable events in the order of time, like journals, chronological tables, or dry and meagre annals.

I say the same of all those modern compositions in which we find rather the heads of history, than any thing that deserves to be called history. Their authors are either abridgers or compilers. The first do neither honour to themselves nor good to mankind: for surely the abridger is in a form below the translater: and the book, at least the history; that wants to be abridged, does not deserve to be read. They have done anciently a great deal of hurt by substituting many a bad book in the place of a good one; and by giving occasion to men, who contented themselves with extracts and abridgments, to neglect, and, through their neglect, to lose the invaluable originals: for which reason I curse CONSTANTINE PORPHYROGENETES as heartily as I do GREGORY. The second are of some use, as far as they contribute to preserve public acts, and dates, and the memory of great events. But they who are thus employed
have

have seldom the means of knowing those private passages on which all public transactions depend, and as seldom the skill and the talents necessary to put what they do know well together: they cannot see the working of the mine, but their industry collects the matter that is thrown out. It is the business, or it should be so, of others to separate the pure ore from the dross, to stamp it into coin, and to enrich not encumber mankind. When there are none sufficient to this task, there may be antiquaries, and there may be journalists or annalists, but there are no historians.

It is worth while to observe the progress that the Romans and the Greeks made towards history. The Romans had journalists or annalists from the very beginning of their state. In the sixth century, or very near it at soonest, they began to have antiquaries, and some attempts were made towards writing of history. I call these first historical productions attempts only or essays: and they were no more, neither among the Romans nor among the Greeks. "Græ- "ci ipsi sic initio scriptitarunt ut noster Cato, ut Pictor, ut Piso." It is Antony, not the triumvir, my lord, but his grandfather the famous orator, who says this in the second book

book of TULLY De oratore; he adds afterwards, " Itaque qualis apud Græcos PHE-
" RECYDES, HELLANICUS, ACUSILAUS, alii-
" que permulti, talis noster CATO, et PIC-
" TOR, et PISO." I know that ANTONY
speaks here strictly of defect of style and
want of oratory. They were " tantummodo
" narratores, non exornatores," as he expresses himself: but as they wanted style and
skill to write in such a manner as might answer all the ends of history, so they wanted
materials. PHERECYDES wrote something
about IPHIGENIA, and the festivals of BACCHUS. HELLANICUS was a poetical historian, and ACUSILAUS engraved genealogies
on plates of brass. PICTOR, who is called by
LIVY " scriptorum antiquissimus," published, I think, some short annals of his own
time. Neither he nor PISO could have sufficient materials for the history of Rome; nor
CATO, I presume, even for the antiquities
of Italy. The Romans, with the other people of that country, were then just rising
out of barbarity, and growing acquainted
with letters; for those that the Grecian colonies might bring into Sicily, and the southern parts of Italy, spread little, or lasted
little, and made in the whole no figure. And
whatever learning might have flourished
among the ancient Etrurians, which was

perhaps

perhaps at moſt nothing better than augury, and divination, and ſuperſtitious rites, which were admired and cultivated in ignorant ages, even that was almoſt entirely worn out of memory. Pedants, who would impoſe all the traditions of the four firſt ages of Rome, for authentic hiſtory, have inſiſted much on certain annals, of which mention is made in the very place I have juſt now quoted. "Ab initio rerum Romana-" rum," ſays the ſame interlocutor, "uſque " ad P. Mucium pontificem maximum, " res omnes ſingulorum annorum manda-" bat literis pontifex maximus, efferebat-" que in album, et proponebat tabulam do-" mi, poteſtas ut eſſet populo cognoſcendi; " idemque etiam nunc annales maximi nomi-" nantur." But, my lord, be pleaſed to take notice, that the very diſtinction I make is made here between a bare annaliſt and an hiſtorian: "erat hiſtoria nihil aliud," in " theſe early days, niſi annalium confectio." Take notice likewiſe, by the way, that Livy, whoſe particular application it had been to ſearch into this matter, affirms poſitively that the greateſt part of all public and private monuments, among which he ſpecifies theſe very annals, had been deſtroyed in the ſack of Rome by the Gauls: and Plutarch cites Clodius for the ſame aſſertion, in the life of Numa Pompilius. Take notice, in the

laſt

last place, of that which is more immediately to our present purpose. These annals could contain nothing more than short minutes or memorandums hung up in a table at the tontiff's house, like the rules of the game in a billiard room, and much such history as we have in the epitomes prefixed to the books of LIVY or of any other historian, in lapidary inscriptions, or in some modern almanacks. Materials for history they were no doubt, but scanty and insufficient; such as those ages could produce when writing and reading were accomplishments so uncommon, that the prætor was directed by law, clavum pangere, to drive a nail into the door of a temple, that the number of years might be reckoned by the number of nails. Such in short as we have in monkish annalists, and other ancient chroniclers of nations now in being: but not such as can entitle the authors of them to be called historians, nor can enable others to write history in that fullness in which it must be written to become a lesson of ethics and politics. The truth is, nations, like men, have their infancy: and the few passages of that time, which they retain, are not such as deserved most to be remembered; but such as, being most proportioned to that age, made the strongest impressions on their minds. In those nations that preserve their dominion

long

long and grow up to manhood, the elegant as well as the neceffary arts and fciences are improved to fome degree of perfection: and hiftory, that was at firft intended only to record the names, or perhaps the general characters of fome famous men, and to tranfmit in grofs the remarkable events of every age to pofterity, is raifed to anfwer another, and a nobler end.

II. Thus it happened among the Greeks, but much more among the Romans, notwithftanding the prejudices in favour of the former even among the latter. I have fometimes thought that Virgil might have juftly afcribed to his countrymen the praife of writing hiftory better, as well as that of affording the noblelt fubjects for it, in thofe famous verfes,* where the different excellencies of the two nations are fo finely touched: but he would have weakened perhaps by lengthening, and have flattened the climax. Open Herodotus, you are en-

---

* Excudent alii fpirantia mollius æra.
Credo equidem: vivos ducent de marmore vultus;
Orabunt caufas melius: cœlique meatus
Defcribent radio, et furgentia fidera dicent:
Tu regere imperio populos, Romane memento:
Hæ tibi erunt artes; pacifque imponere morem,
Parcere fubjectis, et debellare fuperbos.

tertained by an agreeable story-teller, who meant to entertain, and nothing more. Read THUCIDIDES or XENOPHON, you are taught indeed as well as entertained: and the statesman or the general, the philosopher or the orator, speaks to you in every page. They wrote on subjects on which they were well informed, and they treated them fully: they maintained the dignity of history, and thought it beneath them to vamp up old traditions, like the writers of their age and country, and to be the trumpeters of a lying antiquity. The Cyropædia of XENOPHON may be objected perhaps; but if he gave it for a romance, not an history, as he might for aught we can tell, it is out of the case: and if he gave it for an history, not a romance, I should prefer his authority to that of HERODOTUS or any other of his countrymen. But however this might be, and whatever merit we may justly ascribe to these two writers, who were almost single in their kind, and who treated but small portions of history; certain it is in general, that the levity as well as loquacity of the Greeks made them incapable of keeping up to the true standard of history: and even POLYBIUS and DIONESIUS of Halicarnassus must bow to the great Roman authors. Many principal men

men of that commonwealth wrote memorials of their own actions and their own times: SYLLA, CÆSAR, LABIENUS, POLLIO, AUGUSTUS, and others. What writers of memorials, what compilers of the materia historica were these? What genius was necessary to finish up the pictures that such masters had sketched? Rome afforded men that were equal to the task. Let the remains, the precious remains of SALLUST, of LIVY, and of TACITUS, witness this truth. When TACITUS wrote, even the appearances of virtue had been long proscribed, and taste was grown corrupt as well as manners. Yet history preserved her integrity, and her lustre. She preserved them in the writings of some whom TACITUS mentions, in none perhaps more than his own; every line of which out-weighs whole pages of such a rhetor as FAMIANUS STRADA. I single him out among the moderns, because he had the foolish presumption to censure TACITUS, and to write history himself: and your lordship will forgive this short excursion in honour of a favourite author.

WHAT a school of private and public virtue had been opened to us at the resurrection of learning, if the latter historians of the Roman common-wealth, and the first of the succeeding monarchy, had come down to us entire? The few that are come down, though broken and imperfect, compose the best body of history that we have, nay the only body of ancient history that deserves to be an object of study. It fails us indeed most at that remarkable and fatal period, where our reasonable curiosity is raised the highest. Livy employed five-and forty books to bring his history down to the end of the sixth century, and the breaking out of the third Punic war: but he employed ninety-five to bring it down from thence to the death of DRUSUS; that is, through the course of one hundred and twenty or thirty years. APION, DION CASSIUS and others, nay even PLUTARCH included, make us but poor amends for what is lost of LIVY. Among all the adventitious helps by which we endeavour to supply this loss in some degree, the best are those that we find scattered up and down in the works of TULLY. His Orations particularly, and his Letters, contain many curious anecdotes and instructive reflections, concerning the intrigues and machinations that were carried on against liberty, from CATILINE's conspiracy to CÆSAR's. The state of the government, the constitution and temper of the several parties,

parties, and the characters of the principal persons who figured at that time on the public stage, are to be seen there in a stronger and truer light than they would have appeared perhaps if he had wrote purposely on this subject, and even in those memorials which he somewhere promises Atticus to write. " Excudam aliquod Heraclidium opus, " quod lateat in thesauris tuis." He would hardly have unmasked in such a work, as freely as in familiar occasional letters, Pompey, Cato, Brutus, nay himself; the four men of Rome, on whose praises he dwelt with the greatest complacency. The age in which Livy flourished abounded with such materials as these: they were fresh, they were authentic; it was easy to procure them, it was safe to employ them. How he did employ them in executing the second part of his design, we may judge by his execution of the first: and, I own to your lordship, I should be glad to exchange, if it were possible, what we have of this history for what we have not. Would you not be glad, my lord, to see, in one stupendous draught, the whole progress of that government from liberty to servitude? the whole series of causes and effects, apparent and real, public and private? those which all men saw, and all good men lamented and opposed at the time; and those which were so disguised to the prejudices, to the partialities of a divided people, and even to the corruption of mankind, that many did not, and that many could pretend they did not discern them, till it was too late to resist them? I am sorry to say it, this part of the Roman story would be not only more curious and more authentic than the former, but of more immediate and more important application to the present state of Britain. But it is lost; the loss is irreparable, and your lordship will not blame me for deploring it.

III. They who set up for scepticism may not regret the loss of such an history: but this I will be bold to assert to them, that an history must be wrote on this plan, and must aim at least at these perfections, or it will answer sufficiently none of the intentions of history. That it will not answer sufficiently the intention I have insisted upon in these letters, that of instructing posterity by the example of former ages, is manifest: and I think it is as manifest, that an history cannot be said even to relate faithfully, and inform us truly, that does not relate fully, and inform us of all that is necessary to make a
true

true judgment concerning the matters contained in it. Naked facts, without the causes that produced them, and the circumstances that accompanied them, are not sufficient to characterise actions or counsels. The nice degrees of wisdom and of folly, of virtue and of vice, will not only be undiscoverable in them; but we must be very often unable to determine under which of these characters they fall in general. The sceptics I am speaking of are therefore guilty of this absurdity: the nearer an history comes to the true idea of history, the better it informs, and the more it instructs us, the more worthy to be rejected it appears to them. I have said and allowed enough to content any reasonable man about the uncertainty of history. I have owned that the best are defective, and I will add in this place an observation which did not, I think, occur to me before. Conjecture is not always distinguished perhaps as it ought to be; so that an ingenious writer may sometimes do very innocently, what a malicious writer does very criminally as often as he dares, and as his malice requires it; he may account for events after they have happened, by a system of causes and conduct that did not really produce them, though it might possibly or even probably have produced them.

But this observation, like several others, becomes a reason for examining and comparing authorities, and for preferring some, not for rejecting all. DAVILA, a noble historian surely, and one whom I should not scruple to confess equal in many respects to LIVY, as I should not scruple to prefer his countryman GUICCIARDIN to THUCYDIDES in every respect: DAVILA, my lord, was accused, from the first publication of his history, or at least was suspected, of too much refinement and subtilty, in developing the secret motives of actions, in laying the causes of events too deep, and deducing them often through a series of progression too complicated, and too artistly wrought. But yet the suspicious person who should reject this historian upon such general inducements as these, would have no grace to oppose his suspicions to the authority of the first duke of EPERNON, who had been an actor, and a principal actor too, in many of the scenes that DAVILA recites. GIRARD, secretary to this duke, and no contemptible biographer, relates, that this history came down to the place where the old man resided in Gasgogny, a little before his death; that he read it to him, that the duke confirmed the truth of the narrations in it, and seemed only surprized by what means the author

could

could be so well informed of the most secret councils and measures of those times.

IV. I have said enough on this head, and your lordship may be induced perhaps, by what I have said, to think with me, that such histories as these, whether ancient or modern, deserve alone to be studied. Let us leave the credulous learned to write history without materials, or to study those who do so; to wrangle about ancient traditions, and to ring different changes on the same set of bells. Let us leave the sceptics, in modern as well as ancient history, to triumph in the notable discovery of the ides of one month mistaken for the calends of another, or in the various dates and contradictory circumstances which they find in weekly gazettes, and monthly mercuries. Whilst they are thus employed, your lordship and I will proceed, if you please, to consider more closely, than we have yet done, the rule mentioned above; that I mean of using discernment and choice in the study of the most authentic history, that of not wandering in the light, which is as necessary as that of not groping in the dark.

MAN is the subject of every history; and to know him well, we must see him
and

and confider him, as hiftory alone can prefent him to us, in every age, in every country, in every ftate, in life and in death. Hiftory therefore of all kinds, of civilized and uncivilized, of ancient and modern nations, in fhort of all hiftory, that defcends to a fufficient detail of human actions and characters, is ufeful to bring us acquainted with our fpecies, nay with ourfelves. To teach and to inculcate the general principles of virtue, and the general rules of wifdom and good policy, which refult from fuch details of actions and characters, comes for the moft part, and always fhould come, exprefsly and directly into the defign of thofe who are capable of giving fuch details: and therefore whilft they narrate as hiftorians, they hint often as philofophers, they put into our hands, as it were, on every proper occafion, the end of a clue, that ferves to remind us of fearching, and to guide us in the fearch of that truth which the example before us either eftablifhes or illuftrates. If a writer neglects this part, we are able however to fupply his neglect by our own attention and induftry: and when he gives us a good hiftory of Peruvians or Mexicans, of Chinefe or Tartars, of Mufcovites or Negroes, we may blame him,

but

but we muſt blame ourſelves much more, if we do not make it a good leſſon of philoſophy. This being the general uſe of hiſtory, it is not to be neglected: Every one may make it, who is able to read and to reflect on what he reads: and every one who makes it will find, in his degree, the benefit that ariſes from an early acquaintance contracted in this manner with mankind. We are not only paſſengers or ſojourners in this world, but we are abſolute ſtrangers at the firſt ſteps we make in it. Our guides are often ignorant, often unfaithful. By this map of the country, which hiſtory ſpreads before us, we may learn, if we pleaſe, to guide ourſelves. In our journey through it, we are beſet on every ſide. We are beſieged ſometimes even in our ſtrongeſt holds. Terrors and temptations, conducted by the paſſions of other men, aſſault us: and our own paſſions, that correſpond with theſe, betray us. Hiſtory is a collection of the journals of thoſe who have travelled through the ſame country, and been expoſed to the ſame accidents; and their good and their ill ſucceſs are equally inſtructive. In this purſuit of knowledge an immenſe field is opened to us: general hiſtories, ſacred and prophane; the hiſtories of particular countries, particular

cular events, particular orders, particular men; memorials, anecdotes, travels. But we muſt not ramble in this field without diſcernment or choice, nor even with theſe muſt we ramble too long.

As to the choice of authors, who have wrote on all theſe various ſubjects, ſo much has been ſaid by learned men concerning all thoſe that deſerve attention, and their ſeveral characters are ſo well eſtabliſhed, that it would be a ſort of pedantic affectation to lead your lordſhip through ſo voluminous, and at the ſame time ſo eaſy, a detail. I paſs it over therefore in order to obſerve, that as ſoon as we have taken this general view of mankind, and of the courſe of human affairs in different ages and different parts of the world, we ought to apply, and, the ſhortneſs of human life conſidered, to confine ourſelves almoſt entirely, in our ſtudy of hiſtory, to ſuch hiſtories as have an immediate relation to our profeſſions, or to our rank and ſituation in the ſociety to which we belong. Let me inſtance in the profeſſion of divinity, as the nobleſt and the moſt important.

(1) I have ſaid ſo much concerning the care which divines of all religions have taken

in the corruption of hiftory, that I fhould have anathemas pronounced againft me, no doubt, in the eaft and the weft, by the dairo, the mufti, and the pope, if thefe letters were fubmitted to ecclefiaftical cenfure; for furely, my lord, the clergy have a better title, than the fons of Apollo, to be called " genus irritabile vatum." What would it be, if I went about to fhew, how many of the Chriftian clergy abufe, by mifreprefentation and falfe quotation, the hiftory they can no longer corrupt? And yet, this tafk would not be even to me, an hard one. But as I mean to fpeak in this place of chriftian divines alone, fo I mean to fpeak of fuch of them particularly as may be called divines without any fneer; of fuch of them, for fome fuch I think theré are, as believe themfelves, and would have mankind believe; not for temporal, but fpiritual intereft, not for the fake of the clergy, but for the fake of mankind. Now it has been long matter of aftonifhment to me, how fuch perfons as thefe could take fo much filly pains to eftablifh myftery on metaphyfics, revelation on philofophy, and matters of fact on abftract reafoning? A religion founded on the authority of a divine miffion, confirmed by prophecies and miracles, appeals to facts: and the facts muft

be

be proved as all other facts that pass for authentic are proved! for faith, so reasonable after this proof is absurd before it. If they are thus proved, the religion will prevail without the assistance of so much profound reasoning: if they are not thus proved, the authority of it will sink in the world, even with this assistance. The divines object in their disputes with atheists, and they object very justly, that these men require improper proofs; proofs that are not suited to the nature of the subject, and then cavil that such proofs are not furnished. But what then do they mean, to fall into the same absurdity themselves in their disputes with theists, and to din improper proofs in ears that are open to proper proofs? The matter is of great moment, my lord, and I make no excuse for the zeal which obliges me to dwell a little on it. A serious and honest application to the study of ecclesiastical history, and every part of prophane history and chronology relative to it, is incumbent on such reverend persons as are here spoken of, on a double account: because history alone can furnish the proper proofs, that the religion they teach is of God; and because the unfair manner, in which these proofs have been and are daily furnished, creates prejudices, and gives advantages

vantages against christianity that require to be removed. No scholar will dare to deny, that false history, as well as sham miracles, has been employed to propagate Christianity formerly: and whoever examines the writers of our own age will find the same abuse of history continued. Many and many instances of this abuse might be produced. It is grown into custom, writers copy one another, and the mistake that was committed, or the falshood that was invented by one, is adopted by hundreds.

ABBADIE says in his famous book, that the gospel of St. MATTHEW is cited by CLEMENS bishop of Rome, a disciple of the Apostles; that BARNABAS cites it in his epistle; that IGNATIUS and POLYCARPE receive it; and that the same fathers, that give testimony for MATTHEW, give it likewise for MARK. Nay your lordship will find, I believe, that the present bishop of London, in his third pastoral letter, speaks to the same effect. I will not trouble you nor myself with any more instances of the same kind. Let this, which occurred to me as I was writing, suffice. It may well suffice; for I presume the fact advanced by the minister and the bishop is a mistake. If the fathers of the first century do mention

tion some passages that are agreeable to what we read in our evangelists, will it follow that these fathers had the same gospels before them? To say so is a manifest abuse of history, and quite inexcusable in writers that knew, or should have known, that these fathers made use of other gospels, wherein such passages might be contained, or they might be preserved in unwritten tradition. Besides which I could almost venture to affirm that these fathers of the first century do not expressly name the gospels we have of MATTHEW, MARK, LUKE, and JOHN, To the true reasons that have been given why those who make divinity their profession, should study history, particularly ecclesiastical history, with an honest and serious application; in order to support christianity against the attacks of unbelievers, and to remove the doubts and prejudices that the unfair proceedings of men of their own order have raised in minds candid but not implicit, willing to be informed, but curious to examine; to these, I say, we may add another consideration, that seems to me of no small importance. Writers of the Roman religion have attempted to shew, that the text of the holy writ is on many accounts insufficient to be the sole criterion of orthodoxy: I apprehend too that

that they have fhewn it. Sure I am that experience, from the firft promulgation of chriftianity to this hour, fhews abundantly with how much eafe and fuccefs the moft oppofite, the moft extravagant, nay the moft impious opinions, and the moft contradictory faiths, may be founded on the fame text, and plaufibly defended by the fame authority. Writers of the reformed religion have erected their batteries againft tradition; and the only difficulty they had to encounter in this enterprize lay in levelling and pointing their cannon fo as to avoid demolifhing in one common ruin, the traditions they retain, and thofe they reject. Each fide has been employed to weaken the caufe and explode the fyftem of his adverfary: and, whilft they have been fo employed, they have jointly laid their axes to the root of chriftianity: for thus men will be apt to reafon upon what they have advanced. " If the text has not " that authenticity, clearnefs, and preci- " fion which are neceffary to eftablifh it as a " divine and a certain rule of faith and " practice; and if the tradition of the " church, from the firft ages of it till the " days of LUTHER and CALVIN, has been " corrupted itfelf, and has ferved to cor- " rupt the faith and practice of chriftians;

" there

"there remains at this time no standard
"at all of christianity. By consequence
"either this religion was not originally of di-
"vine institution, or else God has not
"provided effectually for preserving the
"genuine purity of it, and the gates of
"hell have actually prevailed, in con-
"tradiction to his promise, against the
"church." The best effect of this reasoning that can be hoped for, is, that men
should fall into theism, and subscribe to the
first proposition: he must be worse than an
atheist who can affirm the last. The dilem-
ma is terrible, my lord. Party-zeal and
private interest have formed it: the common interest of christianity is deeply concerned to solve it. Now, I presume, it can
never be solved without a more accurate
examination, not only of the christian but
of the Jewish system, than learned men have
been hitherto impartial enough and saga-
cious enough to take, or honest enough to
communicate. Whilst the authenticity and
sense of the text of the Bible remain as difputable, and whilst the tradition of the
church remains as problematical, to say no
worse, as the immense labours of the christian divines in several communions have
made them appear to be; christianity may
lean on the civil and ecclesiastical power,
and

and be supported by the forcible influence of education: but the proper force of religion, that force which subdues the mind and awes the conscience by conviction, will be wanting.

I had reason therefore to produce divinity, as one instance of those professions that require a particular application to the study of some particular parts of history: and since I have said so much on the subject in my zeal for christianity, I will add this further. The resurrection of letters was a fatal period; the christian system has been attacked, and wounded too, very severely since that time. The defence has been better made indeed by modern divines, than it had been by ancient fathers and apologists. The moderns have invented new methods of defence, and have abandoned some posts that were not tenable: but still there are others, in defending which they lie under great disadvantages. Such are various facts, piously believed in former times, but on which the truth of christianity has been rested very imprudently in more enlightened ages; because the falsity of some, and the gross improbability of others are so evident, that, instead of answering the purpose for which they

LETTER V.

were invented, they have rendered the whole tenor of ecclesiastical history and tradition precarious, ever since a strict but just application of the rules of criticism has been made to them, I touch these things lightly; but if your lordship reflects upon them, you will find reason perhaps to think as I do, that it is high time the clergy in all christian communions should join their forces, and establish those historical facts, which are the foundations of the whole system, on clear and unquestionable historical authority, such as they require in all cases of moment from others; reject candidly what cannot be thus established; and pursue their enquiries in the same spirit of truth through all the ages of the church; without any regard to historians, fathers, or councils, more than they are strictly entitled to on the face of what they have transmitted to us on their own consistency, and on the concurrence of other authority. Our pastors would be thus, I presume, much better employed than they generally are. Those of the clergy who make religion merely a trade, who regard nothing more than the subsistence it affords them, or in higher life the wealth and power they enjoy by the means of it, may say to themselves, that it will last their time, or that

policy

policy and reason of state will preserve the form of a church when the spirit of religion is extinct. But those whom I mentioned above, those who act for spiritual not temporal ends, and are desirous that men should believe and practise the doctrines of christianity, as well as go to church and pay tithes, will feel and own the weight of such considerations as these; and agree, that however the people have been, and may be still amused, yet christianity has been in decay ever since the resurrection of letters; and that it cannot be supported as it was supported before that æra, nor by any other way than that which I propose, and which a due application to the study of history, chronology, and criticism, would enable our divines to pursue, no doubt, with success.

I might instance, in other professions, the obligation men lie under of applying themselves to certain parts of history, and I can hardly forbear doing it in that of the law; in it's nature the noblest and most beneficial to mankind, in its abuse and debasement the most sordid and the most pernicious. A lawyer now is nothing more, I speak of ninety-nine in an hundred at least, to use some of Tully's words, " nisi leguleius qui-
" dam

LETTER V.

" dam cautus, et acutus præco actionum,
" cantor formularum, auceps syllabarum."
But there have been lawyers that were orators,
philosophers, historians: there have been
BACONS and CLARENDONS, my lord. There
will be none such any more, till, in some
better age, true ambition or the love of
fame prevails over avarice; and till men find
leisure and encouragement to prepare themselves for the exercise of this profession, by
climbing up to the " vantage ground," so
my lord BACON calls it, of science: instead
of groveling all their lives below, in a mean
but gainful application to all the little arts
of chicane. Till this happen, the profession of the law will scarce deserve to be
ranked among the learned professions: and
whenever it happens, one of the vantage
grounds, to which men must climb, is metaphysical, and the other, historical knowledge. They must pry into the secret recesses of the human heart, and become well
acquainted with the whole moral world, that
they may discover the abstract reason of all
laws: and they must trace the laws of particular states, especially of their own, from
the first rough sketches to the more perfect
draughts; from the first causes or occasions
that produced them, through all the effects, good and bad, that they produced.
But

Of the STUDY of HISTORY.

But I am running infenfibly into a fubject, which would detain me too long from one that relates more immediately to your lordfhip, and with which I intend to conclude this long letter.

(2) I PASS from the confideration of thofe profeffions to which particular parts or kinds of hiftory feem to belong: and I come to fpeak of the ftudy of hiftory, as a neceffary mean to prepare men for the difcharge of that duty which they owe to their country, and which is common to all the members of every fociety that is conftituted according to the rules of right reafon, and with a due regard to the common good. I have met, in St. REAL's works, or fome other French book, with a ridicule caft on private men who make hiftory a political ftudy, or who apply themfelves in any manner to affairs of ftate. But the reflection is too general. In governments fo arbitrary by their conftitution, that the will of the prince is not only the fupreme but the fole law, it is fo far from being a duty that it may be dangerous, and muft be impertinent in men, who are not called by the prince to the adminiftration of public affairs, to concern themfelves about it, or to fit themfelves for it. The fole vocation

there is the favour of the court; and whatever defignation God makes by the talents he beftows, though it may ferve, which it feldom ever does, to direct the choice of the prince, yet I prefume that it cannot become a reafon to particular men, or create a duty on them, to devote themfelves to the public fervice. Look on the Turkifh government, fee a fellow taken, from rowing in a common paffage-boat, by the caprice of the prince: fee him invefted next day with all the power the foldans took under the caliphs, or the mayors of the palace under the fucceffors of CLOVIS: fee a whole empire governed by the ignorance, inexperience, and arbitrary will of this tyrant, and a few other fubordinate tyrants, as ignorant and unexperienced as himfelf. In France indeed, though an abfolute government, things go a little better. Arts and fciences are encouraged, and here and there an example may be found of a man who has rifen by fome extraordinary talents, amidft innumerable examples of men who have arrived at the greateft honours and higheft pofts by no other merit than that of affiduous fawning, attendances, or of fkill in fome defpicable puerile amufement; in training wafps, for inftance, to take regular flights like hawks, and ftoop at flies. The nobility

lity of France, like the children of tribute among the ancient Saracens and modern Turks, are set apart for wars. They are bred to make love, to hunt, and to fight: and, if any of them should acquire knowledge superior to this, they would acquire that which might be prejudicial to themselves, but could not become beneficial to their country. The affairs of state are trusted to other hands. Some have risen to them by drudging long in business: some have been made ministers almost in the cradle: and the whole power of the government has been abandoned to others in the dotage of life. There is a monarchy, an absolute monarchy too, I mean that of China, wherein the administration of the government is carried on, under the direction of the prince, ever since the dominion of the Tartars has been established, by several classes of Mandarins, and according to the deliberation and advice of several orders of councils: the admission to which classes and orders depends on the abilities of the candidates, as their rise in them depends on the behaviour they hold, and the improvements they make afterwards. Under such a government, it is neither impertinent nor ridiculous, in any of the subjects who are invited by their circumstances, or pushed
to

to it by their talents, to make the history of their own and of other countries a political study, and to fit themselves by this and all other ways for the service of the public. It is not dangerous neither; or an honour, that outweighs the danger, attends it: since private men have a right by the ancient constitution of this government, as well as councils of state, to represent to the prince the abuses of his administration. But still men have not there the same occasion to concern themselves in the affairs of the state, as the nature of a free government gives to the members of it. In our own country, for in our own the forms of a free government at least are hitherto preserved, men are not only designed for the public service by the circumstances of their situation, and their talents, all which may happen in others: but they are designed to it by their birth in many cases, and in all cases they may dedicate themseves to this service, and take, in different degrees, some share in it, whether they are called to it by the prince or no. In absolute governments, all public service is to the prince, and he nominates all those that serve the public. In free governments, there is a distinct and a principal service due to the state. Even the king, of such a limited monarchy as ours, is but the

the firſt ſervant of the people. Among his ſubjects ſome are appointed by the conſtitution, and others are elected by the people, to carry on the exerciſe of the legiſlative power jointly with him, and to controul the executive power independently on him. Thus your lordſhip is born a member of that order of men, in whom a third part of the ſupreme power of the government reſides: and your right to the exerciſe of the power belonging to this order not being yet opened, you are choſen into another body of men, who have different power and a different conſtitution, but who poſſeſs another third part of the ſupreme legiſlative authority, for as long a time as the commiſſion or truſt delegated to them by the people laſts. Free-men, who are neither born to the firſt, nor elected to the laſt, have a right however to complain, to repreſent, to petition, and, I add, even to do more in caſes of the utmoſt extremity. For ſure there cannot be a greater abſurdity, than to affirm, that the people have a remedy in reſiſtance, when their prince attempts to enſlave them; but that they have none, when their repreſentatives ſell themſelves and them.

THE ſum of what I have been ſaying is, that, in free governments, the public ſervice
is

is not confined to those whom the prince appoints to different posts in the administration under him; that there the care of the state is the care of multitudes; that many are called to it in a particular manner by their rank, and by other circumstances of their situation; and that even those whom the prince appoints are not only answerable to him, but like him, and before him, to the nation, for their behaviour in their several posts. It can never be impertinent nor ridiculous therefore in such a country, whatever it might be in the habit of St. Real's, which was Savoy I think; or in Peru, under the Incas, where, Garcilasso de la Vega says, it was lawful for none but the nobility to study—for men of all degrees to instruct themselves in those affairs wherein they may be actors, or judges of those that act, or controulers of those that judge. On the contrary it is incumbent on every man to instruct himself, as well as the means and opportunities he has permitted, concerning the nature and interests of the governments, and those rights and duties that belong to him, or to his superiors, or to his inferiors. This in general; but in particular, it is certain that the obligations under which we lie to serve our country increase, in proportion to the ranks we hold, and the other circumstances

stances of birth, fortune, and situation that call us to this service; and, above all, to the talents which God has given us to perform it.

It is in this view, that I shall address to your lordship, whatever I have further to say on the study of history.

LETTER VI.

From what period modern history is peculiarly useful to the service of our country, viz.

From the end of the fifteenth century to the present.

The division of this into three particular periods:

In order to a sketch of the history and state of Europe from that time.

SINCE then you are, my lord, by your birth, by the nature of our government, and by the talents God has given you, attached for life to the service of your country; since genius alone cannot enable you to go through this service with honour to yourself, and advantage to your country; whether you support, or whether you oppose the administrations that arise; since a
great

great stock of knowledge, acquired betimes and continually improved, is necessary to this end; and since one part of this stock must be collected from the study of history, as the other part is to be gained by observation and experience; I come now to speak to your lordship of such history as has an immediate relation to the great duty and business of your life, and of the method to be observed in this study. The notes I have by me, which were of some little use thus far, serve me no farther, and I have no books to consult. No matter; I shall be able to explain my thoughts without their assistance, and less liable to be tedious. I hope to be as full and as exact on memory alone, as the manner in which I shall treat the subject, requires me to be.

I say then, that however closely affairs are linked together in the progression of governments, and how much soever events that follow, are dependant on those that precede, the whole connection diminishes to sight as the chain lengthens; till at last it seems to be broken, and the links that are continued from that point, bear no proportion nor any similitude to the former. I would not be understood to speak only of those great changes, that are wrought by a

cor-

concurrence of extraordinary events; for inſtance the expulſion of one nation, the deſtruction of one government, and the eſtabliſhment of another: but even of thoſe that are wrought in the ſame governments and among the ſame people, ſlowly and almoſt imperceptibly, by the neceſſary effects of time, and flux condition of human affairs. When ſuch changes as theſe happen in ſeveral ſtates about the ſame time, and conſequently affect other ſtates by their vicinity, and by many different relations which they frequently bear to one another; then is one of thoſe periods formed, at which the chain ſpoken of is ſo broken as to have little or no real or viſible connection with that which we ſee continue. A new ſituation different from the former, begets new intereſts in the ſame proportion of difference; not in this or that particular ſtate alone, but in all thoſe that are concerned by vicinity or other relations, as I ſaid juſt now, in one general ſyſtem of policy. New intereſts beget new maxims of government, and new methods of conduct. Theſe, in their turns, beget new manners, new habits, new cuſtoms. The longer this new conſtitution of affairs continues, the more will this difference increaſe: and although ſome analogy may remain long between what preceded and what succeeded such a period, yet will this analogy soon become an object of mere curiosity, not of profitable enquiry. Such a period therefore is, in the true sense of the words, an epocha or an æra, a point of time at which you stop, or from which you reckon forward. I say forward; because we are not to study in the present case, as chronologers compute, backward. Should we persist to carry our researches much higher, and to push them even to some other period of the same kind, we should misemploy our time; the causes then laid having spent themselves, the series of effects derived from them being over, and our concern in both consequently at an end. But a new system of causes and effects, that subsists in our time, and whereof our conduct is to be a part, arising at the last period, and all that passes in our time being dependent on what has passed since that period, or being immediately relative to it, we are extremely concerned to be well informed about all those passages. To be entirely ignorant about the ages that precede this æra would be shameful. Nay some indulgence may be had to a temperate curiosity in the review of them. But to be learned about them is a ridiculous affectation in any man who means to be useful to the present age.

age. Down to this æra let us read hiftory; from this æra, and down to our own time, let us ftudy it.

The end of the fifteenth century feems to be juft fuch a period as I have been defcribing, for thofe who live in the eighteenth, and who inhabit the weftern parts of Europe. A little before, or a little after this point of time, all thofe events happened, and all thofe revolutions began, that have produced fo vaft a change in the manners, cuftoms, and interefts of particular nations, and in the whole policy, ecclefiaftical and civil, of thefe parts of the world. I muft defcend here into fome detail, not of hiftories, collections, or memorials; for all thefe are well enough known: and though the contents are in the heads of few, the books are in the hands of many. But inftead of fhewing your lordfhip where to look, I fhall contribute more to your entertainment and inftruction, by marking out, as well as my memory will ferve me to do it, what you are to look for, and by furnifhing a kind of clue to your ftudies. I fhall give, according to cuftom, the firft place to religion,

LETTER VI.

A view of the ecclesiastical government of Europe from the beginning of the sixteenth century.

OBSERVE then, my lord, that the demolition of the papal throne was not attempted with success till the beginning of the sixteenth century. If you are curious to cast your eyes back, you will find BERENGER in the eleventh, who was soon silenced; ARNOLDUS in the same, who was soon hanged; VALDO in the twelfth, and our WICKLIFF in the fourteenth, as well as others perhaps whom I do not recollect. Sometimes the doctrines of the church were alone attacked; and sometimes the doctrine, the discipline and the usurpations of the pope. But little fires, kindled in corners of a dark world, were soon stifled by that great abettor of christian unity, the hangman. When they spread and blazed out, as in the case of the Albigeois and of the Hussites, armies were raised to extinguish them by torrents of blood; and such saints as DOMINIC, with the crucifix in their hands, instigated the troops to the utmost barbarity. Your lordship will find that the church of Rome was maintained by such charitable and salutary means among others, till the period spoken of: and you will be curious, I am sure, to enquire how this period came to be more fatal to her than any former conjuncture. A multitude of circumstances which you will easily trace in the histories of the fifteenth and sixteenth centuries, to go no further back, concurred to bring about this great event: and a multitude of others as easy to be traced, concurred to hinder the demolition from becoming total, and to prop the tottering fabric. Among these circumstances, there is one less complicated and more obvious than others, which was of principal and universal influence. The art of printing had been invented about forty or fifty years before the period we fix: from that time, the resurrection of letters hastened on apace; and at this period they had made great progress, and were cultivated with great application. MAHOMET the second drove them out of the east into the west; and the popes proved worse politicians than the mufties in this respect. NICHOLAS the fifth, encouraged learning, and learned men. SIXTUS the fourth was, if I mistake not, a great collector of books at least: and LEO the tenth was the patron of every art and science. The magicians themselves broke the charm by which they had bound mankind for so many ages: and the adventure of that knight-errant, who, thinking himself happy in the arms of a celestial nymph, found that he was the miserable slave of an infernal hag, was in some sort renewed. As soon as the means of acquiring and spreading information grew common, it is no wonder that a system was unravelled, which could not have been woven with success in any ages, but those of gross ignorance, and credulous superstition. I might point out to your lordship many other immediate causes, some general like this that I have mentioned, and some particular. The great schism, for instance, that ended in the begining of the fifteenth century, and in the council of Constance, had occasioned prodigious scandal. Two or three vicars of CHRIST, two or three infallible heads of the church. roaming about the world at a time, furnished matter of ridicule as well as scandal: and whilst they appealed, for so they did in effect, to the laity, and reproached and excommunicated one another, they taught the world what to think of the institution, as well as exercise of the papal authority. The same lesson was taught by the council of Pisa, that preceded, and by that of Basle,

that

that followed the Council of Conſtance. The horrid crimes of ALEXANDER the ſixth, the ſaucy ambition of JULIUS the ſecond, the immenſe profuſion and ſcandalous exactions of LEO the tenth; all theſe events and characters, following in a continued ſeries from the beginning of one century, prepared the way for the revolution that happened in the beginning of the next. The ſtate of Germany, the ſtate of England, and that of the North, were particular cauſes, in theſe ſeveral countries, of this revolution. Such were many remarkable events that happened about the ſame time, and a little before it, in theſe and in other nations; and ſuch were likewiſe the characters of many of the princes of that age, ſome of whom favoured the reformation like the elector of Saxony, on a principle of conſcience; and moſt of whom favoured it, juſt as others oppoſed it, on a principle of intereſt. This your lordſhip will diſcover manifeſtly to have been the caſe; and the ſole difference you will find between HENRY the eighth and FRANCIS the firſt, one of whom ſeparated from the pope, as the other adhered to him, is this: HENRY the eighth divided, with the ſecular clergy and his people, the ſpoil of the pope, and his ſatellites, the monks; FRANCIS the firſt divided, with the pope, the spoil of his clergy, secular and regular, and of his people. With the same impartial eye that your lordship surveys the abuses of religion, and the corruptions of the church as well as court of Rome, which brought on the reformation at this period; you will observe the characters and conduct of those who began, who propagated, and who favoured the reformation: and from your observation of these, as well as of the unsystematical manner in which it was carried on at same time in various places, and of the want of concert, nay even of charity, among the reformers, you will learn what to think of the several religions that unite in their opposition to the Roman, and yet hate one another most heartily; what to think of the several sects that have sprouted, like suckers, from the same great roots; and what the true principles are of protestant ecclesiastical policy. This policy had no being till LUTHER made his establishment in Germany; till ZWINGLIUS began another in Switzerland, which CALVIN carried on, and, like AMERICUS VESPUTIUS who followed CHRISTOPHER COLUMBUS, robbed the first adventurer of his honour; and till the reformation in our country was perfected under EDWARD the sixth and ELIZABETH.

Even

Even popish ecclesiastical policy is no longer the same since that æra. His holiness is no longer at the head of the whole western church: and to keep the part that adheres to him, he is obliged to loosen their chains, and to lighten his yoke. The spirit and pretensions of his court are the same, but not the power. He governs by expedient and management more, and by authority less. His decrees and his briefs are in danger of being refused, explained away, or evaded, unless he negociates their acceptance before he gives them, governs in concert with his flock, and feeds his sheep according to their humour and interest. In short, his excommunications, that made the greatest emperors tremble, are despised by the lowest members of his own communion; and the remaining attachment to him has been, from this æra, rather a political expedient to preserve an appearance of unity, than a principle of conscience; whatever some bigotted princes may have thought, whatever ambitious prelates and hireling scribblers may have taught, and whatever a people, worked up to enthusiasm by fanatical preachers, may have acted. Proofs of this would be easy to draw, not only from the conduct of such princes, as FERDINAND the first, and MAXIMILIAN the second, who could scarce be esteemed

esteemed papists though they continued in the pope's communion: but even from that of princes who persecuted their protestant subjects with great violence. Enough has been said, I think to shew your lordship how little need there is of going up higher than the beginning of the sixteenth century in the study of history, to acquire all the knowledge necessary at this time in ecclesiastical policy, or in civil policy as far as it is relative to this. Historical monuments of this sort are in every man's hand, the facts are sufficiently verified, and the entire scenes lie open to our observation: even that scene of solemn refined banter exhibited in the council of Trent, imposes on no man who reads PAOLO, as well as PALLAVICINI, and the letters of VARGAS.

A view of the civil government of Europe in the beginning of the sixteenth century.

I. In FRANCE.

A VERY little higher need we go, to observe those great changes in the civil constitutions of the principal nations of Europe, in the partition of power among them, and by consequence in the whole system of European policy, which have operated so strongly for more than two centuries, and which operate still. I will not affront the memory of our HENRY the seventh so much as to compare him to LEWIS the eleventh: and yet I perceive some resemblance between them; which would perhaps appear greater if PHILIP of Commines had wrote the History of HENRY as well as that of LEWIS; or if my lord BACON had wrote that of LEWIS as well as that of HENRY. This prince came to the crown of England a little before the close of the fifteenth century: and LEWIS began his reign in France about twenty years sooner. These reigns make remarkable periods in the histories of both nations.

To reduce the power, privileges, and poſſeſſions of the nobility, and to increaſe the wealth and authority of the crown, was the principal object of both. In this their ſucceſs was ſo great, that the conſtitutions of the two governments have had, ſince that time, more reſemblance, in name and in form than in reality, to the conſtitutions that prevailed before. Lewis the eleventh was the firſt, ſay the French, " qui mit " les rois hors de page." The independency of the nobility had rendered the ſtate of his predeceſſors very dependent, and their power precarious. They were the ſovereigns of great vaſſals; but theſe vaſſals were ſo powerful, that one of them was ſometimes able, and two or three of them always, to give law to the ſovereign. Before Lewis came to the crown, the Engliſh had been driven out of their poſſeſſions in France, by the poor character of Henry the ſixth, the domeſtic troubles of his reign, and the defection of the houſe of Burgundy from his alliance, much more than by the ability of Charles the ſeventh, who ſeems to have been neither a greater hero nor a greater politician than Henry the ſixth; and even than by the vigour and union of the French nobility in

his

his service. After Lewis came to the crown, Edward the fourth made a shew of carrying the war again into France: but he soon returned home, and your lordship will not be at a loss to find much better reasons for his doing so, in the situation of his affairs and the characters of his allies, than those which Philip of Commines draws from the artifice of Lewis, from his good cheer, and his pensions. Now from this time our pretensions on France were in effect given up: and Charles the bold, the last prince of the house of Burgundy, being killed, Lewis had no vassal able to molest him. He re-united the duchy of Burgundy and Artois to his crown, he acquired Provence by gift, and his son Britany by marriage: and thus France grew, in the course of a few years, into that great and compact body which we behold at this time. The History of France before this period, is like that of Germany, a complicated history of several states and several interests; sometimes concurring like members of the same monarchy, and sometimes warring on one another. Since this period, the history of France is the history of one state under a more uniform and orderly government; the history of a monarchy wherein in the prince is poffeffor of fome, as well as lord of all the great fieffees: and the authority of many tyrants centering in one, though, the people are not become more free, yet the whole fyftem of domeftic policy is entirely changed. Peace at home is better fecured, and the nation grown fitter to carry war abroad. The governors of great provinces and of ftrong fortreffes have oppofed their king, and taken arms againft his authority and commiffion fince that time: but yet there is no more refemblance between the authority and pretenfions of thefe governors, or the nature and occafions of thefe difputes, and the authority and pretenfions of the vaffals of the crown in former days, or the nature and occafions of their difputes with the prince and with one another, than there is between the ancient and the prefent peers of France. In a word, the conftitution is fo altered, that any knowledge we can acquire about it, in the hiftory that precedes this period, will ferve to little purpofe in our ftudy of the hiftory that follows it, and to lefs purpofe ftill in affifting us to judge of what paffes in the prefent age. The kings of France fince that time, more mafters at home, have been able to exert themfelves more

more abroad: and they began to do so immediately; for CHARLES the eighth, son and successor of LEWIS the eleventh, formed great designs of foreign conquests, though they were disappointed by his inability, by the levity of the nation, and by other causes. LEWIS the twelfth and FRANCIS the first, but especially FRANCIS, meddled deep in the affairs of Europe: and though the superior genius of FERDINAND called the catholic, and the star of CHARLES the fifth prevailed against them, yet the efforts they made, shew sufficiently how the strength and importance of this monarchy were increased in their time. From whence we may date likewise the rivalship of the house of France, for we may reckon that of Valois and that of Bourbon as one upon this occasion, and the house of Austria; that continues at this day, and that has cost so much blood and so much treasure in the course of it.

II. In ENGLAND.

THOUGH the power and influence of the nobility sunk in the great change that began under HENRY the seventh in England, as they did in that which began under LEWIS the eleventh in France; yet the new constitutions that these changes produced were very different. In France the lords alone lost, the king alone gained; the clergy held their possessions and their immunities, and the people remained in a state of mitigated slavery. But in England the people gained as well as the crown. The commons had already a share in the legislature; so that the power and influence of the lords being broke by HENRY the seventh, and the property of the commons increasing by the sale that his son made of church lands, the power of the latter increased of course by this change in a constitution, the forms whereof were favourable to them. The union of the roses put an end to the civil wars of York and Lancaster, that had succeeded those we commonly call the barons wars, and the humour of warring in France,

France, that had lafted near four hundred years under the Normans and Plantagenets, for plunder as well as conqueft was fpent. Our temple of JANUS was fhut by HENRY the feventh. We neither laid wafte our own nor other countries any longer: and wife laws and a wife government changed infenfibly the manners, and gave a new turn to the fpirit of our people. We were no longer the free-booters we had been. Our nation maintained her reputation in arms whenever the public intereft or the public authority required it; but war ceafed to be, what it had been, our principal and almoft our fole profeffion. The arts of peace prevailed among us. We became hufbandmen, manufacturers and merchants, and we emulated neighbouring nations in literature. It is from this time that we ought to ftudy the hiftory of our country, my lord, with the utmoft application. We are not much concerned to know with critical accuracy what were the ancient forms of our parliaments concerning which, however, there is little room for difpute from the reign of HENRY the third at leaft; nor in fhort the whole fyftem of our civil conftitution before HENRY the feventh, and of our ecclefiaftical conftitution

LETTER VI.

stitution before HENRY the eighth. But he who has not studied and acquired a thorough knowledge of them both, from these periods down to the present time, in all the variety of events by which they have been affected, will be very unfit to judge or to take care of either. Just as little are we concerned to know, in any nice detail, what the conduct of our princes, relatively to their neighbours on the continent, was before this period, and at a time when the partition of power and a multitude of other circumstances rendered the whole political system of Europe, so vastly different from that which has existed since. But he who has not traced this conduct from the period we fix, down to the present age, wants a principal part of the knowledge that every English minister of state should have. Ignorance in the respects here spoken of is the less pardonable, because we have more, and more authentic, means of information concerning this, than concerning any other period. Anecdotes enough to glut the curiosity of some persons, and to silence all the captious cavils of others, will never be furnished by any portion of history; nor indeed can they according to the nature and
course

course of human affairs: but he who is content to read and obferve, like a fenator and a ftatefman, will find in our own and in foreign hiftorians as much information as he wants, concerning the affairs of our ifland, her fortune at home, and her conduct abroad, from the fifteenth century to the eighteenth. I refer to foreign hiftorians, as well as to our own, for this feries of our own hiftory; not only becaufe it is reafonable to fee in what manner the hiftorians of other countries have related the tranfactions wherein we have been concerned, and what judgment they have made of our conduct, domeftic and foreign, but for another reafon likewife. Our nation has furnifhed as ample and as important matter, good and bad, for hiftory, as any nation under the fun: and yet we muft yield the palm in writing hiftory moft certainly to the Italians and to the French, and, I fear, even to the Germans. The only two pieces of hiftory we have, in any refpect to be compared with the ancient, are, the reign of HENRY the feventh by my lord BACON, and the Hiftory of our civil war in the laft century by your noble anceftor my lord chancellor CLARENDON. But we have no general hiftory to be compared with some of other countries: neither have we, which I lament much more, particular histories, except the two I have mentioned, nor writers of memorials nor collectors of monuments and anecdotes, to vie in number or in merit with those that foreign nations can boast; from COMMINES, GUICCIARDIN, DU BELLAY, PAOLO, DAVILA, THUANUS, and a multitude of others, down through the whole period that I propose to your lordship. But although this be true, to our shame; yet it is true likewise that we want no necessary means of information. They lie open to our industry, and our discernment. Foreign writers are for the most part scarce worth reading when they speak of our domestic affairs: nor are our English writers for the most part of greater value when they speak of foreign affairs. In this mutual defect, the writers of other countries are, I think, more excusable than ours: for the nature of our government, the political principles in which we are bred, our distinct interests as islanders, and the complicated various interests and humours of our parties, all these are so peculiar to ourselves, and so different from the notions, manners, and habits of other nations, that it is not wonderful they should be puzzled

or

or should fall into error, when they undertake to give relations of events that result from all these, or to pass any judgment upon them. But as these historians are mutually defective, so they mutually supply each other's defects. We must compare them therefore, make use of our discernment, and draw our conclusions from both. If we proceed in this manner, we have an ample fund of history in our power, from whence to collect sufficient authentic information; and we must proceed in this manner, even with our own historians of different religions, sects, and parties, or run the risque of being misled by domestic ignorance and prejudice in this case, as well as by foreign ignorance and prejudice in the other.

LETTER VI.

III. In SPAIN and the Empire.

SPAIN figured little in Europe till the latter part of the fifteenth century; till Castile and Arragon were united by the marriage of FERDINAND and ISABELLA; till the total expulsion of the Moors, and till the discovery of the West Indies. After this, not only Spain took a new form, and grew into immense power; but, the heir of FERDINAND and ISABELLA being heir likewise of the houses of Burgundy and Austria, such an extent of dominion accrued to him by all these successions, and such an addition of rank and authority by his election to the empire, as no prince had been master of in Europe from the days of CHARLES the great. It is proper to observe here how the policy of the Germans altered in the choice of an emperor, because the effects of this alteration have been great. When RODOLPHUS of Hapsburgh was chose in the year one thousand two hundred and seventy, or about that time, the poverty and the low estate of this prince, who had been marshal of the court to a king of Bohemia, was an inducement to elect him. The disorderly

orderly and lawlefs ftate of the empire made the princes of it in thofe days unwilling to have a more powerful head. But a contrary maxim took place at this æra: CHARLES the fifth and FRANCIS the firft, the two moft powerful princes of Europe, were the fole candidates; for the elector of Saxony, who is faid to have declined, was rather unable to ftand in competition with them: and CHARLES was chofen by the unanimous fuffrages of the electoral college if I miftake not. Another CHARLES, CHARLES the fourth, who was made emperor illegally enough on the depofition of LEWIS of Bavaria, and about one hundred and fifty years before, feems to me to have contributed doubly to eftablifh this maxim; by the wife conftitutions that he procured to pafs, that united the empire in a more orderly form and better fyftem of government; and by alienating the imperial revenues to fuch a degree, that they were no longer fufficient to fupport an emperor who had not great revenues of his own. The fame maxim and other circumftances have concurred to keep the empire in this family ever fince, as it had been often before; and this family having large dominions in the empire, and larger pretenfions, as well as dominions, out of it, the other states of Europe, France, Spain and England particularly, have been more concerned since this period in the affairs of Germany, than they were before it: and by confequence the hiftory of Germany, from the beginning of the fixteenth century, is of importance, and a neceffary part of that knowledge which your lordfhip defires to acquire.

The Dutch commonwealth was not formed till near a century later. But as foon as it was formed, nay even whilft it was forming, thefe provinces, that were loft to obfervation among the many that compofed the dominions of Burgundy and Auftria, became fo confiderable a part of the political fyftem of Europe, that their hiftory muft be ftudied by every man who would inform himfelf of this fyftem.

Soon after this ftate had taken being, others of a more ancient original began to mingle in thofe difputes and wars, thofe councils, negociations, and treaties, that are to be the principal objects of your lordfhip's application in the ftudy of hiftory. That of the northern crowns deferves your attention little, before the laft century.
Till

Till the election of FREDERICK the first to the crown of Denmark, and till that wonderful revolution which the first GUSTAVUS brought about in Sweden, it is nothing more than a confused rhapsody of events, in which the great kingdoms and states of Europe neither had any concern, nor took any part. From the time I have mentioned, the northern crowns have turned their counsels and their arms often southwards, and Sweden particularly, with prodigious effect.

To what purpose should I trouble your lordship with the mention of histories of other nations? they are either such as have no relation to the knowledge you would acquire, like that of the Poles, the Muscovites, or the Turks; or they are such as, having an occasional or a secondary relation to it, fall of course into your scheme; like the history of Italy for instance, which is sometimes a part of that of France, sometimes of that of Spain, and sometimes of that of Germany. The thread of history, that you are to keep, is that of the nations who are, and must always be concerned in the same scenes of action with your own These are the principal nations of the weſt. Things that have no immediate relation to your own country, or to them, are either too remote, or too minute, to employ much of your time: and their hiſtory and your own is, for all your purpoſes, the whole hiſtory of Europe.

THE two great powers, that of France and that of Auſtria, being formed, and a rivalſhip eſtabliſhed by conſequence between them; it began to be the intereſt of their neighbours to oppoſe the ſtrongeſt and moſt enterpriſing of the two, and to be the ally and friend of the weakeſt. From hence aroſe the notion of a balance of power in Europe, on the equal poize of which the ſafety and tranquillity of all muſt depend. To deſtroy the equality of this balance has been the aim of each of theſe rivals in his turn: and to hinder it from being deſtroyed, by preventing too much power from falling into one ſcale, has been the principle of all the wiſe councils of Europe, relative to France and to the houſe of Auſtria, through the whole period that began at the æra we have fixed, and ſubſiſts at this hour. To make a careful and juſt obſervation, therefore, of the riſe and decline of theſe powers, in the

two

two last centuries and in the present; of the projects which their ambition formed; of the means they employed to carry these projects on with success; of the means employed by others to defeat them; of the issue of all these endeavours in war and in negociation; and particularly, to bring your observations home to your own country and your own use, of the conduct that England held, to her honour or dishonour, to her advantage or disadvantage, in every one of the numerous and important conjunctures that happened—ought to be the principal subject of your lordship's attention in reading and reflecting on this part of modern history.

Now to this purpose you will find it of great use, my lord, when you have a general plan of the history in your mind, to go over the whole again in another method; which I propose to be this. Divide the entire period into such particular periods as the general course of affairs will mark out to you sufficiently, by the rise of new conjunctures, of different schemes of conduct, and of different theatres of action. Examine this period of history as you would

examine

examine a tragedy or a comedy; that is, take first the idea or a general notion of the whole, and after that examine every act and every scene apart. Consider them in themselves, and consider them relatively to one another. Read this history as you would that of any ancient period; but study it afterwards, as it would not be worth your while to study the other; nay as you could not have it in your power the means of studying the other, if the study was really worth your while. The former part of this period abounds in great historians: and the latter part is so modern, that even tradition is authentic enough to supply the want of good history, if we are curious to enquire, and if we hearken to the living with the same impartiality and freedom of judgment as we read the dead: and he that does one will do the other. The whole period abounds in memorials, in collections of public acts and monuments of private letters, and of treaties. All these must come into your plan of study, my lord; many not to be read through, but all to be consulted and compared. They must not lead you, I think, to your enquiries, but your enquiries must lead you to them. By joining history and that which we call the

mate-

materia historica together in this manner, and by drawing your information from both, your lordship will acquire not only that knowledge, which many have in some degree, of the great transactions that have passed, and the great events that have happened in Europe during this period, and of their immediate and obvious causes and consequences; but your lordship will acquire a much superior knowledge, and such a one as very few men possess almost in any degree, a knowledge of the true political system of Europe during this time. You will see it in it's primitive principles, in the constitutions of governments, the situations of countries, their national and true interests, the characters and the religion of people, and other permanent circumstances. You will trace it through all its fluctuations, and observe how the objects vary seldom, but the means perpetually, according to the different characters of princes and of those who govern; the different abilities of those who serve; the course of accidents, and a multitude of other irregular and contingent circumstances.

The particular periods into which the whole period should be divided, in my opinion,

opinion, are thefe. 1. From the fifteenth to the end of the fixteenth century. 2. From thence to the Pyrenean treaty. 3. From thence down to the prefent time.

YOUR lordfhip will find this divifion as apt and as proper, relatively to the particular hiftories of England, France, Spain, and Germany, the principal nations concerned, as it is relatively to the general hiftory of Europe.

THE death of queen ELIZABETH, and the acceffion of king JAMES the firft, made a vaft alteration in the government of our nation at home, and in her conduct abroad, about the end of the firft of thefe periods. The wars that religion occafioned, and ambition fomented in France, through the reigns of FRANCIS the fecond, CHARLES the ninth, HENRY the third, and a part of HENRY the fourth, ended: and the furies of the league were crufhed by this great prince, about the fame time. PHILIP the fecond of SPAIN marks this period likewife by his death, and by the exhaufted condition in which he left the monarchy he governed: which took the lead no longer in difturbing the peace of mankind, but acted

a fea second part in abetting the bigotry and ambition of FERDINAND the second and the third. The thirty years war, that devasted Germany did not begin till the eighteenth year of the seventeenth century, but the feeds of it were sowing some time before, and even at the end of the sixteenth. FERDINAND the first and MAXIMILIAN had shewn much lenity and moderation in the disputes and troubles that arose on account of religion. Under RODOLPHUS and MATTHIAS, as the succession of their cousin FERDINAND approached, the fires that were covered began to smoke and to sparkle; and if the war did not begin with this century, the preparation for it, and the expectation of it did.

THE second period ends in one thousand six hundred and sixty, the year of the restoration of CHARLES the second to the throne of England; when our civil wars, and all the disorders which CROMWELL's usurpation had produced, were over: and therefore a remarkable point of time, with respect to our country. It is no less remarkable with respect to Germany, Spain, and France.

As to Germany; the ambitious projects of the German branch of Austria had been entirely defeated, the peace of the empire had been restored, and almost a new constitution formed, or an old one revived, by the treaties of Westphalia; nay the imperial eagle was not only fallen, but her wings were clipped.

As to Spain; the Spanish branch was fallen as low twelve years afterwards, that is, in the year one thousand six hundred and sixty. PHILIP the second left his successors a ruined monarchy. He left them something worse; he left them his example and his principles of government, founded in ambition, in pride, in ignorance, in bigotry, and all the pedantry of state. I have read somewhere or other, that the war of the Low Countries alone cost him, by his own confession, five hundred and sixty-four millions, a prodigious sum in what species soever he reckoned. PHILIP the third and PHILIP the fourth followed his example and his principles of government, at home and abroad. At home, there was much form, but no good order, no œconomy, nor wisdom of policy in the state.

The

church continued to devour the state, and that monster the inquisition to dispeople the country, even more than perpetual war, and all the numerous colonies that Spain had sent to the West Indies: for your lordship will find that Philip the third drove more than nine hundred thousand Moriscoes out of his dominions by one edict, with such circumstances of inhumanity in the execution of it, as Spaniards alone could exercise, and that tribunal who had provoked this unhappy race to revolt, could alone approve. Abroad, the conduct of these princes was directed by the same wild spirit of ambition: rash in undertaking though slow to execute, and obstinate in pursuing, though unable to succeed, they opened a new sluice to let out the little life and vigour that remained in their monarchy. Philip the second is said to have been piqued against his uncle Ferdinand, for refusing to yield the empire to him on the abdication of Charles the fifth. Certain it is, that as much as he loved to disturb the peace of mankind, and to meddle in every quarrel that had the appearance of supporting the Roman and oppressing every other church, he meddled little in the affairs of Germany. But, Ferdinand and Maxi-

MILIAN dead, and the offspring of MAXI-
MILIAN extinct, the kings of Spain espoused
the interests of the other branch of their
family, entertained remote views of ambition in favour of their own branch, even
on that side, and made all the enterprizes
of FERDINAND of Gratz, both before and
after his elevation to the empire, the common cause of the house of Austria. What
compleated their ruin was this, they knew
not how to lose, nor when to yield. They
acknowledged the independency of the
Dutch commonwealth, and became the allies
of their ancient subjects, at the treaty
of Munster: but they would not forego their
usurped claim on Portugal, and they persisted
to carry on singly the war against France.
Thus they were reduced to such a lowness
of power as can hardly be parelleled in any
other case: and PHILIP the fourth was
obliged at last to conclude a peace, on terms
repugnant to his inclination, to that of his
people, to the interest of Spain, and to that
of all Europe, in the Pyrenean treaty.

As to France; this æra of the entire
fall of the Spanish power is likewise that
from which we may reckon that France
grew as formidable, as we have seen her, to
her

her neighbours, in power and pretensions. HENRY the fourth meditated great designs, and prepared to act a great part in Europe in the very beginning of this period, when RAVAILLAC stabbed him. His designs died with him, and are rather guessed at than known; for surely those which his historian PEREFIXE, and the compilers of SULLY's memorials ascribe to him, of a christian commonwealth divided into fifteen states, and of a senate to decide all differences, and to maintain this new constitution of Europe, are too chimerical to have been really his: but his general design of abasing the house of Austria, and establishing the superior power in that of Bourbon, was taken up, about twenty years after his death, by RICHELIEU, and was pursued by him and by MAZARIN with so much ability and success, that it was effected entirely by the treaties of Westphalia, and by the Pyrenean treaty: that is, at the end of the second of those periods I have presumed to propose to your lordship.

WHEN the third, in which we now are, will end, and what circumstances will mark the end of it, I know not: but this I know, that the great events and revolutions, which

LETTER VI.

have happened in the courfe of it, intereft us ftill more nearly than thofe of the two precedent periods. I intended to have drawn up an elenchus or fummary of the three, but I doubted, on further reflection, whether my memory would enable me to do it with exactnefs enough: and I faw that, if I was able to do it, the deduction would be immeafurably long. Something of this kind however it may be reafonable to attempt, in fpeaking of the laft period: which may hereafter occafion a further trouble to your lordfhip.

But to give you fome breathing time, I will poftpone it at prefent, and am in the mean while,

My Lord,

Your, &c.

LETTER VII.

A sketch of the state and history of Europe, from the Pyrenean treaty in one thousand six hundred and fifty nine, to the year one thousand six hundred and eighty eight.

THE first observation I shall make on this third period of modern history is, that as the ambition of CHARLES the fifth, who united the whole formidable power of Austria in himself, and the restless temper, the cruelty, and bigotry of PHILIP the second, were principally objects of the attention and solicitude of the councils of Europe, in the first of these periods; and as the ambition of FERDINAND the second, and the third, who aimed at nothing less than

than extirpating the proteſtant intereſt, and under that pretence ſubduing the liberties of Germany, were objects of the ſame kind in the ſecond; ſo an oppoſition to the growing power of France, or to ſpeak more properly, to the exorbitant ambition of the houſe of Bourbon, has been the principal affair of Europe, during the greateſt part of the preſent period. The deſign of aſpiring to univerſal monarchy, was imputed to CHARLES the fifth, as ſoon as he began to give proofs of his ambition and capacity. The ſame deſign was imputed to LEWIS the fourteenth, as ſoon as he began to feel his own ſtrength, and the weakneſs of his neighbours. Neither of theſe princes was induced, I believe, by the flattery of his courtiers, or the apprehenſions of his adverſaries, to entertain ſo chimerical a deſign as this would have been, even in that falſe ſenſe wherein the word univerſal is ſo often underſtood: and I miſtake very much if either of them was of a character, or in circumſtances, to undertake it. Both of them had ſtrong deſires to raiſe their families higher, and to extend their dominions farther; but neither of them had that bold and adventurous ambition which makes a conqueror and

and an hero. These apprehensions however were given wisely, and taken usefully. They cannot be given nor taken too soon when such powers as these arise; because when such powers as these are besieged as it were early, by the common policy and watchfulness of their neighbours, each of them may in his turn of strength sally forth, and gain a little ground; but none of them will be able to push their conquests far, and much less to consummate the entire projects of their ambition. Besides the occasional opposition that was given to CHARLES the fifth, by our HENRY the eighth, according to the different moods of humour he was in; by the popes, according to the several turns of their private interest, and by the princes of Germany according to the occasions or pretences that religion or civil liberty furnished, he had from his first setting out a rival and an enemy in FRANCIS the first, who did not maintain his cause " in " forma pauperis," if I may use such an expression: as we have seen the house of Austria, sue, in our days, for dominion, at the gate of every palace in Europe. FRANCIS the first was the principal in his own quarrels, paid his own armies, fought his

his own battles; and though his valour alone did not hinder CHARLES the fifth from subduing all Europe, as BAYLE, a better philologer than politician, somewhere asserts, but a multitude of other circumstances easily to be traced in history; yet he contributed by his victories, and even by his defeats, to waste the strength and check the course of that growing power. LEWIS the fourteenth had no rival of this kind in the house of Austria, nor indeed any enemy of this importance to combat, till the prince of Orange became king of Great Britain: and he had great advantages in many other respects, which it is necessary to consider, in order to make a true judgment on the affairs of Europe from the year one thousand six hundred and sixty. You will discover the first of these advantages, and such as were productive of all the rest, in the conduct of RICHELIEU and of MAZARIN. RICHELIEU formed the great design, and laid the foundations: MAZARIN pursued the design, and raised the superstructure. If I do not deceive myself extremely, there are few passages in history that deserve your lordship's attention more than the conduct that the first and greatest of these
ministers

ministers held, in laying the foundations I speak of. You will observe how he helped to embroil affairs on every side, and to keep the house of Austria at bay as it were; how he entered into the quarrels of Italy against Spain, into that concerning the Valteline, and that concerning the succession of Mantua; without engaging so deep as to divert him from another great object of his policy, subduing Rochelle and disarming the Huguenots. You will observe how he turned himself, after this was done, to stop the progress of FERDINAND in Germany. Whilst Spain fomented discontents in the court, and disorders in the kingdom of France, by all possible means, even by taking engagements with the duke of ROHAN, and for supporting the protestants; RICHELIEU abetted the same interest in Germany against FERDINAND; and in the Low Countries against Spain. The emperor was become almost the master in Germany. CHRISTIAN the fourth, king of Denmark, had been at the head of a league, wherein the United Provinces, Sweden, and Lower Saxony entered, to oppose his progress: but CHRISTIAN had been defeated by TILLY and VALSTEIN, and obliged to conclude a treaty at Lubec, where FERDINAND gave him the law. It was then that GUSTAVUS ADOLPHUS, with whom RICHELIEU made an alliance, entered into this war, and soon turned the fortune of it. The French minister had not yet engaged his master openly in the war; but when the Dutch grew impatient, and threatened to renew their truce with Spain, unless France declared; when the king of SWEDEN was killed, and the battle of Nordlingen lost; when Saxony had turned again to the side of the emperor, and Brandenburgh, and so many others had followed this example, that Hesse almost alone persisted in the Swedish alliance; then RICHELIEU engaged his master, and profited of every circumstance which the conjuncture afforded, to engage him with advantage. For, first, he had a double advantage by engaging so late: that of coming fresh into the quarrel against a wearied and almost exhausted enemy: and that of yielding to the impatience of his friends, who, pressed by their necessities and by the want they had of France, gave this minister an opportunity of laying those claims, and establishing those pretensions, in all his treaties with

Hol-

Holland, Sweden, and the princes and ſtates of the empire, on which he had projected the future aggrandiſement of France. The manner in which he engaged, and the air that he gave to his engagement, were advantages of the ſecond ſort, advantages of reputation and credit; yet were theſe of no ſmall ment in the courſe of the war, and operated ſtrongly in favour of France, as he deſigned they ſhould, even after his death, and at and after the treaties of Weſtphalia. He varniſhed ambition with the moſt plauſible and popular pretences. The elector of TREVES had put himſelf under the protection of France: and, if I remember right, he made this ſtep when the emperor could not protect him againſt the Swedes, whom he had reaſon to apprehend. No matter, the governor of Luxemburgh was ordered to ſurprize TREVES, and to ſeize the elector. He executed his orders with ſucceſs, and carried this prince priſoner into Brabant. RICHELIEU ſeized the lucky circumſtance; he reclaimed the elector: and on the refuſal of the cardinal infant, the war was declared. France, you ſee, appeared the common friend of liberty, the defender

of

of it in the Low Countries againſt the king of Spain, and in Germany againſt the emperor, as well as the protector of the princes of the empire, many of whoſe eſtates had been illegally invaded, and whoſe perſons were no longer ſafe from violence even in their own palaces. All theſe appearances were kept up in the negociations at Munſter, where Mazarin reaped what Richelieu had ſowed. The demands that France made for herſelf were very great; but the conjuncture was favourable, and ſhe improved it to the utmoſt. No figure could be more flattering than her's, at the head of theſe negociations; nor more mortifying than the emperor's, through the whole courſe of the treaty. The princes and ſtates of the empire had been treated as vaſſals by the emperor: France determined then to treat with him on this occaſion as ſovereigns, and ſupported them in this determination. Whilſt Sweden ſeemed concerned for the proteſtant intereſt alone, and ſhewed no other regard, as ſhe had no other alliance; France affected to be impartial alike to the proteſtant and to the papiſt, and to have no intereſt at heart but the common intereſt

interest of the Germanic body. Her demands were exceffive, but they were to be fatisfied principally out of the emperor's patrimonial dominions. It had been the art of her minifters to eftablifh this general maxim on many particular experiences, that the grandeur of France was a real, and would be a conftant fecurity to the rights and liberties of the empire againft the emperor: and it is no wonder therefore, this maxim prevailing, injuries, refentments, and jealoufies being frefh on one fide, and fervices, obligations, and confidence on the other, that the Germans were not unwilling France fhould extend her empire on this fide of the Rhine, whilft Sweden did the fame on this fide of the Baltic. Thefe treaties, and the immenfe credit and influence that France had acquired by them in the empire, put it out of the power of one branch of the houfe of Auftria to return the obligations of affiftance to the other, in the war that continued between France and Spain, till the Pyrenean treaty. By this treaty the fuperiority of the houfe of Bourbon over the houfe of Auftria was not only compleated and confirmed, but the great defign of uniting

the

the Spanish and the French monarchies under the former was laid.

THE third period therefore begins by a great change of the balance of power in Europe, and by the prospect of one much greater and more fatal. Before I descend into the particulars I intend to mention, of the course of affairs, and of the political conduct of the great powers of Europe in this third period; give me leave to cast my eyes once more back on the second. The reflection I am going to make seems to me important, and leads to all that is to follow.

THE Dutch made their peace separately at Munster with Spain, who acknowledged then the sovereignty and independency of their commonwealth. The French, who had been, after our ELIZABETH, their principal support, reproached them severely for this breach of faith. They excused themselves in the best manner, and by the best reasons, they could. All this your lordship will find in the monuments of that time. But I think it not improbable that they had a motive you will not find there,

and

and which it was not proper to give as a reason or excuse to the French. Might not the wise men amongst them consider even then, besides the immediate advantages that accrued by this treaty to their commonwealth, that the imperial power was fallen; that the power of Spain was vastly reduced; that the house of Austria was nothing more than the shadow of a great name, and that the house of Bourbon was advancing, by large strides, to a degree of power as exorbitant, and as formidable as that of the other family had been in the hands of CHARLES the fifth, of PHILIP the second, and lately of the two FERDINANDS? might they not foresee, even then, what happened in the course of very few years, when they were obliged, for their own security, to assist their old enemies the Spaniards against their old friends the French? I think they might. Our CHARLES the first was no great politician, and yet he seemed to discern that the balance of power was turning in favour of France, some years before the treaties of Westphalia. He refused to be neuter, and threatened to take part with Spain, if the French pursued the design of besieging Dunkirk and
Grave-

Graveline, according to a concert taken between them and the Dutch, and in purfuance of a treaty for dividing the Spanifh Low Countries, which RICHELIEU had negociated. CROMWELL either did not difcern this turn of the balance of power, long afterwards when it was much more vifible; or, difcerning it, he was induced by reafons of private intereft to act againft the general intereft of Europe. CROMWELL joined with France againft Spain, and though he got Jamaica and Dunkirk, he drove the Spaniards into a neceffity of making a peace with France, that has difturbed the peace of the world almoft fourfcore years, and the confequences of which have well-nigh beggared in our times the nation he enflaved in his. There is a tradition, I have heard it from perfons who lived in thofe days, and I believe it came from THURLOE, that CROMWELL was in treaty with Spain, and ready to turn his arms againft France when he died. If this fact was certain, as little as I honour his memory, I fhould have fome regret that he died fo foon. But whatever his intentions were, we muft charge the Pyrenean treaty, ty, and the fatal consequences of it, in a great measure to his account. The Spaniards abhorred the thought of marrying their Infanta to Lewis the fourteenth. It was on this point that they broke the negociation Lionne had begun: and your lordship will perceive, that if they resumed it afterwards, and offered the marriage they had before rejected, Cromwell's league with France was a principal inducement to this alteration of their resolutions.

The precise point at which the scales of power turn like that of the solstice in either tropic, is imperceptible to common observation: and, in one case as in the other, some progress must be made in the new direction, before the change is perceived. They who are in the sinking scale, for in the political balance of power, unlike to all others, the scale that is empty sinks, and that which is full rises; they who are in the sinking scale do not easily come off from the habitual prejudices of superior wealth, or power, or skill, or courage, nor from the confidence that these prejudices inspire. They who are in the rising scale do not immediately feel their strength, nor assume that confidence in it which successful experience gives them afterwards. They who are the most concerned to watch the variations of this balance, mis-judge often in the same manner, and from the same prejudices. They continue to dread a power no longer able to hurt them, or they continue to have no apprehensions of a power that grows daily more formidable. Spain verified the first observation at the end of the second period, when, proud and poor, and enterprizing and feeble, she still thought herself a match for France. France verified the second observation at the beginning of the third period, when the triple alliance stopped the progress of her arms, which alliances much more considerable were not able to effect afterwards. The other principal powers of Europe, in their turns, have verified the third observation in both it's parts, through the whole course of this period.

When Lewis the fourteenth took the adminiſtration of affairs into his own hands, about the year one thouſand ſix hundred and ſixty, he was in the prime of his age, and had, what princes ſeldom have, the advantages of youth and thoſe of experience together. Their education is generally bad; for which reaſon royal birth, that gives a right to the throne among other people, gave an abſolute excluſion from it among the Marmalukes. His was, in all reſpects, except one, as bad as that of other princes. He jeſted ſometimes on his own ignorance; and there were other defects in his character, owing to his education, which he did not ſee. But Mazarin had initiated him betimes into the myſteries of his policy. He had ſeen a great part of thoſe foundations laid, on which he was to raiſe the fabric of his future grandeur: and as Mazarin finiſhed the work that Richelieu began, he had the leſſons of one, and the examples of both, to inſtruct him. He had acquired habits of ſecrecy and method, in buſineſs; of reſerve, diſcretion, decency, and dignity, in behaviour. If he was not the greateſt king, he was

the best actor of majesty at least, that
ever filled a throne. He by no means
wanted that courage which is commonly called bravery, though the want of it
was imputed to him in the midst of
his greatest triumphs: nor that other
courage, less ostentatious and more rare-
ly found, calm, steady, persevering resolution: which seems to arise less from
the temper of the body, and is therefore called courage of the mind. He
had them both most certainly, and I
could produce unquestionable anecdotes
in proof. He was, in one word, much
superior to any prince with whom he
had to do, when he began to govern.
He was surrounded with great cap-
tains bred in former wars, and with
great ministers bred in the same school
as himself. They who had worked
under MAZARIN, worked on the same
plan under him; and as they had the
advantage of genius, and experience
over most of the ministers of other
countries, so they had another advantage
over those who were equal or superior to them: the advantage of serving
a master whose absolute power was established; and the advantage of a situation wherein they might exert their
whole

whole capacity without contradiction; over that, for instance, wherein your lordship's great grand father was placed, at the same time, in England, and JOHN DE WIT in Holland. Among these ministers, COLBERT must be mentioned particularly upon this occasion; because it was he who improved the wealth, and consequently the power of France extremely, by the order he put into the finances, and by the encouragement he gave to trade and manufactures. The soil, the climate, the situation of France, the ingenuity, the industry, the vivacity of her inhabitants are such; she has so little want of the product of other countries, and other countries have so many real or imaginary wants to be supplied by her; that when she is not at war with all her neighbours, when her domestic quiet is preserved, and any tolerable administration of government prevails, she must grow rich at the expence of those who trade, and even of those who do not open a trade, with her. Her bawbles, her modes, the follies and extravagancies of her luxury, cost England, about the time we are speaking of, little less than eight hundred thousand pounds sterling a year, and other nations in their proportions. COLBERT made the most of all these advantageous circumstances, and whilst he filled the national spunge, he taught his successors how to squeeze it; a secret that he repented having discovered, they say, when he saw the immense sums that were necessary to supply the growing magnificence of his master.

THIS was the character of LEWIS the fourteenth, and this was the state of his kingdom at the beginning of the present period. If his power was great, his pretensions were still greater. He had renounced, and the Infanta with his consent had renounced, all right to the succession of Spain, in the strongest terms that the precaution of the councils of Madrid could contrive. No matter; he consented to these renunciations, but your lordship will find by the letters of MAZARIN, and by other memorials, that he acted on the contrary principle, from the first, which he avowed soon afterwards. Such a power, and such pretensions

tenfions fhould have given, one would think, an immediate alarm to the reft of Europe. PHILIP the fourth was broken and decayed, like the monarchy he governed. One of his fons died, as I remember, during the negociations that preceded the year one thoufand fix hundred and fixty: and the furvivor, who was CHARLES the fecond, rather languifhed, than lived, from the cradle to the grave. So dangerous a contingency therefore, as the union of the two monarchies of France and Spain, being in view forty years together; one would imagine that the principal powers of Europe had the means of preventing it conftantly in view during the fame time. But it was otherwife. France acted very fyftematically from the year one thoufand fix hundred and fixty, to the death of king CHARLES the fecond of Spain. She never loft fight of her great object, the fucceffion to the whole Spanifh monarchy; and fhe accepted the will of the king of SPAIN in favour of the duke of ANJOU. As fhe never loft fight of her great object during this time, fo fhe loft no opportunity of increafing creasing her power, while she waited for that of succeeding in. her pretensions. The two branches of Austria were in no condition of making a considerable opposition to her designs and attempts. Holland, who of all other powers was the most concerned to oppose them, was at that time under two influences that hindered her from pursuing her true interest. Her true interest was to have used her utmost endeavours to unite closely and intimately with England on the restoration of king CHARLES. She did the very contrary. JOHN DE WIT, at the head of the Louvestein faction, governed. The interest of his party was to keep the house of Orange down; he courted therefore the friendship of France, and neglected that of England. The alliance between our nation and the Dutch was renewed, I think, in one thousand six hundred and sixty two; but the latter had made a defensive league with France a little before, on the supposition principally of a war with England. The war became inevitable very soon. CROMWELL had chastised them for their usurpations in trade,

and

and the outrages and cruelties they had committed; but he had not cured them. The same spirit continued in the Dutch, the same resentments in the English: and the pique of merchants became the pique of nations. France entered into the war on the side of Holland; but the little assistance she gave the Dutch shewed plainly enough that her intention was to make these two powers waste their strength against one another, whilst she extended her conquests in the Spanish Low Countries. Her invasion of these provinces obliged DE WIT to change his conduct. Hitherto he had been attached to France in the closest manner, had led his republic to serve all the purposes of France, and had renewed with the marshal D'ESTRADES a project of dividing the Spanish Netherlands between France and Holland, that had been taken up formerly, when RICHELIEU made use of it to flatter their ambition, and to engage them to prolong the war against Spain. A project not unlike to that which was held out to them by the famous preliminaries, and the extravagant barrierrier-treaty, in one thoufand feven hundred and nine; and which engaged them to continue a war on the principle of ambition, into which they had entered with more reafonable and more moderate views.

As the private intereft of the two DE WITS hindered that common-wealth from being on her guard, as early as fhe ought to have been, againft France; fo the miftaken policy of the court of England, and the fhort views, and the profufe temper of the prince who governed, gave great advantages to LEWIS the fourteenth in the purfuit of his defigns. He bought Dunkirk: and your lordfhip knows how great a clamour was raifed on that occafion againft your noble anceftor; as if he alone had been anfwerable for the meafure, and his intereft had been concerned in it. I have heard our late friend Mr. GEORGE CLARK, quote a witnefs, who was quite unexceptionable, but I cannot recall his name at prefent, who, many years after all thefe tranfactions, and the death of my lord CLARENDON, affirmed, that the earl of SANDWICH

wich had owned to him, that he himself gave his opinion, among many others,
officers, and ministers, for selling Dunkirk. Their reasons could not be good, I
presume to say; but several, that might
be plausible at that time, are easily guef-
sed. A prince like king Charles, who
would have made as many bad bargains
as any young spendthrift, for money,
finding himself thus backed, we may
assure ourselves, was peremptorily determined to sell: and whatever your great
grandfather's opinion was, this I am able
to pronounce upon my own experience,
that his treaty for the sale is no proof he
was of opinion to sell. When the resolution of selling was once taken, to
whom could the sale be made? To the
Dutch? No. This measure would have
been at least as impolitic, and, in
that moment, perhaps more odious
than the other. To the Spaniards?
They were unable to buy: and, as
low as their power was sunk, the principle of opposing it still prevailed. I
have sometimes thought that the Spaniards, who were forced to make peace
with Portugal, and to renounce all
claim

claim to that crown, four or five years afterwards, might have been induced to take this refolution then, if the regaining Dunkirk without any expence had been a condition propofed to them; and that the Portuguefe, who, notwithftanding their alliance with England and the indirect fuccours that France afforded them, were little able, after the treaty efpecially, to fupport a war againft Spain, might have been induced to pay the price of Dunkirk, for fo great an advantage as immediate peace with Spain, and the extinction of all foreign pretences on their crown. But this fpeculation concerning events fo long ago paffed is not much to the purpofe here. I proceed therefore to obferve, that notwithftanding the fale of Dunkirk, and the fecret leanings of our court to that of France, yet England was firft to take the alarm, when LEWIS the fourteenth invaded the Spanifh Netherlands in one thoufand fix hundred and fixty feven: and the triple alliance was the work of an Englifh minifter. It was time to take this alarm; for from the moment that the king of FRANCE claimed a right to the county of Burgundy, the dutchy

of

of Brabant, and other portions of the Low Countries as devolved on his queen by the death of her father PHILIP the fourth, he pulled off the mask entirely. Volumes were written to establish, and to refute this supposed right. Your lordship no doubt will look into a controversy that has employed so many pens and so many swords; and I believe you will think it was sufficiently bold in the French, to argue from customs, that regulated the course of private successions in certain provinces to a right of succeeding to the sovereignty of those provinces; and to assert the divisibility of the Spanish monarchy, with the same breath with which they asserted the indivisibility of their own; although the proofs in one case were just as good as the proofs in the other, and the fundamental law of indivisibility was at least as good a law in Spain, as either this or the Salique law was in France. But however proper it might be for the French and Austrian pens to enter into long discussions, and to appeal, on this great occasion, to the rest of Europe; the rest of Europe had a short objection to make to the plea of France, which

which no sophisms, no quirks of law, could evade. Spain accepted the renunciations as a real security: France gave them as such to Spain, and in effect to the rest of Europe. If they had not been thus given, and thus taken, the Spaniards would not have married their Infanta to the king of FRANCE, whatever distress they might have endured by the prolongation of the war. These renunciations were renunciations of all rights whatsoever to the whole Spanish monarchy, and to every part of it. The provinces claimed by France at this time were parts of it. To claim them, was therefore to claim the whole; for if the renunciations were no bar to the rights accruing to MARY THERESA on the death of her father PHILIP the fourth, neither could they be any to the rights that would accrue to her, and her children, on the death of her brother CHARLES the second: an unhealthful youth, and who at this instant was in immediate danger of dying; for to all the complicated distempers he brought into the world with him, the small-pox was added. Your lordship sees how the fatal contingency of uniting the two mon-

monarchies of France and Spain ſtared mankind in the face; and yet nothing, that I can remember, was done to prevent it: not ſo much as a guarantee given, or a declaration made to aſſert the validity of theſe renunciations, and for ſecuring the effect of them. The triple alliance indeed ſtopped the progreſs of the French arms, and produced the treaty of Aix la Chapelle. But England, Sweden, and Holland, the contracting powers in this alliance, ſeemed to look, and probably did look, no farther. France kept a great and important part of what ſhe had ſurprized or raviſhed, or purchaſed; for we cannot ſay with any propriety that ſhe conquered: and the Spaniards were obliged to ſet all they ſaved to the account of gain. The German branch of Auſtria had been reduced very low in power and in credit under FERDINAND the third, by the treaties of Weſtphalia, as I have ſaid already. LEWIS the fourteenth maintained, during many years, the influence theſe treaties had given him among the princes and ſtates of the empire. The famous capitulation made at Franckfort on the election of LEOPOLD, who ſucceeded FERDINAND about the year one thouſand ſix hundred and
fifty

fifty seven, was encouraged by the intrigues of France: and the power of France was looked upon as the sole power that could ratify and secure effectually the observation of the conditions then made. The league of the Rhine was not renewed I believe after the year one thousand six hundred and sixty six; but though this league was not renewed, yet some of these princes and states continued in their old engagement with France: whilst others took new engagements on particular occasions, according as private and sometimes very paltry interests, and the emissaries of France in all their little courts, disposed them. In short the princes of Germany shewed no alarm at the growing ambition and power of Lewis the fourteenth, but contributed to encourage one, and to confirm the other. In such a state of things the German branch was little able to assist the Spanish branch against France, either in the war that ended by the Pyrenean treaty, or in that we are speaking of here, the short war that began in one thousand six hundred and sixty seven, and was ended by the treaty of Aix la Chapelle, in one thousand six hundred and sixty eight. But it was not this alone that disabled the emperor from acting

with

with vigour in the cause of his family then, nor that has rendered the house of Austria a dead weight upon all her allies ever since. Bigotry, and its inseparable companion, cruelty, as well as the tyranny and avarice of the court of Vienna, created in those days, and has maintained in ours, almost a perpetual diversion of the imperial arms from all effectual opposition to France. I mean to speak of the troubles in Hungary. Whatever they became in their progress, they were caused originally by the usurpations and persecutions of the emperor, and when the Hungarians were called rebels first, they were called so for no other reason than this, that they would not be slaves. The dominion of the emperor being less supportable than that of the Turks, this unhappy people opened a door to the latter to infest the empire, instead of making their country what it had been before, a barrier against the Ottoman power. France became a sure, though secret ally of the Turks, as well as the Hungarians, and has found her account in it, by keeping the emperor in perpetual alarms on that side, while she has ravaged the empire and the Low Countries on the other. Thus we saw, thirty two years ago, the arms of France and Bavaria in possession of Passau, and the malcontents of Hungary in the suburbs of Vienna. In a word, when Lewis the fourteenth made the first essay of his power, by the war of one thousand six hundred and sixty seven, and founded, as it were, the councils of Europe concerning his pretensions on the Spanish succession, he found his power to be great beyond what his neighbours or even he perhaps thought it: great by the wealth, and greater by the united spirit of his people; greater still by the ill policy, and divided interests that governed those who had a superior common interest to oppose him. He found that the members of the triple alliance did not see, or seeing did not think proper to own that they saw, the injustice, and the consequence of his pretensions. They contented themselves to give to Spain an act of guaranty for securing the execution of the treaty of Aix la Chapelle. He knew even then how ill the guarantee would be observed by two of them at least, by England and by Sweden. The treaty itself was nothing more than a composition between the bully and the bullied. Tournay, and Lisle, and Doway, and other places that I have forgot, were yielded to him: and he restored the county of Burgundy, according to the option that Spain made, against

against the interest and expectation too of the Dutch, when an option was forced upon her. The king of SPAIN compounded for his possession: but the emperor compounded at the same time for his succession, by a private eventual treaty of partition, which the commander of GREMONVILLE and the count of AVERSBERG signed at Vienna. The same LEOPOLD, who exclaimed so loudly, in one thousand six hundred and ninety eight, against any partition of the Spanish monarchy, and refused to submit to that which England and Holland had then made, made one himself in one thousand six hundred and sixty eight, with so little regard to these two powers, that the whole ten provinces were thrown into the lot of France.

THERE is no room to wonder if such experience as LEWIS the fourteenth had upon this occasion, and such a face of affairs in Europe, raising his hopes, raised his ambition: and if, in making peace at Aix la Chapelle, he meditated a new war, the war of one thousand six hundred and seventy two; the preparations he made for it, by negociations in all parts, by alliances whereever he found ingression, and by the increase

crease of his forces, were equally proofs of ability, industry, and power. I shall not descend into these particulars: your lordship will find them pretty well detailed in the memorials of that time. But one of the alliances he made I must mention, though I mention it with the utmost regret and indignation. England was fatally engaged to act a part in this conspiracy against the peace and the liberty of Europe, nay, against her own peace and her own liberty; for a bubble's part it was, equally wicked and impolitic. Forgive the terms I use, my lord: none can be too strong. The principles of the triple alliance just and wise, and worthy of a king of England, were laid aside. Then, the progress of the French arms was to be checked, the ten provinces were to be saved, and by saving them, the barrier of Holland was to be preserved. Now, we joined our counsels and our arms to those of France, in a project that could not be carried on at all, as it was easy to foresee, and as the event shewed, unless it was carried on against Spain, the emperor, and most of the princes of Germany, as well as the Dutch; and which could not be carried on successfully, without leaving the ten provinces entirely at the mercy of France and giving her pretence and

and opportunity of ravaging the empire, and extending her conquests on the Rhine. The medal of VAN BEUNINGHEN, and other pretences that France took for attacking the states of the Low Countries, were ridiculous. They imposed on no one: and the true object of LEWIS the fourteenth was manifest to all. But what could a king of England mean? CHARLES the second had reasons of resentment against the Dutch, and just ones too no doubt. Among the rest, it was not easy for him to forget the affront he had suffered, and the loss he had sustained, when, depending on the peace that was ready to be signed, and that was signed at Breda in July, he neglected to fit out his fleet; and when that of Holland, commanded by RUYTER, with CORNELIUS DE WIT on board as deputy or commissioner of the states, burnt his ships at Chatham in June. The famous perpetual edict, as it was called, but did not prove in the event, against the election of a state-holder, which JOHN DE WIT promoted, carried, and obliged the prince of Orange to swear to maintain a very few days after the conclusion of the peace at Breda, might be another motive in the breast of king CHARLES the second: as it was certainly a pretence of revenge on the Dutch, or at least on the DE WITS and the Louveſtein faction, that ruled almoſt deſpotically in that commonwealth. But it is plain that neither theſe reaſons, nor others of a more ancient date, determined him to this alliance with France; ſince he contracted the triple alliance within four or five months after the two events, I have mentioned, happened. What then did he mean? Did he mean to acquire one of the ſeven provinces, and divide them, as the Dutch had twice treated for the diviſion of the ten, with France? I believe not; but this I believe, that his inclinations were favourable to the popiſh intereſt in general, and that he meant to make himſelf more abſolute at home; that he thought it neceſſary to this end to humble the Dutch, to reduce their power, and perhaps to change the form of their government; to deprive his ſubjects of the correſpondence with a neighbouring proteſtant and free ſtate, and of all hope of ſuccour and ſupport from thence in their oppoſition to him; in a word, to abet the deſigns of France on the continent, that France might abet his deſigns on his own kingdom. This, I ſay, I believe; and this I ſhould venture to affirm, if I had in my hands to produce, and was at liberty to quote, the private relations I have read formerly, drawn

up

up by those who were no enemies to such designs, and on the authority of those who were parties to them. But whatever king CHARLES the second meant, certain it is that his conduct established the superiority of France in Europe.

BUT this charge, however, must not be confined to him alone. Those who were nearer the danger, those who were exposed to the immediate attacks of France, and even those who were her rivals for the same succession, have either assisted her, or engaged to remain neuters, a strange fatality prevailed, and produced such a conjuncture as can hardly be paralleled in history. Your lordship will observe with astonishment even in the beginning of the year one thousand six hundred and seventy two, all the neighbours of France acting as if they had nothing to fear from her, and some as if they had much to hope, by helping her to oppress the Dutch and sharing with her the spoils of that commonwealth. "Delenda est Carthago," was the cry in England, and seemed too a maxim on the continent.

IN the course of the same year, you will observe that all these powers took the alarm, and began to unite in opposition to France. Even England thought it time to interpose in favour of the Dutch. The consequences of this alarm, of this sudden turn in the policy of Europe and of that which happened by the massacre of the DE WITS, and the elevation of the prince of ORANGE, in the government of the seven provinces, saved these provinces, and stopped the rapid progress of the arms of France. LEWIS the fourteenth indeed surprised the seven provinces in this war, as he had surprised the ten in that of one thousand six hundred and sixty seven, and ravaged defenceless countries with armies sufficient to conquer them, if they had been prepared to resist. In the war of one thousand six hundred and seventy two, he had little less than one hundred and fifty thousand men on foot, besides the bodies of English, Swiss, Italians, and Swedes, that amounted to thirty or forty thousand more. With this mighty force he took forty places in forty days, imposed extravagant conditions of peace, played the monarch a little while at Utrecht; and as soon as the Dutch recovered from their consternation, and, animated by the example of the prince of Orange and the hopes of succour, refused these conditions, he went back to Versailles, failles, and left his generals to carry on his enterprize: which they did with so little success, that Grave and Maestricht alone remained to him of all the boasted conquests he had made; and even these he offered two years afterwards to restore, if by that concession he could have prevailed on the Dutch at that time to make peace with him. But they were not yet disposed to abandon their allies; for allies now they had. The emperor and the king of Spain had engaged in the quarrel against France, and many of the princes of the empire had done the same. Not all. The Bavarian continued obstinate in his neutrality, and to mention no more, the Swedes made a great diversion in favour of France in the empire; where the duke of Hanover abetted their designs as much as he could, for he was a zealous partisan of France, though the other princes of his house acted for the common cause. I descend into no more particulars. The war that Lewis the fourteenth kindled by attacking in so violent a manner the Dutch commonwealth, and by making so arbitrary an use of his first success, became general, in the Low Countries, in Spain, in Sicily, on the upper and lower Rhine, in Denmark, in Sweden, and in the provinces of Germany belonging to these two crowns;

on the Mediterranean, the Ocean, and the Baltic. France fupported this war with advantage on every fide: and when your lordfhip confiders in what manner it was carried on againft her, you will not be furprifed that fhe did fo. Spain had fpirit, but too little ftrength to maintain her power in Sicily, where Meffina had revolted; to defend her frontier on that fide of the Pyrenees; and to refift the great efforts of the French in the Low Countries. The empire was divided; and, even among the princes who acted againft France, there was neither union in their councils, nor concert in their projects, nor order in preparations, nor vigour in execution: and, to fay the truth, there was not, in the whole confederacy, a man whofe abilities could make him a match for the prince of CONDE or the marfhal of TURENNE; nor many who were in any degree equal to LUXEMBURG, CREQUI, SCHOMBERG, and other generals of inferior note, who commanded the armies of France. The emperor took this very time to make new invafions on the liberties of Hungary, and to oppref's his proteftant fubjects. The prince of ORANGE alone acted with invincible firmnefs, like a patriot, and a hero. Neither the feductions of France nor thofe of England,
                                                        neither

neither the temptations of ambition nor those of private interest could make him swerve from the true interest of his country, nor from the common interest of Europe. He had raised more sieges, and lost more battles, it was said, than any general of his age had done. Be it so. But his defeats were manifestly due in a great measure to circumstances independent on him: and that spirit, which even these defeats could not depress, was all his own. He had difficulties in his own commonwealth; the governors of the Spanish Low Countries crossed his measures sometimes: the German allies disappointed and broke them often: and it is not improbable that he was frequently betrayed. He was so perhaps even by SOUCHES, the imperial general: a Frenchman according to BAYLE, and a pensioner of Louvois according to common report, and very strong appearances. He had not yet credit and authority sufficient to make him a centre of union to a whole confederacy, the soul that animated and directed so great a body. He came to be such afterwards; but at the time spoken of he could not take so great a part upon him. No other prince or general was equal to it; and the consequences of this defect appeared almost in every operation. France was surrounded

rounded by a multitude of enemies, all intent to demolish her power. But, like the builders of Babel, they spoke different languages; and as those could not build, these could not demolish, for want of understanding one another. France improved this advantage by her arms, and more by her negociations. Nimeghen was, after Cologn, the scene of these. England was the mediating power, and I know not whether our Charles the second did not serve her purposes more usefully in the latter, and under the character of mediator, than he did or could have done by joining his arms to her's, and acting as her ally. The Dutch were induced to sign a treaty with him, that broke the confederacy, and gave great advantage to France: for the purport of it was to oblige France and Spain to make peace on a plan to be proposed to them, and no mention was made in it of the other allies that I remember. The Dutch were glad to get out of an expensive war. France promised to restore Maestricht to them, and Maestricht was the only place that remained unrecovered of all they had lost. They dropped Spain at Nimeghen, as they had dropped France at Munster, but many circumstances concurred to give a much worse grace to their abandoning of Spain, than

than to their abandoning of France. I
need not fpecify them. This only I would
obferve: when they made a feparate
peace at Munfter, they left an ally who
was in condition to carry on the war alone
with advantage, and they prefumed to impofe no terms upon him: when they made
a feparate peace at Nimehegen, they abandoned an ally who was in no condition to
carry on the war alone, and who was reduced to accept whatever terms the common enemy prefcribed. In their great diftrefs in one thoufand fix hundred and feventy three, they engaged to reftore Maef-
tricht to the Spaniards as foon as it fhould
be retaken: it was not retaken, and they
accepted it for themfelves as the price of
the feparate peace they made with France.
The Dutch had engaged farther, to make
neither peace nor truce with the king of
FRANCE, till that prince confented to reftore
to Spain all he had conquered fince the
Pyrenean treaty. But, far from keeping
this promife in any tolerable degree, LEWIS
the fourteenth acquired, by the plan impofed on Spain at Nimeghen, befides the
county of Burgundy, fo many other countries and towns on the fide of the ten Spanifh provinces, that thefe, added to the
places he kept of thofe which had been
yielded

yielded to him by the treaty of Aix la Chapelle (for some of little consequence he restored) put into his hands the principal strength of that barrier, against which we goaded ourselves almost to death in the last great war; and made good the saying of the marshal of Schomberg, that to attack this barrier was to take the beast by his horns. I know very well what may be said to excuse the Dutch. The emperor was more intent to tyrannize his subjects on one side, than to defend them on the other. He attempted little against France, and the little he did attempt was ill ordered, and worse executed. The assistance of the princes of Germany was often uncertain, and always expensive. Spain was already indebted to Holland for great sums; greater still must be advanced to her if the war continued: and experience shewed that France was able, and would continue, to prevail against her present enemies. The triple league had stopped her progress, and obliged her to abandon the county of Burgundy; but Sweden was now engaged in the war on the side of France, as England had been in the beginning of it: and England was now privately favourable to her interests, as Sweden had been in the beginning of it. The whole

whole ten provinces would have been subdued in the course of a few campaigns more: and it was better for Spain and the Dutch too, that part should be saved by accepting a sort of composition, than the whole be risqued by refusing it. This might be alledged to excuse the conduct of the States General, in imposing hard terms on Spain; in making none for their other allies, and in signing alone: by which steps they gave France an opportunity that she improved with great dexterity of management, the opportunity of treating with the confederates one by one, and of beating them by detail in the cabinet, if I may so say, as she had often done in the field. I shall not compare these reasons, which were but two well founded in fact, and must appear plausible at least, with other considerations that might be, and were at the time, insisted upon. I confine myself to a few observations, which every knowing and impartial man must admit. Your lordship will observe, first, that the fatal principle of compounding with Lewis the fourteenth, from the time that his pretensions, his power, and the use he made of it, began to threaten Europe, prevailed still more at Nimeghen than it had prevailed at Aix: so that although he did not obtain to the full,

all

all he attempted, yet the dominions of France were by common consent, on every treaty, more and more extended; her barriers on all sides were more and more strengthened; those of her neighbours were more and more weakened; and that power, which was to assert one day, against the rest of Europe, the pretended rights of the house of Bourbon to the Spanish monarchy was more and more established, and rendered truly formidable in such hands at least, during the course of the first eighteen years of the period. Your lordship will please to observe in the second place, that the extreme weakness of one branch of Austria, and the miserable conduct of both; the poverty of some of the princes of the empire, and the disunion, and, to speak plainly, the mercenary policy of all of them; in short, the confined views, the false notions, and, to speak as plainly of my own as of other nations, the iniquity of the councils of England, not only hindered the growth of this power from being stopped in time, but nursed it up into strength almost insuperable by any future confederacy. A third observation is this: If the excuses made for the conduct of the Dutch at Nimeghen are not sufficient, they too must come in for their share in this

con-

condemnation, even after the death of the DE WITS; as they were to be condemned moſt juſtly, during that adminiſtration, for abetting and favouring France. If theſe excuſes, grounded on their inability to purſue any longer a war, the principal profit of which was to accrue to their confederates, for that was the caſe after the year one thouſand ſix hundred and ſeventy three, or one thouſand ſix hundred and ſeventy four, and the principal burden of which was thrown on them by their confederates; if theſe are ſufficient, they ſhould not have acted for decency's ſake as well as out of good policy, the part they did act in one thouſand ſeven hundred and eleven, and one thouſand ſeven hundred and twelve, towards the late queen, who had complaints of the ſame kind, in a much higher degree, and with circumſtances much more aggravating, to make of them, of the emperor, and of all the princes of Germany; and who was far from treating them, and their other allies, at that time as they treated Spain and their other allies in one thouſand ſix hundred and ſeventy eight. Immediately after the Dutch had made their peace, that of Spain was ſigned with France. The emperor's treaty with this crown and that of Sweden was concluded in the following

lowing year: and Lewis the fourteenth being now at liberty to assist his ally, whilst he had tied up the powers with whom he had treated from assisting theirs, he soon forced the king of Denmark and the elector of Brandenburg to restore all they had taken from the Swedes, and to conclude the peace of the north. In all these treaties he gave the law, and he was now at the highest point of his grandeur. He continued at this point for several years, and in this heighth of his power he prepared those alliances against it, under the weight of which he was at last well-nigh oppressed; and might have been reduced as low as the general interest of Europe required, if some of the causes, which worked now, had not continued to work in his favour, and if his enemies had not proved, in their turn of fortune, as insatiable as prosperity had rendered him.

After he had made peace with all the powers with whom he had been in war, he continued to vex both Spain and the empire, and to extend his conquests in the Low Countries, and on the Rhine, both by the pen and the sword. He erected the chambers of Metz and of Brisach, where his own subjects were prosecutors, witnesses, and

and judges all at once. Upon the decisions of these tribunals, he seized into his own hands, under the notion of dependencies and the pretence of re-unions, whatever towns or districts of country tempted his ambition, or suited his conveniency: and added, by these and by other means, in the midst of peace, more territories to those the late treaties had yielded to him, than he could have got by continuing the war. He acted afterwards, in the support of all this, without any bounds or limits. His glory was a reason for attacking Holland in one thousand six hundred and seventy two, and his conveniency a reason for many of the attacks he made on others afterwards. He took Luxemburg by force: he stole Strasburgh; he bought Caffal: and, whilst he waited the opportunity of acquiring to his family the crown of Spain, he was not without thoughts, nor hopes perhaps, of bringing into it the imperial crown likewise. Some of the cruelties he exercised in the empire may be ascribed to his disappointment in this view: I say some of them, because in the war ended by the treaty of Nimeghen, he had already exercised many. Though the French writers endeavour to slide over them, to palliate them, and to impute them particularly to the English that were in their service, for even this one of their writers has the front to advance: yet these cruelties unheard of among civilized nations, must be granted to have been ordered by the counsels, and executed by the arms of France, in the Palatinate, and in other parts.

If LEWIS the fourteenth could have contented himself with the acquisitions that were confirmed to him by the treaties of one thousand six hundred and seventy eight, and one thousand six hundred and seventy nine, and with the authority and reputation which he then gained; it is plain that he would have prevented the alliances that were afterwards formed against him; and that he might have regained his credit amongst the princes of the empire, where he had one family-alliance by the marriage of his brother to the daughter of the elector Palatine, and another by that of his son to the sister of the elector of Bavaria; where Sweden was closely attached to him, and where the same principles of private interest would have soon attached others as closely. He might have remained not only the principal, but the directing power of Europe, and have held this rank with all the glory imaginable, till the death of the king

king of Spain, or some other object of great ambition, had determined him to act another part. But, instead of this, he continued to vex and provoke all those who were, unhappily for them, his neighbours, and that, in many instances for trifles. An example of this kind occurs to me. On the death of the duke of Deux Ponts, he seized that little inconsiderable dutchy, without any regard to the indisputable right of the king of Sweden, to the services that crown had rendered him, or to the want he might have of that alliance hereafter. The consequence was, that Sweden entered, with the emperor the king of Spain, the elector of Bavaria, and the States General, into the alliance of guaranty, as it was called, about the year one thousand six hundred and eighty three, and into the famous league of Ausburg, in one thousand six hundred and eighty six.

Since I have mentioned this league, and since we may date from it a more general and a more concerted opposition to France than there had been before; give me leave to recall some of the reflections that have presented themselves to my mind, in considering what I have read, and what I have heard related, concerning the passages of that

that time. They will be of use to form our judgment concerning later paffages. If the king of FRANCE became an object of averfion on account of any invafions he made, any deviations from public faith, any barbarities exercifed where his arms prevailed, or the perfecution of his proteftant fubjects; the emperor deferved to be fuch an object, at leaft as much as he, on the fame accounts. The emperor was fo too, but with this difference relatively to the political fyftem of the weft: the Auftrian ambition and bigotry exerted themfelves in diftant countries, whofe interefts were not confidered as a part of this fyftem; for, otherwife there would have been as much reafon for affifting the people of Hungary and of Tranfylvania againft the emperor, as there had been formerly for affifting the people of the feven united provinces againft Spain, or as there have been lately for affifting them againft France: but the ambition and bigotry of LEWIS the fourteenth were exerted in the Low Countries, on the Rhine, in Italy, and in Spain, in the very midft of this fyftem, if I may fay fo, and with fuccefs that could not fail to fubvert it in time. The power of the houfe of Auftria, that had been feared too long, was feared no longer: and that of the houfe of
Bourbon,

Bourbon, by having been feared too late, was now grown terrible. The emperor was so intent on the eſtabliſhment of his abſolute power in Hungary, that he expoſed the empire doubly to deſolation and ruin for the ſake of it. He left the frontier almoſt quite defenceleſs on the ſide of the Rhine, againſt the inroads and ravages of France: and by ſhewing no mercy to the Hungarians, nor keeping any faith with them, he forced that miſerable people into alliances with the Turk, who invaded the empire, and beſieged Vienna. Even this event had no effect upon him. Your lordſhip will find, that Sobieski king of Poland, who had forced the Turks to raiſe the ſiege, and had fixed the imperial crown that tottered on his head, could not prevail on him to take thoſe meaſures by which alone it was poſſible to cover the empire, to ſecure the King of Spain, and to reduce that power who was probably one day to diſpute with him this prince's ſucceſſion. Tekeli and the malecontents made ſuch demands as none but a tyrant could refuſe, the preſervation of their ancient privileges, liberty of conſcience, the convocation of a free diet or parliament, and others of leſs importance. All was in vain. The war continued with them, and with the Turks, and

and France was left at liberty to push her enterprizes almost without oppofition, againſt Germany and the Low Countries. The diſtreſs in both was ſo great, that the States General ſaw no other expedient for ſtopping the progreſs of the French arms, than a ceſſation of hoſtilities, or a truce of twenty years; which they negociated, and which was accepted by the emperor and the king of SPAIN on the terms that LEWIS the fourteenth thought fit to offer. By theſe terms he was to remain in full and quiet poſſeſſion of all he had acquired ſince the years one thouſand ſix hundred and ſeventy eight, and one thouſand ſix hundred and ſeventy nine; among which acquiſitions that of Luxemburg and that of Straſburg were comprehended. The conditions of this truce were ſo advantageous to France, that all their intrigues were employed to obtain a definitive treaty of peace upon the ſame conditions. But this was neither the intereſt nor the intention of the other contracting powers. The imperial arms had been very ſuccefsful againſt the Turks. This ſuccefs as well as the troubles that followed upon it in the Ottaman armies, and at the Porte, gave a reaſonable expectation of concluding a peace on that ſide: and, this peace concluded, the emperor, and the

the empire, and the king of Spain would have been in a much better posture to treat with France. With these views, that were wise and just, the league of Ausburg was made between the emperor, the kings of Spain and Sweden, as princes of the empire, and the other circles and princes. This league was purely defensive. An express article declared it to be so: and as it had no other regard, it was not only conformable to the laws and constitutions of the empire, and to the practice of all nations, but even to the terms of the act of truce so lately concluded. This pretence therefore for breaking the truce, seizing the electorate of Cologn, invading the Palatinate, besieging Philipsburg, and carrying unexpected and undeclared war into the empire, could not be supported: nor is it possible to read the reasons published by France at this time, and drawn from her fears of the imperial power, without laughter. As little pretence was there to complain, that the emperor refused to convert at once the truce into a definitive treaty; since, if he had done so, he would have confirmed in a lump, and without any discussion, all the arbitrary decrees of those chambers, or courts, that France had erected to cover her usurpations; and would have given up
al-

almost a sixth part of the provinces of the empire, that France one way or other had possessed herself of. The pretensions of the Dutchess of ORLEANS on the succession of her father, and her brother, which were disputed by the then elector Palatine, and were to be determined by the laws and customs of the empire, afforded as little pretence for beginning this war, as any of the former allegations. The exclusion of the cardinal of FURSTENBERG, who had been elected to the archbishoprick of Cologn, was capable of being aggravated: but even in this case his most Christian majesty opposed his judgment and his authority against the judgment and authority of that holy father, whose eldest son he was proud to be called. In short, the true reason why LEWIS the fourteenth began that cruel war with the empire, two years after he had concluded a cessation of hostilities for twenty, was this: he resolved to keep what he had got; and therefore he resolved to encourage the Turks to continue the war. He did this effectually, by invading Germany at the very instant when the Sultan was suing for peace. Notwithstanding this, the Turks were in treaty again the following year: and good policy should have obliged the emperor, since he could not hope to carry on this war and that

against

against France, at the same time with vigour and effect, to conclude a peace with the least dangerous enemy of the two. The decision of this dispute with France could not be deferred, his designs against the Hungarians were in part accomplished, for his son was declared king, and the settlement of that crown in his family was made; and the rest of these, as well as those that he formed against the Turks, might be deferred. But the councils of Vienna judged differently, and insisted even at this critical moment on the most exorbitant terms; on some of such a nature, that the Turks shewed more humanity and a better sense of religion in refusing, than they in asking them. Thus the war went on in Hungary, and proved a constant diversion in favour of France, during the whole course of that which Lewis the fourteenth began at this time: for the treaty of Carlowitz was posterior to that of Ryswic. The empire, Spain, England, and Holland engaged in the war with France, and on them the emperor left the burden of it. In the short war of one thousand six hundred and sixty seven, he was not so much as a party, and instead of assisting the king of Spain, which, it must be owned, he was in no good condition of doing, he bargained for dividing that

that prince's fucceffion, as I have obferved above. In the war of one thoufand fix hundred and feventy two he made fome feeble efforts. In this of one thoufand fix hundred and eighty eight he did ftill lefs; and in the war which broke out at the beginning of the prefent century he did nothing, at leaft after the firft campaign in Italy, and after the engagements that England and Holland took by the grand alliance. In a word, from the time that an oppofition to France became a common caufe in Europe, the houfe of Auftria has been a clog upon it in many inftances, and of confiderable affiftance to it in none. The acceffion of England to this caufe, which was brought about by the revolution of one thoufand fix hundred and eighty eight, might have made amends, and more than amends, one would think, for this defect, and have thrown fuperiority of power and of fuccefs on the fide of the confederates, with whom fhe took part againft France. This, I fay, might be imagined, without over-rating the power of England, or undervaluing that of France; and it was imagined at that time. How it proved otherwife in the event; how France came triumphant out of the war that ended by the treaty of Ryfwic, and though fhe gave

up

up a great deal, yet preserved the greatest and the best part of her conquest and acquisitions made since the treaties of Westphalia, and the Pyrenées; how she acquired, by the gift of Spain, that whole monarchy for one of her princes, though she had no reason to expect the least part of it without a war at one time, nor the great lot of it even by a war at any time; in short, how she wound up advantageously the ambitious system she had been fifty years in waving; how she concluded a war, in which she was defeated on every side, and wholly exhausted, with little diminution of the provinces and barriers acquired to France, and with the quiet possession of Spain and the Indies to a prince of the house of Bourbon: all this, my lord, will be the subject of your researches, when you come down to the latter part of the last period of modern history.

LETTER VIII.

The same subject continued from the year one thousand six hundred and eighty-eight.

YOUR lordship will find that the objects proposed by the alliance of one thousand six hundred and eighty nine between the emperor and the States, to which England acceded, and which was the foundation of the whole confederacy then formed, were no less than to restore all things to the terms of the Westphalian and Pyrenean treaties, by the war; and to preserve them in that state, after the war, by a defensive alliance and guaranty of the same confederate powers against France. The particular as well as general meaning of this engagement was plain enough: and if it had not been so, the sense of it would have been sufficiently determined, by that separate article, in which England and Holland obliged themselves to assist the " house
of

"of Austria, in taking and keeping pos-
"session of the Spanish monarchy, when-
"ever the case should happen of the death
"of CHARLES the second, without lawful
"heirs." This engagement was double,
and thereby relative to the whole political
system of Europe, alike affected by the
power and pretensions of France. Hitherto the power of France had been alone
regarded, and her pretensions seemed to
have been forgot: or to what purpose
should they have been remembered, whilst
Europe was so unhappily constituted, that
the states, at whose expence she encreased
her power, and their friends and allies,
thought that they did enough upon every
occasion if they made some tolerable composition with her? They who were not in
circumstances to refuse confirming present,
were little likely to take effectual measures
against future usurpations. But now, as the
alarm was greater than ever, by the outrages that France had committed, and the
intrigues she had carried on; by the little
regard she had shewn to public faith, and
by the airs of authority she had assumed
twenty years together: so was the spirit
against her raised to an higher pitch, and
the means of reducing her power, or at
least of checking it, were increased. The
princes

princes and states who had neglected or favoured the growth of this power, which all of them had done in their turns, saw their error; saw the necessity of repairing it, and saw that unless they could check the power of France by uniting a power superior to her's, it would be impossible to hinder her from succeeding in her great designs on the Spanish succession. The court of England had submitted, not many years before, to abet her usurpations, and the king of England had stooped to be her pensioner. But the crime was not national. On the contrary, the nation had cried out loudly against it, even whilst it was committing: and as soon as ever the abdication of King JAMES, and the elevation of the prince of ORANGE to the throne of England happened, the nation engaged with all imaginable zeal in the common cause of Europe, to reduce the exorbitant power of France, to prevent her future and to revenge her past attempts; for even a spirit of revenge prevailed, and the war was a war of anger as well as of interest.

UNHAPPILY this zeal was neither well conducted, nor well seconded. It was zeal without success in the first of the two wars that followed the year one thoufand fix hundred and eighty-eight; and zeal without knowledge, in both of them. I enter into no detail concerning the events of thefe two wars. This only I obferve on the firft of them, that the treaties of Ryfwic were far from anfwering the ends propofed and the engagements taken by the firft grand alliance. The power of France, with refpect to extent of dominions and ftrength of barrier, was not reduced to the terms of the Pyrenean treaty, no not to thofe of the treaty of Nimeghen. Lorrain was reftored indeed with very confiderable referves, and the places taken or ufurped on the other fide of the Rhine: but then Strafburg was yielded up abfolutely to France by the emperor, and by the empire. The conceffions to Spain were great, but fo were the conquefts and the encroachments made upon her by France, fince the treaty of Nimeghen: and fhe got little at Ryfwic, I believe nothing more than fhe had faved at Nimeghen before. All thefe conceffions, however, as well as the acknowledgment of King WILLIAM, and others made by LEWIS the fourteenth after he had taken Ath and Barcelona, even during the courfe of the negociations, compared with the loffes and repeated defeats

of

of the allies and the ill state of the confederacy, surprised the generality of mankind, who had not been accustomed to so much moderation and generosity on the part of this prince. But the pretensions of the house of Bourbon on the Spanish succession remained the same. Nothing had been done to weaken them; nothing was prepared to oppose them: and the opening of this succession was visibly at hand: for CHARLES the second had been in immediate danger of dying about this time. His death could not be a remote event: and all the good queen's endeavours to be got with child had proved ineffectual. The league dissolved, all the forces of the confederates dispersed, and many disbanded; France continuing armed, her forces by sea and land encreased and held in readiness to act on all sides, it was plain that the confederates had failed in the first object of the grand alliance, that of reducing the power of France; by succeeding in which alone they could have been able to keep the second engagement, that of securing the succession of Spain to the house of Austria.

AFTER this peace, what remained to be done? In the whole nature of things there
remained

remained but three. To abandon all care, of the Spanish succession was one; to compound with France upon this succession was another; and to prepare, like her, during the interval of peace, to make an advantageous war whenever CHARLES the second should die, was a third. Now the first of these was to leave Spain, and in leaving Spain, to leave all Europe in some sort at the mercy of France; since whatever disposition the Spaniards should make of their crown, they were quite unable to support it against France; since the emperor could do little without his alliance; and since Bavaria, the third pretender, could do still less, and might find, in such a case, his account perhaps better in treating with the house of Bourbon than with that of Austria. More needs not be said on this head; but on the other two, which I shall consider together, several facts are proper to be mentioned, and several reflections necessary to be made.

WE might have counter-worked, no doubt, in their own methods of policy, the councils of France, who made peace to dissolve the confederacy, and great concessions, with very suspicious generosity, to gain the Spaniards: we might have waited,
like

like them, that is in arms, the death of CHARLES the second, and have fortified in the mean time the difpofitions of the king, the court, and people of Spain, againft the pretenfions of France: we might have made the peace which was made fome time after that, between the emperor and the Turks, and have obliged the former at any rate to have fecured the peace of Hungary, and to have prepared by thefe and other expedients, for the war that would inevitably break out on the death of the king of SPAIN.

BUT all fuch meafures were rendered impracticable, by the emperor chiefly. Experience had fhewn, that the powers who engaged in alliance with him muft expect to take the whole burden of his caufe upon themfelves; and that Hungary would maintain a perpetual diverfion in favour of France, fince he could not refolve to lighten the tyrannical yoke he had eftablifhed in that country and in Tranfilvania, nor his minifters to part with the immenfe confifcations they had appropriated to themfelves. Paft experience fhewed this: and the experience that followed, confirmed it very fatally. But further; there was not only little affiftance to be expected from him by

those who should engage in his quarrel: he did them hurt of another kind, and deprived them of many advantages by false measures of policy and unskilful negociations. Whilst the death of CHARLES the second was expected almost daily, the court of Vienna seemed to have forgot the court of Madrid, and all the pretensions on that crown. When the count D'HARRACH was sent thither, the imperial councils did something worse. The king of SPAIN was ready to declare the arch-duke CHARLES his successor; he was desirous to have this young prince sent into Spain: the bent of the people was in favour of Austria, or it had been so, and might have been easily turned the same way again: at court no cabal was yet formed in favour of Bourbon, and a very weak intrigue was on foot in favour of the electorial prince of BAVARIA. Not only CHARLES might have been on the spot ready to reap the succession, but a German army might have been there to defend it; for the court of Madrid insisted on having twelve thousand of these troops, and, rather than not to have them offered to contribute to the payment of them privately: because it would have been too unpopular among the Spaniards, and too prejudicial to the Austrian interest, to have
had

had it known that the emperor declined the payment of a body of his own troops that were demanded to secure that monarchy to his son. These proposals were half refused, and half evaded: and in return to the offer of the crown of Spain to the archduke, the imperial councils asked the government of Milan for him. They thought it a point of deep policy to secure the Italian provinces, and to leave to England and Holland the care of the Low Countries, of Spain, and the Indies. By declining these proposals, the house of Austria renounced in some sort the whole succession: at least she gave England and Holland reasons, whatever engagements these powers had taken, to refuse the harder task of putting her into possession by force; when she might, and would not, procure to the English and Dutch, and her other allies, the easier task of defending her in this possession.

I said that the measures mentioned above were rendered impracticable, by the emperor chiefly, because they were rendered so likewise by other cirumstances at the same conjuncture. A principal one I shall mention, and it shall be drawn from the state of our own country, and the disposition of our people. Let us take this up from

from king WILLIAM's acceſſion to our crown. During the whole progreſs that LEWIS the fourteenth made towards ſuch exorbitant power, as gave him well grounded hopes of acquiring at laſt to his family the Spaniſh monarchy, England had been either an idle ſpectator of all that paſſed on the continent, or a faint and uncertain ally againſt France, or a warm and ſure ally on her ſide, or a partial mediator between her and the powers confederated in their common defence. The revolution produced as great a change in our foreign conduct as in our domeſtic eſtabliſhment: and our nation engaged with great ſpirit in the war of one thouſand ſix hundred and eighty eight. But then this ſpirit was raſh, preſumptuous and ignorant, ill conducted at home, and ill ſeconded abroad: all which has been touched already. We had waged no long wars on the continent, nor been very deeply concerned in foreign confederacies, ſince the fourteenth and fifteenth centuries. The hiſtory of EDWARD the third, however, and of the firſt twelve or fifteen years of HENRY the ſixth might have taught us ſome general but uſeful leſſons, drawn from remote times, but applicable to the preſent. So might the example of HENRY the eighth, who ſquandered away

great

great fums for the profit of taking a town or the honour of having an emperor in his pay; and who divided afterwards by treaty the kingdom of France between himfelf and Charles the fifth, with fuccefs fo little anfwerable to fuch an undertaking, that it is hard to believe his imperial and Englifh majefty were both in earneft. If they were fo, they were both the bubbles of their prefumption. But it feems more likely that Henry the eighth was bubbled on this occafion by the great hopes that Charles held out to flatter his vanity: as he had been bubbled by his father-in-law, Ferdinand, at the beginning of his reign, in the war of Navarre. But thefe reflections were not made, nor had we enough confidered the example of Elizabeth, the laft of our princes who had made any confiderable figure abroad, and from whom we might have learned to act with vigour, but to engage with caution, and always to proportion our affiftance according to our abilities, and the real neceffities of our allies. The frontiers of France were now fo fortified, her commerce and her naval force were fo encreafed, her armies were grown fo numerous, her troops were fo difciplined, fo inured to war, and fo animated by a long courfe of fuccefsful campaigns,

paigns, that they who looked on the situation of Europe could not fail to see how difficult the enterprize of reducing her power was become. Difficult as it was, we were obliged on ever account, and by reasons of all kinds, to engage in it: but then we should have engaged with more forecast, and have conducted ourself in the management of it, not with less alacrity and spirit, but with more order, more œconomy, and a better application of our efforts. But they who governed were glad to engage us at any rate: and we entered on this great scheme of action, as our nation is too apt to do, hurried on by the ruling passion of the day. I have been told by several, who were on the stage of the world at this time, that the generality of our people believed, and were encouraged to believe, the war could not be long, if the king was vigorously supported: and there in a humdrum speech of a speaker, of the house of commons, I think, who humbly desired his majesty to take this opportunity of reconquering his ancient dutchy of Acquitain. We were soon awakened from these gaudy dreams. In seven or eight years no impression had been made on France that was besieged as it were on every side: and after repeated defeats in the

Low

Low Countries, where king WILLIAM laid the principal stress of the war, his sole triumph was the retaking of Namur, that had been taken by the French a few years before. Unsustained by success abroad, we are not to wonder that the spirit flagged at home; nor that the discontents of those who were averse to the established government uniting with the far greater number of those who disliked the administration, inflamed the general discontents of the nation, oppressed with taxes, pillaged by usurers, plundered at sea, and disappointed at land. As we run into extremes always, some would have continued this war at any rate, even at the same rate: but it was not possible they should prevail in such a situation of affairs, and such a disposition of minds. They who got by the war, and made immense fortunes by the necessities of the public, were not so numerous nor so powerful, as they have been since. The moneyed interest was not yet a rival able to cope with the landed interest, either in the nation or in parliament. The great corporations that had been erected more to serve the turn of party, than for any real national use, aimed indeed even then at the strength and influence which they have since acquired in the legislature; but they had not made the same progress by promoting national corruption,

tion, as they and the court have made since. In short, the other extreme prevailed. The generality of people grew as fond of getting out of the war, as they had been of entering into it: and thus far perhaps, considering how it had been conducted, they were not much to be blamed. But this was not all; for when king WILLIAM had made the peace, our martial spirit became at once so pacific, that we seemed resolved to meddle no more in the affairs of the continent, at least to employ our arms no more in the quarrels that might arise there: and accordingly we reduced our troops in England to seven thousand men.

I HAVE sometimes considered, in reflecting on these passages, what I should have done, if I had sat in parliament at that time; and have been forced to own myself, that I should have voted for disbanding the army then; as I voted in the following parliament for censuring the partition-treaties. I am forced to own this, because I remember how imperfect my notions were of the situation of Europe in that extraordinary crisis, and how much I saw the true interest of my own country in an half light. But, my lord, I own it with some shame; because in truth nothing could be more absurd than the conduct we held. What! because

because we had not reduced the power of France by the war, nor excluded the house of Bourbon from the Spanish succession, nor compounded with her upon it by the peace; and because the house of Austria had not helped herself, nor put it into our power to help her with more advantage and better prospect of success—were we to leave that whole succession open to the invasions of France, and to suffer even the contingency to subsist, of seeing those monarchies united? What! because it was become extravagant, after the trials so lately made, to think ourselves any longer engaged by treaty or obliged by good policy, to put the house of Austria in possession of the whole Spanish monarchy, and to defend her in this possession by force of arms, were we to leave the whole at the mercy of France? If we were not to do so, if we were not to do one of the three things that I said above remained to be done, and if the emperor put it out of our power to do another of them with advantage; were we to put it still more out of our power, and to wait unarmed for the death of the king of SPAIN? In fine, if we had not the prospect of disputing with France, so successfully as we might have had it, the Spanish succession, whenever it should be open; were we not only to shew by disarming, that we would not dispute it at all, but to censure likewise the second of the three things mentioned above, and which king WILLIAM put in practice, the compounding with France, to prevent if possible a war, in which we were averse to engage?

ALLOW me to push these reflections a little further, and to observe to your lordship, that if the proposal of sending the archduke into Spain had been accepted in time by the imperial court, and taken effect and become a measure of the confederacy, that war indeed would have been protracted; but France could not have hindered the passage of this prince and his German forces: and our fleet would have been better employed in escorting them, and in covering the coasts of Spain and of the dominions of that crown both in Europe and in America, than it was in so many unmeaning expeditions from the battle of La Hogue to the end of the war. France indeed would have made her utmost efforts to have had satisfaction on her pretensions, as ill-founded as they were. She would have ended that war, as we began the next, when we demanded a reasonable satisfaction for the emperor: and though I think that the allies would

would have had, in very many respects, more advantages in defending Spain, than in attacking France; yet, upon a supposition that the defence would have been as ill conducted as the attack was, and that by consequence, whether CHARLES the second had lived to the conclusion of this war, or had died before it, the war must have ended in some partition or other; this partition would have been made by the Spaniards themselves. They had been forced to compound with France on her former pretensions, and they must and they would have compounded on these, with an Austrian prince on the throne, just as they compounded, and probably much better than they compounded, on the pretensions we supported against them, when they had a prince of Bourbon on their throne. France could not have distressed the Spaniards, nor have over run their monarchy, if they had been united; and they would have been united in this case, and supported by the whole confederacy: as we distressed both France and them, over-run their monarchy in one hemisphere, and might have done so in both, when they were disunited, and supported by France alone. France would not have acted, in such negociations, the ridiculous part which the emperor acted in
those

those that led to the peace of Utrecht, nor have made her bargain worse by neglecting to make it in time. But the war ending as it did, though I cannot see how king WILLIAM could avoid leaving the crown of Spain and that entire monarchy at the discretion of LEWIS the fourteenth, otherwise than by compounding to prevent a new war he was in no sort prepared to make; yet it is undeniable, that, by consenting to a partition of their monarchy, he threw the Spaniards into the arms of France. The first partition might have taken place, perhaps, if the electoral prince of BAVARIA had lived, whom the French and Spaniards too would have seen much more willingly than the archduke on the throne of Spain. For among all the parties into which that court was divided in one thousand six hundred and ninety eight, when this treaty was made, that of Austria was grown the weakest, by the disgust taken at a German queen, and at the rapacity and insolence of her favourites. The French were looked upon with esteem and kindness at Madrid; but the Germans were become, or growing to be, objects of contempt to the ministers, and of aversion to the people. The electoral prince died in one thousand six hundred and ninety nine. The star of Austria, so fatal to all those

those who were obstacles to the ambition of that house, prevailed; as the elector expressed himself in the first pangs of his grief. The state of things changed very much by his death The archduke was to have Spain and the Indies, according to a second partition: and the Spaniards, who had expressed great resentment at the first, were pushed beyond their bearing by this. They soon appeared to be so; for the second treaty of partition was signed in March one thousand seven hundred; and the will was made, to the best of my remembrance, in the October following. I shall not enter here into many particulars concerning these great events. They will be related faithfully, and I hope fully explained, in a work which your lordship may take the trouble very probably from perusing some time or other, and which I shall rather leave, than give to the public. Something however must be said more, to continue and wind up this summary of the latter period of modern history.

FRANCE then saw her advantage, and improved it no doubt, though not in the manner, nor with the circumstances, that some lying scribblers of memorials and anecdotes have advanced. She had sent one of the ablest

ablest men of her court to that of MADRID, the marshal of HARCOURT, and she had stipulated in the second treaty of partition, that the archduke should go neither into Spain nor the dutchy of Milan, during the life of CHARLES the second. She was willing to have her option between a treaty and a will. By the acceptation of the will, all king WILLIAM's measures were broke. He was unprepared for war as much as when he made these treaties to prevent one; and if he meant in making them, what some wise, but refining men have suspected, and what I confess I see no reason to believe, only to gain time by the difficulty of executing them, and to prepare for making war, whenever the death of the king of SPAIN should alarm mankind, and rouse his own subjects out of their inactivity and neglect of foreign interests: if so, he was disappointed in that too; for France took possession of the whole monarchy at once, and with universal concurrence, at least without opposition or difficulty, in favour of the duke of ANJOU. By what has been observed, or hinted rather, very shortly, and I fear a little confusedly, it is plain, that reducing the power of France, and securing the whole Spanish succession to the house of Austria, were two points that king
WILLIAM

WILLIAM, at the head of the British and Dutch commonwealths and of the greatest confederacy Europe had seen, was obliged to give up. All the acquisitions that France cared to keep for the maintenance of her power were confirmed to her by the treaty of Ryswic: and king WILLIAM allowed, indirectly at least, the pretensions of the house of Bourbon to the Spanish succession, as LEWIS the fourteenth allowed, in the same manner, those of the house of Austria, by the treaties of partition. Strange situation! in which no expedient remained to prepare for an event, visibly so near, and of such vast importance as the death of the king of SPAIN, but a partition of his monarchy, without his consent, or his knowledge! If king WILLIAM had not made this partition, the emperor would have made one, and with as little regard to trade, to the barrier of the seven provinces, or to the general system of Europe, as had been shewed by him when he made the private treaty with France already mentioned, in one thousand six hundred and sixty eight. The ministers of Vienna were not wanting to insinuate to those of France overtures of a separate treaty, as more conducive to their common interests than the accession of his imperial majesty to that of partition.

But the councils of Verſailles judged very reaſonably, that a partition made with England and Holland would be more effectual than any other, if a partition was to take place: and that ſuch a partition would be juſt as effectual as one made with the emperor, to furniſh arguments to the emiſſaries of France, and motives to the Spaniſh councils, if a will in favour of France could be obtained. I repeat it again; I cannot ſee what king WILLIAM could do in ſuch circumſtances as he found himſelf in after thirty years ſtruggle, except what he did: neither can I ſee how he could do what he did, eſpecially. after the reſentment expreſſed by the Spaniards, and the furious memorial preſented by CANALES on the concluſion of the firſt treaty of partition, without apprehending that the conſequence would be a will in favour of France. He was in the worſt of all political circumſtances, and that wherein no one good meaſure remains to be taken; and out of which he left the two nations, at the head of whom he had been ſo long, to fight and negociate themſelves and their confederates, as well as they could.

WHEN this will was made and accepted, LEWIS the fourteenth had ſucceeded, and the

the powers in oppofition to him had failed, in all the great objects of intereft an dambition, which they had kept in fight for more than forty years; that is, from the beginning of the prefent period. The actors changed their parts in the tragedy that followed. The power, that had fo long and fo cruelly attacked, was now to defend, the Spanifh monarchy: and the powers, that had fo long defended, were now to attack it. Let us fee how this was brought about: and that we may fee it the better, and make a better judgment of all that paffed from the death of CHARLES the fecond to the peace of Utrecht, let us go back to the time of his death, and confider the circumftances that formed this complicated ftate of affairs in three views; a view of right, a view of policy, and a view of power.

The right of fucceeding to the crown of Spain would have been undoubtedly in the children of MARIA THERESA, that is, in the houfe of Bourbon; if this right had not been barred by the folemn renunciations fo often mentioned. The pretenfions of the houfe of Auftria were founded on thefe renunciations, on the ratification of them by the Pyrenean treaty, and the confirmation of them by the will of PHILIP the fourth.

The pretenfions of the houfe of Bourbon were founded on a fuppofition, it was indeed no more, and a vain one too, that thefe renunciations were in their nature null. On this foot the difpute of right ftood during the life of Charles the fecond, and on the fame it would have continued to ftand even after his death, if the renunciations had remained unfhaken; if his will, like that of his father, had confirmed them, and had left the crown, in purfuance of them, to the houfe of Auftria. But the will of Charles the fecond, annulling thefe renunciations, took away the fole foundation of the Auftrian pretenfions; for, however this act might be obtained, it was juft as valid as his father's, and was confirmed by the univerfal concurrence of the Spanifh nation to the new fettlement he made of that crown. Let it be, as I think it ought to be, granted, that the true heirs could not claim againft renunciations that were, if I may fay fo, conditions of their birth: but Charles the fecond had certainly as good a right to change the courfe of fucceffion agreeable to the order of nature and the conftitution of that monarchy, after his true heirs were born, as Philip the fourth had to change it, contrary to this order and this conftitution, before they were born, or at any

any other time. He had as good a right, in short, to difpenfe with the Pyrenean treaty, and to fet it afide in this refpect, as his father had to make it: fo that the renunciations being annulled by that party to the Pyrenean treaty who had exacted them, they could be deemed no longer binding, by virtue of this treaty, on the party who had made them. The fole queftion that remained therefore between thefe rival houfes, as to right, was this, whether the engagements taken by Lewis the fourteenth in the partition treaties obliged him to adhere to the terms of the laft of them in all events, and to deprive his family of the fucceffion, which the king of Spain opened, and the Spanifh nation offered to them; rather than to depart from a compofition he had made, on pretenfions that were difputable then, but were now out of difpute? It may be faid, and it was faid, that the treaties of partition being abfolute, without any condition or exception relative to any difpofition the king of Spain had made, or might make of his fucceffion, in favour of Bourbon or Auftria; the difpofition made by his will, in favour of the duke of Anjou, could not affect the engagements fo lately taken by Lewis the fourteenth in thefe treaties, nor difpenfe with a literal ob-

observation of them. This might be true on strict principles of justice; but I apprehend that none of these powers who exclaimed so loudly against the perfidy of France in this case, would have been more scrupulous in a parallel case. The maxim 'summum jusest summa injuria' would have been quoted, and the rigid letter of treaties would have been softened by an equitable interpretation of their spirit and intention. His imperial majesty, above all, had not the least colour of right to exclaim against France on this occasion; for in general, if his family was to be stripped of all the dominions they have acquired by breach of faith, and means much worse than the acceptation of the will, even allowing all the invidious circumstances imputed to the conduct of France to be true, the Austrian family would sink from their present grandeur to that low state they were in two or three centuries ago. In particular, the emperor, who had constantly refused to accede to the treaties of partition, or to submit to the dispositions made by them, had not the least plausible pretence to object to Lewis the fourteenth, that he departed from them. Thus, I think, the right of the two houses stood on the death of Charles the second. The right of the Spaniards, an independent nation, to regulate their own succession, or to receive the prince whom the dying monarch had called to it; and the right of England and Holland to regulate the succession, to divide, and parcel out this monarchy in different lots, it would be equally foolish to go about to establish. One is too evident, the other too absurd, to admit of any proof. But enough has been said concerning right, which was in truth little regarded by any of the parties concerned immediately or remotely in the whole course of these proceedings. Particular interests were alone regarded, and these were pursued as ambition, fear, resentment, and vanity directed: I mean the ambition of the two houses contending for superiority of power; the fear of England and Holland, lest this superiority should become too great in either; the resentment of Spain at the dismemberment of that monarchy projected by the partition-treaties; and the vanity of that nation, as well as the princes of the house of Bourbon: for as vanity mingled with resentment to make the will, vanity had a great share in determining the acceptation of it.

LET us now confider the fame conjuncture in a view of policy. The policy of the Spanifh councils was this. They could not brook that their monarchy fhould be divided: and this principle is expreffed ftrongly in the will of CHARLES the fecond, where he exhorts his fubjects not to fuffer any difmemberment or diminution of a monarchy founded by his predeceffors with fo much glory. Too weak to hinder this difmemberment by their own ftrength, too well apprifed of the little force and little views of the court of Vienna, and their old allies having engaged to procure this difmemberment even by force of arms; nothing remained for them to do, upon this principle, but to detach France from the engagements of the partition treaties, by giving their whole monarchy to a prince of the houfe of Bourbon. As much as may have been faid concerning the negociations of France to obtain a will in her favour, and yet to keep in referve the advantages ftipulated for her by the partition-treaties, if fuch a will could not be obtained, and though I am perfuaded that the marfhal of HARCOURT, who helped to procure this will, made his court to LEWIS the fourteenth as much as the marfhal of TALLARD,
who

who negociated the partitions; yet it is certain, that the acceptation of the will was not a meafure definitely taken at Verfailles when the king of Spain died. The alternative divided thofe councils, and, without entering at this time into the arguments urged on each fide, adhering to the partitions feemed the caufe of France, accepting the will that of the houfe of Bourbon.

It has been faid by men of great weight in the councils of Spain, and was faid at that time by men as little fond of the houfe of Bourbon, or of the French nation, as their fathers had been; that if England and Holland had not formed a confederacy and begun a war, they would have made PHILIP the fifth as good a Spaniard as any of the preceding PHILIPS, and not have endured the influence of French councils in the adminiftration of their government: but that we threw them entirely into the hands of France when we began the war, becaufe the fleets and armies of this crown being neceffary to their defence, they could not avoid fubmitting to this influence as long as the fame neceffity continued; and, in fact, we have feen that the influence lafted no longer. But notwithftanding this, it muft be confeffed, that a war was unavoidable.

able. The immediate securing of commerce and of barriers, the preventing an union of the two monarchies in some future time, and the preservation of a certain degree at least of equality in the scales of power, were points too important to England, Holland, and the rest of Europe, to be rested on the moderation of French, and the vigour of Spanish councils, under a prince of the house of France. If satisfaction to the house of Austria, to whose rights England and Holland shewed no great regard whilst they were better founded than they were since the will, had been alone concerned; a drop of blood spilt, or five shillings spent in the quarrel, would have been too much profusion. But this was properly the scale into which it became the common interest to throw all the weight that could be taken out of that of Bourbon. And therefore your lordship will find, that when negociations with D'AVAUX were set on foot in Holland to prevent a war, or rather on our part to gain time to prepare for it, in which view the Dutch and we had both acknowledged PHILIP king of SPAIN; the great article we insisted on was, that reasonable satisfaction should be given the emperor, upon his pretensions founded on the treaty of partition. We could

could do no otherwife; and France who offered to make the treaty of Ryfwic the foundation of that treaty, could do no otherwife than refufe to confent that the treaty of partition fhould be fo, after accepting the will, and thereby engaging to oppofe all partition or difmemberment of the Spanifh monarchy. I fhould mention none of the other demands of England and Holland, if I could neglect to point out to your lordfhip's obfervation, that the fame artifice was employed at this time, to perplex the more a negociation that could not fucceed on other accounts, as we faw employed in the courfe of the war, by the Englifh and Dutch minifters, to prevent the fuccefs of negociations that might, and ought to have fucceeded. The demand I mean, is that of " a liberty not only to explain the terms " propofed, but to increafe or amplify " them in the courfe of the negociation." I do not remember the words, but this is the fenfe, and this was the meaning of the confederates in both cafes.

In the former, king WILLIAM was determined to begin the war by all the rules of good policy; fince he could not obtain, nay fince France could not grant in that conjuncture, nor without being forced to it by a war, what he was obliged by thefe

very

very rules to demand. He intended therefore nothing by this negociation, if it may be called such, but to preserve forms and appearances, and perhaps, which many have suspected, to have time to prepare, as I hinted just now, both abroad and at home. Many things concurred to favour his preparations abroad. The alarm, that had been given by the acceptation of the will, was increased by every step that France made to secure the effect of it. Thus, for instance, the surprising and seizing the Dutch troops, in the same night, and at the same hour, that were dispersed in the garrisons of the Spanish Netherlands, was not excused by the necessity of securing those places to the obedience of Philip, nor softened by the immediate dismission of those troops. The impression it made was much the same as those of the surprises and seizures of France in former usurpations. No one knew then, that the sovereignty of the ten provinces was to be yielded up to the elector of BAVARIA: and every one saw that there remained no longer any barrier between France and the seven provinces. At home, the disposition of the nation was absolutely turned to a war with France, on the death of king JAMES the second, by the acknowledgment LEWIS the fourteenth made

made of his son as king of England. I know what has been said in excuse for this measure, taken as I believe, on female importunity; but certainly without any regard to public faith, to the true interest of France in those circumstances, or to the true interest of the prince thus acknowledged, in any. It was said, that the treaty of Ryswic obliging his most christian majesty only not to disturb king WILLIAM in his possession, he might, without any violation of it, have acknowledged this prince as king of England; according to the political casuistry of the French, and the example of France, who finds no fault with the powers that treat with the kings of England, although the kings of England retain the title of kings of France; as well as the example of Spain, who makes no complaints that other states treat with the kings of France, although the kings of France retain the title of Navarre. But besides, that the examples are not apposite, because no other powers acknowledge in form the king of England to be king of France, nor the king of France, to be king of Navarre; with what face could the French excuse this measure? Could they excuse it by urging that they adhered to the strict letter of one article of the treaty of Ryswic, against the plain meaning

ing of that very article, and againſt the whole tenor of that treaty : in the ſame breath with which they juſtified the acceptation of the will, by pretending they adhered to the ſuppoſed ſpirit and general intention of the treaties of partition, in contradiction to the letter, to the ſpecific engagements, and to the whole purport of thoſe treaties ? This part of the conduct of Lewis the fourteenth may appear juſtly the more ſurpriſing, becauſe in moſt other parts of his conduct at the ſame time, and in ſome to his diſadvantage, he acted cautiouſly, endeavoured to calm the minds of his neighbours, to reconcile Europe to his grandſon's elevation, and to avoid all ſhew of beginning hoſtilities.

Though king William was determined to engage in a war with France and Spain, yet the ſame good policy, that determined him to engage, determined him not to engage too deeply. The engagement taken in the grand alliance of one thouſand ſeven hundred and one is, " To procure an equi-
" table and reaſonable ſatisfaction to his
" imperial majeſty for his pretenſion to the
" Spaniſh ſucceſſion; and ſufficient ſecu-
" rity to the king of England, and the
" States General, for their dominions, and
" for the navigation and commerce of their
" ſubjects,

"subjects, and to prevent the union of the "two monarchies of France and Spain." As king of England, as ftateholder of Holland, he neither could, nor did engage any further. It may be difputed perhaps among fpeculative politicians, whether the balance of power in Europe would have been better preferved by that fcheme of partition, which the treaties, and particularly the laft of them, propofed, or by that which the grand alliance propofed to be the object of the war? I think there is little room for fuch a difpute, as I fhall have occafion to fay hereafter more exprefly. In this place I fhall only fay, that the object of this war, which king WILLIAM meditated, and queen ANNE waged, was a partition, by which a prince of the houfe of Bourbon, already acknowleged by us and the Dutch as king of Spain, was to be left on the throne of that difmembered monarchy. The wifdom of thofe councils faw that the peace of Europe might be reftored, and fecured on this foot, and that the liberties of Europe would be in no danger.

THE fcales of the balance of power will never be exactly poized, nor in the precife point of equality either difcernible or neceffary to be difcerned. It is fufficient in this,

this, as in other human affairs, that the deviation be not to great. Some there will always be. A constant attention to these deviations is therefore necessary. When they are little, their increase may be easily prevented by early care and the precautions that good policy suggests. But when they become great for want of this care and these precautions, or by the force of unforeseen events, more vigour is to be exerted, and greater efforts to be made. But even in such cases, much reflection is necessary on all the circumstances that form the conjuncture; lest, by attacking with ill success, the deviation be confirmed, and the power that is deemed already exorbitant become more so; and lest, by attacking with good success, whilst one scale is pillaged, too much weight of power be thrown into the other. In such cases, he who has considered, in the histories of former ages, the strange revolutions that time produces, and the perpetual flux and reflux of public as well as private fortunes, of kingdoms and states as well as of those who govern or are governed in them, will incline to think, that if the scales can be brought back by a war, nearly, though not exactly, to the point they were at before this great deviation from it, the rest may be left to
accidents,

accidents, and to the use that good policy is able to make of them.

When Charles the fifth was at the heighth of his power, and in the zenith of his glory, when a king of France and a pope were at once his prisoners; it must be allowed, that, his situation and that of his neighbours compared, they had as much at least to fear from him and from the house of Austria, as the neighbours of Lewis the fourteenth had to fear from him and from the house of Bourbon, when, after all his other success, one of his grandchildren was placed on the Spanish throne. And yet among all the conditions of the several leagues against Charles the fifth, I do not remember that it was ever stipulated, that " no peace should be made with " him as long as he continued to be empe- " ror and king of Spain; nor as long as " any Austrian prince continued capable of " uniting on his head the Imperial and Spa- " nish crowns."

If your lordship makes the application, you will find that the difference of some circumstances does not hinder this example from being very apposite, and strong to the present purpose. Charles the fifth was emperor and king of Spain; but neither was Lewis the fourteenth king of Spain, nor Philip the fifth king of France. That had happened in one instance, which it was apprehended might happen in the other. It had happened, and it was reasonably to be apprehended that it might happen again, and that the Imperial and Spanish crowns might continue, not only in the same family, but on the same heads; for measures were taken to secure the succession of both to Philip the son of Charles. We do not find however that any confederacy was formed, any engagement taken, or any war made, to remove or prevent this great evil. The princes and states of Europe contented themselves to oppose the designs of Charles the fifth, and to check the growth of his power occasionally, and as interest invited, or necessity forced them to do; not constantly. They did perhaps too little against him, and sometimes too much for him: but if they did too little of one kind, time and accident did the rest. Distinct dominions, and different pretensions, created contrary interests in the house of Austria: and on the abdication of Charles the fifth, his brother succeeded, not his son, to the empire. The house of Austria divided into a German and a Spanish branch: and if the two branches came to have a mutual influence on one another, and frequently a common interest, it was not till one of them had fallen from grandeur, and till the other was rather aiming at it, than in possession of it. In short, PHILIP was excluded from the imperial throne by so natural a progression of causes and effects, arising not only in Germany but in his own family, that if a treaty had been made to exclude him from it in favour of FERDINAND, such a treaty might have been said very probably to have executed itself.

THE precaution I have mentioned, and that was neglected in this case without any detriment to the common cause of Europe, was not neglected in the grand alliance of one thousand seven hundred and one. For in that, one of the ends proposed by the war, is to obtain an effectual security against the contingent union of the crowns of France and Spain. The will of CHARLES the second provides against the same contingency: and this great principle of preventing too much dominion and power from falling to the lot of either of the families of Bourbon or Austria, seemed to be agreed on all sides; since in the partition-treaty the same precaution was taken against an union of the Imperial and Spanish crowns. King WILLIAM was enough piqued against France. His ancient prejudices were strong and well founded. He had been worsted in war, over-reached in negociation, and personally affronted by her. England and Holland were sufficiently alarmed and animated, and a party was not wanting, even in our island, ready to approve any engagements he would have taken against France and Spain, and in favour of the house of Austria; though we were less concerned, by any national interest, than any other power that took part in the war, either then or afterwards. But this prince was far from taking a part beyond that which the particular interests of England and Holland, and the general interest of Europe, necessarily required. Pique must have no more a place than affection, in deliberations of this kind. To have engaged to dethrone PHILIP, out of resentment to LEWIS the fourteenth, would have been a resolution worthy of CHARLES the twelfth, king of Sweden, who sacrificed his country, his people, and himself at last, to his revenge. To have engaged to conquer the Spanish monarchy for the house of Austria, or to go, in favour of that family,

mily, one step beyond those that were necessary to keep this house on a foot of rivalry with the other, would have been, as I have hinted, to act the part of a vassal, not of an ally. The former pawns his state, and ruins his subjects, for the interest of his superior lord, perhaps for his lord's humour, or his passion: the latter goes no further than his own interest carries him; nor makes war for those of another, nor even for his own, if they are remote and contingent, as if he fought pro aris et focis, for his religion, his liberty, and his property. Agreeably to these principles of good policy, we entered into the war that began on the death of CHARLES the second: but we soon departed from them, as I shall have occasion to observe in considering the state of things, at this remarkable juncture, in a view of strength.

LET me recall here what I have said somewhere else. They who are in the sinking scale of the balance of power do not easily, nor soon, come off from the habitual prejudices of superiority over their neighbours, nor from the confidence that such prejudices inspire. From the year one thousand six hundred and sixty seven, to the end of that century, France had been constantly in arms, and her arms had been successful. She had sustained a war, without any confederates against the principal powers of Europe confederated against her, and had finished it with advantage on every side, just before the death of the king of SPAIN. She continued armed after the peace, by sea and land. She increased her forces, while other nations reduced theirs, and was ready to defend, or to invade her neighbours, whilst, their confederacy being dissolved, they were in no condition to invade her, and in a bad one to defend themselves. Spain and France had now one common cause. The electors of BAVARIA and COLOGNE supported it in Germany, the duke of SAVOY was an ally, the duke of MANTUA a vassal of the two crowns in Italy. In a word, appearances were formidable on that side; and if a distrust of strength, on the side of the confederacy, had induced England and Holland to compound with France for a partition of the Spanish succession, there seemed to be still greater reason for this distrust after the acceptation of the will, the peaceable and ready submission, of the entire monarchy of Spain to PHILIP, and all the measures taken to secure him in this possession. Such appearances might well impose. They did

so

so on many, and on none more than on the French themselves, who engaged with great confidence and spirit in the war; when they found it, as they might well expect it would be, unavoidable. The strength of France however, though great, was not so great as the French thought it, nor equal to the efforts they undertook to make. Their engagement, to maintain the Spanish monarchy entire under the dominion of PHILIP, exceeded their strength. Our engagement, to procure some out-skirts of it for the house of Austria, was not in the same disproportion to our strength. If I speak positively on this occasion, yet I cannot be accused of presumption; because, how disputable soever these points might be when they were points of political speculation, they are such no longer, and the judgment I make is dictated to me by experience. France threw herself into the sinking scale, when she accepted the will. Her scale continued to sink during the whole course of the war, and might have been kept by the peace as low as the true interest of Europe required. What I remember to have heard the duke of MARLBOROUGH say, before he went to take on him the command of the army in the Low Countries in one thousand seven hundred and two, proved true.

true. The French mis-reckoned very much, if they made the same comparison between their troops and those of their enemies, as they had made in precedent wars. Those that had been opposed to them, in the last, were raw for the most part when it began, the British particularly: but they had been disciplined, if I may say so, by their defeats. They were grown to be veteran at the peace of Ryswic, and though many had been disbanded, yet they had been disbanded lately: so that even these were easily formed a new, and the spirit that had been raised continued in all. Supplies of men to recruit the armies were more abundant on the side of the confederacy, than on that of the two crowns: a necessary consequence of which it seemed to be, that those of the former would grow better, and those of the latter worse, in a long, extensive, and bloody war. I believe it proved so; and if my memory does not deceive me, the French were forced very early to send recruits to their armies, as they send slaves to their gallies. A comparison between those who were to direct their councils, and to conduct the armies on both sides, is a task it would become me little to undertake. The event shewed, that if France had had her CONDE, her TURENNE, or her LUX-
EMBURG,

EMBURG, to oppofe to the confederates: the confederates might have oppofed to her, with equal confidence, their EUGENE of Savoy, their MARLBOROUGH, or their STARENBERG. But there is one obfervation I cannot forbear to make. The alliances were concluded, the quotas were fettled, and the feafon for taking the field approached, when king WILLIAM died. The event could not fail to occafion fome confternation on one fide, and to give fome hopes on the other; for, notwithstanding the ill fuccefs with which he made war generally, he was looked upon as the fole centre of union that could keep together the great confederacy then forming: and how much the French feared, from his life, had appeared a few years before, in the extravagant and indecent joy they expreffed on a falfe report of his death. A fhort time fhewed how vain the fears of fome and the hopes of others were. By his death, the duke of MARLBOROUGH was raifed to the head of the army, and indeed of the confederacy: where he, a new, a private man, a fubject, acquired by merit and by management a more deciding influence, than high birth, confirmed authority, and even the crown of Great Britain, had given to king WILLIAM. Not only all the parts of of that vaſt machine, the grand alliance, were kept more compact and entire; but a more rapid and vigorous motion was given to the whole: and, inſtead of languiſhing out difaſtrous campaigns, we ſaw every ſcene of the war full of action. All thoſe wherein he appeared, and many of thoſe wherein he was not then an actor, but abettor however of their action, were crowned with the moſt triumphant ſucceſs. I take with pleaſure this opportunity of doing juſtice to that great man, whoſe faults I knew, whoſe virtues I admired; and whoſe memory, as the greateſt general and as the greateſt miniſter that our country or perhaps any other has produced, I honour. But beſides this, the obſervation I have made comes into my ſubject, ſince it ſerves to point out to your lordſhip the proof of what I ſaid above, that France undertook too much, when ſhe undertook to maintain the Spaniſh monarchy entire in the poſſeſſion of PHILIP: and that we undertook no more than what was proportionable to our ſtrength, when we undertook to weaken that monarchy by diſmembering it, in the hands of a prince of the houſe of Bourbon, which we had been difabled by ill fortune and worſe conduct to keep out of them. It may be ſaid that the great ſucceſs of the confederates

against

against France proves that their generals were superior to her's, but not that their forces and their national strength were so; that with the same force with which she was beaten, she might have been victorious; that if she had been so, or if the success of the war had varied, or been less decisive against her in Germany, in the Low Countries, and in Italy, as it was in Spain, her strength would have appeared sufficient, and that of the confederacy insufficient. Many things may be urged to destroy this reasoning: I content myself with one. France could not long have made even the unsuccessful efforts she did make, if England and Holland had done what it is undeniable they had strength to do; if besides pillaging, I do not say conquering, the Spanish West Indies, they had hindered the French from going to the South Sea; as they did annually during the whole course of the war without the least molestation, and from whence they imported into France in that time as much silver and gold as the whole species of that kingdom amounted to. With this immense and constant supply of wealth France was reduced in effect to bankruptcy before the end of the war. How much sooner must she have been so, if this supply had been kept

kept from her? The confession of France herself is on my side. She confessed her inability to support what she had undertaken, when she sued for peace as early as the year one thousand seven hundred and six. She made her utmost efforts to answer the expectation of the Spaniards, and to keep their monarchy entire. When experience had made it evident that this was beyond her power, she thought herself justified to the Spanish nation, in consenting to a partition, and was ready to conclude a peace with the allies on the principles of their grand alliance. But as France seemed to flatter herself, till experience made her desirous to abandon an enterprize that exceeded her strength; you will find, my lord, that her enemies began to flatter themselves in their turn, and to form designs and take engagements that exceeded theirs. Great Britain was drawn into these engagements little by little; for I do not remember any parliamentary declaration for continuing the war till PHILIP should be dethroned, before the year one thousand seven hundred and six: and then such a declaration was judged necessary to second the resolution of our ministers and our allies, in departing from the principles of the grand alliance, and in proposing not only

only the reduction of the French, but the conquest of the Spanish monarchy, as the objects of the war. This new plan had taken place, and we had begun to act upon it, two years before, when the treaty with Portugal was concluded, and the arch-duke CHARLES, now emperor, was sent into Portugal first, and into Catalonia afterwards, and was acknowledged and supported as king of Spain.

WHEN your lordship peruses the anecdotes of the times here spoken of, and considers the course and event of the great war which broke out on the death of the king of Spain, CHARLES the second, and was ended by the treaties of Utrecht and Radstat; you will find, that in order to form a true judgment on the whole you must consider very attentively the great change made by the new plan that I have mentioned; and compare it with the plan of the grand alliance, relatively to the general interest of Europe, and the particular interest of your own country. It will not, because it cannot, be denied, that all the ends of the grand alliance might have been obtained by a peace in one thousand seven hundred and six. I need not recall the events of that, and of the precedent years
of

of the war. Not only the arms of France had been defeated on every side; but the inward state of that kingdom was already more exhausted than it had ever been. She went on indeed, but she staggered and reeled under the burden of the war. Our condition, I speak of Great Britain, was not quite so bad; but the charge of the war increased annually upon us. It was evident that this charge must continue to increase, and it was no less evident that our nation was unable to bear it without falling soon into such distress, and contracting such debts, as we have seen and felt, and still feel. The Dutch neither restrained their trade, nor over-loaded it with taxes. They soon altered the proportion of their quotas, and were deficient even after this alteration in them. But, however, it must be allowed that they exerted their whole strength; and they and we paid the whole charge of the war. Since therefore by such efforts as could not be continued any longer, without oppressing and impoverishing these nations to a degree that no interest except that of their very being, nor any engagement of assisting an alliance *totis viribus* can require, France was reduced, and all the ends of the war were become attainable; it will be worth your lordship's lordship's while to consider why the true use was not made of the success of the confederates against France and Spain, and why a peace was not concluded in the fifth year of the war. When your lordship considers this, you will compare in your thoughts what the state of Europe would have been, and that of your own country might have been, if the plan of the grand alliance had been pursued: with the possible as well as certain, the contingent as well as necessary, consequences of changing this plan in the manner it was changed. You will be of opinion, I think, and it seems to me, after more than twenty years of recollection, re-examination, and reflection, that impartial posterity must be of the same opinion; you will be of opinion, I think, that the war was wise and just before the change, because necessary to maintain that equality among the powers of Europe, on which the public peace and common prosperity depends: and that it was unwise and unjust after this change, because unnecessary to this end, and directed to other and to contrary ends. You will be guided by undeniable facts to discover, through all the false colours which have been laid, and which deceived many at the time, that the war, after this change, became a war of paffion, of ambition, of avarice, and of private intereft; the private intereft of particular perfons and particular ftates; to which the general intereft of Europe was facrificed fo entirely; that if the terms infifted on by the confederates had been granted, nay if even thofe which France was reduced to grant, in one thoufand feven hundred and ten, had been accepted, fuch a new fyftem of power would have been created as might have expofed the balance of this power to deviations, and the peace of Europe to troubles, not inferior to thofe that the war was defigned, when it began, to prevent. Whilft you obferve this in general, you will find particular occafion to lament the fate of Great Britain in the midft of triumphs that have been founded fo high. She had triumphed indeed to the year one thoufand feven hundred and fix inclufively: but what were her triumphs afterwards? what was her fuccefs after fhe proceeded on the new plan? I fhall fay fomething on that head immediately. Here let me only fay, that the glory of taking towns, and winning battles, is to be meafured by the utility that refults from thofe victories. Victories, that bring honour to the arms, may bring fhame to the councils, of a nation. To win a battle, to

take

take a town, is the glory of a general, and of an army. Of this glory we had a very large fhare in the courfe of the war. But the glory of a nation is to proportion the ends fhe propofes, to her intereft and her ftrength; the means fhe employs to the ends fhe propofes, and the vigour fhe exerts to both. Of this glory, I apprehend, we have had very little to boaft, at any time, and particularly in the great conjuncture of which I am fpeaking. The reafons of ambition, avarice, and private intereft, which engaged the princes and ftates of the confederacy to depart from the principles of the grand alliance, were no reafons for Great Britain. She neither expected nor defired any thing more than what fhe might have obtained by adhering to thofe principles. What hurried our nation then, with fo much fpirit and ardour, into thofe of the new plan? Your lordfhip will anfwer this queftion to yourfelf, I believe, by the prejudices and rafhnefs of party; by the influence that the firft fuccefles of the confederate arms gave to our minifters: and the popularity they gave, if I may fay fo, to the war; by ancient and frefh refentments, which the unjuft and violent ufurpations, in fhort the whole conduct of Lewis the fourteenth, for forty years together,

gether, his haughty treatment of other princes and ſtates, and even the ſtyle of his court, had created; and, to mention no more, by a notion, groundleſs but prevalent, that he was and would be maſter as long as his grandſon was king of Spain, and that there could be no effectual meaſure taken, though the grand alliance ſuppoſed that there might, to prevent a future union of the two monarchies, as long as a prince of the houſe of Bourbon ſat on the Spaniſh throne. That ſuch a notion ſhould have prevailed, in the firſt confuſion of thoughts which the death and will of CHARLES the ſecond produced, among the generality of men, who ſaw the fleets and armies of France take poſſeſſion of all the parts of the Spaniſh monarchy, is not to be wondered at by thoſe that conſider how ill the generality of mankind are informed, how incapable they are of judging; and yet how ready to pronounce judgment; in fine, how inconſiderately they follow one another in any popular opinion which the heads of party broach, or to which the firſt appearances of things have given occaſion. But, even at this time, the councils of England and Holland did not entertain this notion. They acted on quite another, as might be ſhewn in many inſtances, if any other beſides that of the grand

grand alliance was neceſſary. When theſe councils therefore ſeemed to entertain this notion afterwards, and acted and took engagements to act upon it, we muſt conclude that they had other motives. They could not have theſe; for they knew, that as the Spaniards had been driven by the two treaties of partition to give their monarchy to a prince of the houſe of Bourbon, ſo they were driven into the arms of France by the war that we made to force a third upon them. If we acted rightly on the principles of the grand alliance, they acted rightly on thoſe of the will: and if we could not avoid making an offenſive war, at the expence of forming and maintaining a vaſt confederacy, they could not avoid purchaſing the protection and aſſiſtance of France in a defenſive war, and eſpecially in the beginning of it, according to what I have ſomewhere obſerved already, by yielding to the authority and admitting the influence of that court in all the affairs of their government. Our miniſters knew therefore, that if any inference was to be drawn from the firſt part of this notion, it was for ſhortening, not prolonging, the war; for delivering the Spaniards as ſoon as poſſible from habits of union and intimacy with France; not for continuing them under the fame neceffity, till by length of time thefe habits fhould be confirmed. As to the latter part of this notion, they knew that it was falfe and filly. GARTH the beft natured ingenious wild man I ever knew, might be in the right when he faid, in fome of his poems at that time,

"——An Auftrian prince alone,
" Is fit to nod upon a Spanifh throne."

The fetting an Auftrian prince upon it was, no doubt, the fureft expedient to prevent an union of the two monarchies of France and Spain; juft as fetting a prince of the houfe of Bourbon on that throne was the fureft expedient to prevent an union of the imperial and Spanifh crowns. But it was equally falfe to fay, in either cafe, that this was the fole expedient. It would be no paradox, but a propofition eafily proved, to advance, that if thefe unions had been effectually provided againft, the general intereft of Europe would have been little concerned whether PHILIP or CHARLES had nodded at Madrid. It would be likewife no paradox to fay, that the contingency of uniting France and Spain under the fame prince appeared more remote, about the middle of the laft great war,

when

when the dethronement of Philip in favour of Charles was made a condition of peace sine qua non, than the contingency of an union of the Imperial and Spanish crowns. Nay, I know not whether it would be a paradox to affirm, that the expedient that was taken, and that was always obvious to be taken, of excluding Philip and his race from the succession of France, by creating an interest in all the other princes of the blood, and by consequence a party in France itself, for their exclusion, whenever the case should happen, was not in its nature more effectual than any that could have been taken: and some must have been taken, not only to exclude Charles from the empire whenever the case should happen that happened soon, the death of his brother Joseph without issue male, but his posterity likewise in all future vacancies of the imperial throne. The expedient that was taken against Philip at the treaty of Utrecht, they who opposed the peace attempted to ridicule; but some of them have had occasion since that time to see, though the case has not happened, how effectual it would have been if it had: and he who should go about to ridicule it after our experience, would only make himself ridiculous. Notwithstanding all this, he, who

who transports himself back to that time, must acknowledge, that the confederated powers in general could not but be of GARTH's mind, and think it more agreeable to the common interest of Europe, that a branch of Austria, than a branch of Bourbon, should gather the Spanish succession, and that the maritime powers, as they are called impertinently enough with respect to the superiority of Great Britain, might think it was for their particular interest to have a prince, dependant for some time at least on them, king of Spain, rather than a prince whose dependance, as long as he stood in any, must be naturally on France. I do not say, as some have done, a prince whose family was an old ally, rather than a prince whose family was an old enemy; because I lay no weight on the gratitude of princes, and am as much persuaded that an Austrian king of Spain would have made us returns of that sort in no other proportion than of his want of us, as I am, that PHILIP and his race will make no other returns of the same sort to France. If this affair had been entire, therefore, on the death of the king of SPAIN; if we had made no partition, nor he any will, the whole monarchy of Spain would have been the prize to be fought for; and our wishes, and such efforts as we were able

able to make, in the moſt unprovided condition imaginable, muſt have been on the ſide of Auſtria. But it was far from being entire. A prince of the houſe of Auſtria might have been on the ſpot, before the king of SPAIN died, to gather his ſucceſſion; but inſtead of this a prince of the houſe of Bourbon was there ſoon afterwards, and took poſeſſion of the whole monarchy, to which he had been called by the late king's will, and by the voice of the Spaniſh nation. The councils of England and Holland therefore preferred very wiſely, by their engagements in the grand alliance, what was more practicable though leſs eligible, to what they deemed more eligible, but ſaw become by the courſe of events, if not abſolutely impracticable, yet an enterprize of more length, more difficulty, and greater expence of blood and treaſure, than theſe nations were able to bear; or than they ought to bear, when their ſecurity and that of the reſt of Europe might be ſufficiently provided for at a cheaper rate. If the confederates could not obtain, by the force of their arms, the ends of the war, laid down in the grand alliance, to what purpoſe would it be to ſtipulate for more? And if they were able to obtain theſe, it was evident that, whilſt they diſmembered the Spaniſh monarchy, they

muſt

must reduce the power of France. This happened; the Low Countries were conquered; the French were driven out of Germany and Italy: and Lewis the fourteenth, who had so long and so lately set mankind at defiance, was reduced to sue for peace.

If it had been granted him in one thousand seven hundred and six, on what foot must it have been granted? The allies had already in their power all the states that were to compose the reasonable satisfaction for the emperor. I say, in their power: because though Naples and Sicily were not actually reduced at that time, yet the expulsion of the French out of Italy, and the disposition of the people of those kingdoms, considered, it was plain the allies might reduce them when they pleased. The confederate arms were superior till then in Spain, and several provinces acknowledged Charles the third. If the rest had been yielded to him by treaty, all that the new plan required had been obtained. If the French would not yet have abandoned Philip, as we had found that the Castilians would not even when our army was at Madrid, all that the old plan, the plan of the grand alliance required, had been obtained? but
still

still France and Spain had given nothing to purchase a peace, and they were in circumstances not to expect it without purchasing it. They would have purchased it, my lord: and France, as well as Spain, would have contributed a larger share of the price, rather than continue the war, in her exhausted state. Such a treaty of peace would have been a third treaty of partition indeed, but vastly preferable to the two former. The great objection to the former was drawn from that considerable increase of dominion, which the crown of France, and not a branch of the house of Bourbon, acquired by them. I know what may be said speciously enough to persuade, that such an increase of dominion would not have augmented, but would rather have weakened the power of France, and what examples may be drawn from history to countenance such an opinion. I know likewise, that the compact figure of France, and the contiguity of all her provinces, make a very essential part of the force of her monarchy. Had the designs of CHARLES the eighth, LEWIS the twelfth, FRANCIS the first, and HENRY the second, succeeded, the dominions of France would have been more extensive, and I believe the strength of her monarchy would have been less. I have sometimes
thought

thought that even the loss of the battle of St. Quentin, which obliged HENRY the second to recall the duke of GUISE with his army out of Italy, was in this respect no unhappy event. But the reasoning which is good, I think, when applied to those times, will not hold when applied to ours, and to the case I consider here; the state of France, the state of her neighbours, and the whole constitution of Europe being so extremely different. The objection therefore to the two treaties of partition had a real weight. The power of France, deemed already exorbitant, would have been increased by this accession of dominion, in the hands of LEWIS the fourteenth: and the use he intended to make of it by keeping Italy and Spain in awe, appears in the article that gave him the ports on the Tuscan coast, and the province of Guipuscoa. This king WILLIAM might, and, I question not, did see; but that prince might think too, that for this very reason LEWIS the fourteenth would adhere, in all events, to the treaty of partition: and that these consequences were more remote, and would be less dangerous, than those of making no partition at all. The partition, even the worst that might have been made, by a treaty of peace in one thousand seven hundred

dred and six, would have been the very reverse of this. France would have been weakened, aud her enemies strengthened, by her concessions on the side of the Low Countries, of Germany, and Savoy. If a prince of her royal family had remained in possession of Spain and the West Indies, no advantage would have accrued to her by it, and effectual bars would have been opposed to an union of the two monarchies. The house of Austria would have had a reasonable satisfaction for that shadow of right, which a former partition gave her. She had no other after the will of CHARLES the second; and this may be justly termed a shadow, since England, Holland, and France could confer no real right to the Spanish succession, nor to any part of it. She had declined acceding to that partition, before France departed from it, and would have preferred the Italian provinces, without Spain and the West-Indies, to Spain and the West Indies without the Italian provinces. The Italian provinces would have fallen to her share by this partition. The particular demands of England and Holland would have suffered no difficulty, and those that we were obliged by treaty to make for others would have been easy to adjust. Would not this have been enough,

my

my lord, for the public security, for the common interest, and for the glory of our arms? To have humbled and reduced, in five campaigns, a power that had disturbed and insulted Europe almost forty years; to have restored, in so short a time, the balance of power in Europe to a sufficient point of equality, after it had been more than fifty years, that is from the treaty of Westphalia, in a gradual deviation from this point; in short, to have retrieved, in one thousand seven hundred and six, a game that was become desperate at the beginning of the century. To have done all this before the war had exhausted our strength, was the utmost sure that any man could desire who intended the public good alone: and no honest reason ever was, nor ever will be given, why the war was protracted any longer; why we neither made peace after a short, vigorous, and successful war, nor put it entirely out of the power of France to continue at any rate a long one. I have said, and it is true, that this had been entirely out of her power, if we had given greater interruption to the commerce of Old and New Spain, and if we had hindered France from importing annually, from the year one thousand seven hundred and two, such immense treasures as she did import

by

by the ships she sent, with the permission of Spain, to the South Sea. It has been advanced, and it is a common opinion, that we were restrained by the jealousy of the Dutch from making use of the liberty given by treaty to them and us, and which, without his imperial majesty's leave, since we entered into the war, we might have taken, of making conquests in the Spanish West-Indies. Be it so. But to go to the South Seas, to trade there if we could, to pillage the West-Indies without making conquests if we could not, and, whether we traded or whether we pillaged, to hinder the French from trading there; was a measure that would have given, one ought to think, no jealousy to the Dutch, who might, and it is to be supposed would, have taken their part in these expeditions; or if it had given them jealousy, what could they have replied when a British minister had told them:
'That it little became them to find fault that
'we traded with, or pillaged the Spaniards
'in the West-Indies to the detriment of
'our common enemy, whilst we connived
'at them who traded with this enemy to
'his and their great advantage, against our
'remonstrances, and in violation of the
'condition upon which we had given the
'first augmentation of our forces in the
'Low

'Low Countries?' We might have pursued this measure notwithstanding any engagement that we took by the treaty with Portugal, if I remember that treaty right: but instead of this, we wasted our forces, and squandered millions after millions in supporting our alliance with this crown, and in pursuing the chimerical project which was made the object of this alliance. I call it chimerical, because it was equally so, to expect a revolution in favour of CHARLES the third on the slender authority of such a trifler as the admiral of Castile; and, when this failed us, to hope to conquer Spain by the assistance of the Portuguese, and the revolt of the Catalans. Yet this was the foundation upon which the new plan of the war was built, and so many ruinous engagements were taken.

THE particular motives of private men, as well as of princes and states, to protract the war, are partly known, and partly guessed, at this time. But whenever that time comes, and I am persuaded it will come, when their secret motives, their secret designs, and intrigues, can be laid open, I presume to say to your lordship that the most confused scene of iniquity, and folly, that it is possible to imagine, will

will appear. In the mean while, if your lordſhip conſiders only the treaty of barrier, as my lord TOWNSHEND ſigned it, without, nay in truth, againſt orders; for the duke of MARLBOROUGH, though joint plenipotentiary, did not: if you conſider the famous preliminaries of one thouſand ſeven hundred and nine, which we made a mock-ſhew of ratifying, though we knew that they would not be accepted; for ſo the marquis of TORCY had told the penſionary before he left the Hague, as the ſaid marquis has aſſured me very often ſince that time: if you enquire into the anecdotes of Gertruydenberg, and if you conſult other authentic papers that are extant, your lordſhip will ſee the policy of the new plan, I think, in this light. Though we had refuſed, before the war began, to enter into engagements for the conqueſt of Spain, yet as ſoon as it began, when the reaſon of things was ſtill the ſame, for the ſucceſs of our firſt campaign cannot be ſaid to have altered it, we entered into theſe very engagements. By the treaty wherein we took theſe engagements firſt, Portugal was brought into the grand alliance; that is, ſhe conſented to employ her formidable forces againſt PHILIP, at the expence of England and Holland, provided we would debar ourſelves from making

making any acquisitions, and the house of Austria promise, that she should acquire many important places in Spain, and an immense extent of country in America. By such bargains as this, the whole confederacy was formed, and held together. Such means were indeed effectual to multiply enemies to France and Spain; but a project so extensive and so difficult as to make many bargains of this kind necessary, and necessary for a great number of years, and for a very uncertain event, was a project into which, for this very reason, England and Holland should not have entered. It is worthy your observation, my lord, that these bad bargains would not have been continued, as they were almost to our immediate ruin, if the war had not been protracted under the pretended necessity of reducing the whole Spanish monarchy to the obedience of the house of Austria. Now, as no other confederate except Portugal was to receive his recompence by any dismemberment of dominions in Old or New Spain, the engagements we took to conquer this whole monarchy had no visible necessary cause, but the procuring the accession of this power, that was already neuter, to the grand alliance. This accession, as I have said before, served only to make us neglect immediate and certain advantages, for remote and uncertain hopes; and chuse to attempt the conquest of the Spanish nation at our own vast expence, whom we might have starved, and by starving reduced both the French and them, at their expence.

I called the necessity of reducing the whole Spanish monarchy to the obedience of the house of Austria, a pretended necessity: and pretended it was, not real, without doubt. But I am apt to think your lordship may go further, and find some reasons to suspect, that the opinion itself of this necessity was not very real, in the minds of those who urged it: in the minds I would say of the able men among them; for that it was real in some of our zealous British politicians, I do them the justice to believe. Your lordship may find reasons to suspect perhaps, that this opinion was set up rather to occasion a diversion of the forces of France, and to furnish pretences for prolonging the war for other ends.

BEFORE the year one thousand seven hundred and ten, the war was kept alive with alternate success in Spain; and it may be be said therefore, that the design of conquering this kingdom continued, as well as the hopes of succeeding. But why then did the States General refuse, in one thousand seven hundred and nine, to admit an article in the barrier-treaty, by which they would have obliged themselves to procure the whole Spanish monarchy to the house of Austria, when that zealous politician my lord TOWNSHEND pressed them to it? If their opinion of the necessity of carrying on the war, till this point could be obtained, was real; why did they risque the immense advantages given them with so much profuse generosity by this treaty, rather than consent to an engagement that was so conformable to their opinion?

AFTER the year one thousand seven hundred and ten, it will not be said, I presume, that the war could be supported in Spain with any prospect of advantage on our side. We had sufficiently experienced how little dependance could be had on the vigour of the Portuguese; and how firmly the Spanish nation in general, the Castilians in particular, were attached to PHILIP. Our armies had been twice at Madrid, this prince had been twice driven from the capital, his rival had been there, none stirred in favour of the

the victorious, all wished and acted for the vanquished. In short, the falshood of all those lures, by which we had been enticed to make war in Spain, had appeared sufficiently in one thousand seven hundred and six; but was so grosly evident in one thousand seven hundred and ten, that Mr. CRAGGS, who was sent towards the end of that year by Mr. STANHOPE into England, on commissions which he executed with much good sense, and much address, owned to me, that in Mr. STANHOPE's opinion, and he was not apt to despond of success, especially in the execution of his own projects, nothing could be done more in Spain, the general attachment of the people to PHILIP and their aversion to CHARLES considered: that armies of twenty or thirty thousand men might walk about that country till dooms-day, so he expressed himself, without effect: that wherever they came, the people would submit to CHARLES the third out of terror, and, as soon as they were gone, proclaim PHILIP the fifth again out of affection: that to conquer Spain required a great army; and to keep it, a greater.

WAS it possible, after this, to think in good earnest of conquering Spain, and could

could they be in good earneſt who continued to hold the ſame language, and to inſiſt on the ſame meaſures? Could they be ſo in the following year, when the emperor Joseph died? Charles was become then the ſole ſurviving male of the houſe of Auſtria, and ſucceeded to the empire as well as to all the hereditary dominions of that family. Could they be in earneſt who maintained, even in this conjuncture, that "no peace could be ſafe, honourable, or "laſting, ſo long as the kingdom of Spain "and the Weſt-Indies remained in the "poſſeſſion of any branch of the houſe of "Bourbon?" Did they mean that Charles ſhould be emperor and king of Spain? In this project they would have had the allies againſt them. Did they mean to call the duke of Savoy to the crown of Spain, or to beſtow it on ſome other prince? In this project they would have had his Imperial majeſty againſt them. In either caſe, the confederacy would have been broken: and how then would they have continued the war? Did they mean nothing, or did they mean ſomething more than they owned; ſomething more than to reduce the exorbitant power of France, and to force the whole Spaniſh monarchy out of the houſe of Bourbon?

Both

Both these ends might have been obtained at Gertruydenberg. Why were they not obtained? Read the preliminaries of one thousand seven hundred and nine, which were made the foundation of this treaty. Inform yourself of what passed there, and observe what followed. Your lordship will remain astonished. I remain so every time I reflect upon them, though I saw these things at no very great distance, even whilst they were in transaction; and though I know most certainly, that France lost, two years before, by the little skill and address of her principal * minister, in answering overtures made during the siege of Lisle by a principal person among the allies, such an opportunity, and such a correspondence, as would have removed some of the obstacles that lay now in her way, have prevented others, and have procured her peace. An equivalent for the thirty-seventh article of the preliminaries, that is, for the cession of Spain and the West Indies, was the point to be discussed at Gertruydenberg. Naples and Sicily, or even Naples and Sardinia would have contented the French, at least they would have accepted them as the equivalent. Buys and Vanderdussen, who

* Chamillard.

treated with them, reported this to the ministers of the allies: and it was upon this occasion that the duke of MARLBOROUGH, as BUYS himself told me, took immediately the lead, and congratulated the assembly on the near approach of a peace; said, that since the French were in this disposition, it was time to consider what further demands should be made upon them, according to the liberty observed in the preliminaries; and exhorted all the ministers of the allies to adjust their several ulterior pretensions, and to prepare their demands.

THIS proceeding, and what followed, put me in mind of that of the Romans with the Carthaginians. The former were resolved to consent to no peace till Carthage was laid in ruins. They set a treaty however on foot, at the request of their old enemy, imposed some terms, and referred them to their generals for the rest. Their generals pursued the same method, and, by reserving still a right of making ulterior demands, they reduced the Carthaginians at last to the necessity of abandoning their city, or of continuing the war after they had given up their arms, their machines, and their fleet, in hopes of peace.

FRANCE

France saw the snare, and resolved to run any risque rather than to be caught in it. We continued to demand, under pretence of securing the cession of Spain and the West Indies, that Lewis the fourteenth should take on him to dethrone his grandson in the space of two months; and, if he did not effect it in that time, that we should be at liberty to renew the war without restoring the places that were to be put into our hands according to the preliminaries; which were the most important places France possessed on the side of the Low Countries. Lewis offered to abandon his grandson; and, if he could not prevail on him to resign, to furnish money to the allies, who might at the expence of France, force him to evacuate Spain. The proposition made by the allies had an air of inhumanity: and the rest of mankind might be shocked to see the grandfather obliged to make war on his grandson. But Lewis the fourteenth had treated mankind with too much inhumanity in his prosperous days, to have any reason to complain even of this proposition. His people indeed, who are apt to have great partiality for their kings, might pity his distress. This happened, and he found his account in it.

Philip must have evacuated Spain, I think, notwithstanding his own obstinacy, the spirit of his queen, and the resolute attachment of the Spaniards, if his grandfather had insisted, and been in earnest to force him. But if this expedient was, as it was, odious, why did we prefer to continue the war against France and Spain, rather than accept the other? Why did we neglect the opportunity of reducing, effectually and immediately, the exorbitant power of France, and of rendering the conquest of Spain practicable? both which might have been brought about, and consequently the avowed ends of the war might have been answered, by accepting the expedient that France offered. "France" it was said, "was not sincere: she meant nothing more "than to amuse, and divide." This reason was given at the time; but some of those who gave it then, I have seen ashamed to insist on it since. France was not in a condition to act the part she had acted in former treaties: and her distress was no bad pledge of her sincerity on this occasion. But there was a better still. The strong places that she must have put into the hands of the allies, would have exposed her, on the least breach of faith, to see, not her frontier alone, but even the provinces that lie behind it, desolated:

lated: and prince Eugene might have had the satisfaction, it is said, I know not how truly, he desired, of marching with the torch in his hand to Versailles.

Your lordship will observe, that the conferences at Gertruydenberg ending in the manner they did, the inflexibility of the allies gave new life and spirit to the French and Spanish nations, distressed and exhausted as they were. The troops of the former withdrawn out of Spain, and the Spaniards left to defend themselves as they could, the Spaniards alone obliged us to retreat from Madrid, and defeated us in our retreat. But your lordship may think perhaps, as I do, that if Lewis the fourteenth had bound himself by a solemn treaty to abandon his grandson, had paid a subsidy to dethrone him, and had consented to acknowledge another king of Spain, the Spaniards would not have exerted the same zeal for Philip; the actions of Almenara and Saragossa might have been decisive, and those of Brihuegha and Villa Viciosa would not have happened. After all these events, how could any reasonable man expect that a war should be supported with advantage in Spain, to which the court of Vienna had contributed nothing from the first,

first, scarce bread to their arch-duke; which Portugal waged faintly and with deficient quotas; and which the Dutch had in a manner renounced, by neglecting to recruit their forces? How was CHARLES to be placed on the Spanish throne, or PHILIP at least to be driven out of it? by the success of the confederate arms in other parts. But what success sufficient to this purpose, could we expect? This question may be answered best, by shewing what success we had.

PORTUGAL and Savoy did nothing before the death of the emperor JOSEPH; and declared in form, as soon as he was dead, that they would carry on the war no longer to set the crown of Spain on the head of CHARLES, since this would be to fight against the very principle they had fought for. The Rhine was a scene of inaction. The sole efforts, that were to bring about the great event of dethroning PHILIP, were those which the duke of MARLBOROUGH was able to make. He took three towns in one thousand seven hundred and ten, Aire, Bethune, and St. Venant: and one, Bouchain, in one thousand seven hundred and eleven. Now this conquest being, in fact the only one the confederates made

that

that year, Bouchain may be faid properly and truly to have coſt our nation very near ſeven millions ſterling; for your lordſhip will find, I believe, that the charge of the war for that year amounted to no leſs. It is true that the duke of MARLBOROUGH had propoſed a very great project, by which incurſions would have been made during the winter into France; the next campaign might have been opened early on our ſide; and ſeveral other great and obvious advantages might have been obtained; but the Dutch refuſed to contribute, even leſs than their proportion, for the queen had offered to take the deficiency on herſelf, to the expence of barracks and forage; and diſappointed by their obſtinacy the whole deſign.

WE were then amuſed with viſionary ſchemes of marching our whole army, in a year or two more, and after a town or two more were taken, directly to Paris, or at leaſt into the heart of France. But was this ſo eaſy or ſo ſure a game? The French expected we would play it. Their generals had viſited the ſeveral poſts they might take, when our army ſhould enter France, to retard, to incommode, to diſtreſs us in our march, and even to make a deciſive ſtand

stand and to give us battle. I take what I
say here from indisputable authority, that
of the persons consulted and employed in
preparing for this great distress. Had we
been beaten, or had we been forced to retire towards our own frontier in the Low
Countries, after penetrating into France,
the hopes on which we protracted the war
would have been disappointed, and, I think,
the most sanguine would have then repented
refusing the offers made at Gertruydenberg.
But if we had beaten the French, for it was
scarce lawful in those days of our presumption to suppose the contrary; would the
whole monarchy of Spain have been our
immediate and certain prize? Suppose, and
I suppose it on good grounds, my lord,
that the French had resolved to defend
their country inch by inch, and that LEWIS
the fourteenth had determined to retire with
his court to Lyons or elsewhere, and to defend the passage of the Loire, when he
could no longer defend that of the Seine,
rather than submit to the terms imposed on
him: what should we have done in this
case? Must we not have accepted such a
peace as we had refused; or have protracted
the war till we had conquered France first,
in order to conquer Spain afterwards? Did
we hope for revolutions in France? We
had

had hoped for them in Spain: and we should have been bubbles of our hopes in both. That there was a spirit raised against the government of Lewis the fourteenth, in his court, nay in his family, and that strange schemes of private ambition were formed and forming there, I cannot doubt: and some effects of this spirit produced perhaps the greatest mortifications that he suffered in the latter part of his reign.

A Light instance of this spirit is all I will quote at this time. I supped, in the year one thousand seven hundred and fifteen, at a house in France, where two* persons of no small figure, who had been in great company that night, arrived very late. The conversation turned on the events of the precedent war, and the negociations of the late peace, in the process of the conversation, one of them † broke loose, and said, directing his discourse to me, "Vous "auriez pu nous écraser dans ce tems là: "pourquoi ne l'avez vous pas fait?" I answered him cooly, "Par ce que dans ce "tems-là nous n'avons plus craint vôtre "puiffance." This anecdote, too trivial for history, may find its place in a letter, and

* The duke de La Feuillade and Mortemar.
† La Feuillade.

may serve to confirm what I have admitted, that there were persons even in France, who expected to find their private account in the distress of their country. But these persons were a few, men of wild imaginations and strong passions, more enterprizing than capable, and of more name than credit. In general, the endeavours of Lewis the fourteenth, and the sacrifices he offered to make in order to obtain a peace, had attached his people more than ever to him: and if Lewis had determined not to go farther than he had offered at Gertruydenberg, in abandoning his grandson, the French nation would not have abandoned him.

But to resume what I have said or hinted already: the necessary consequences of protracting the war in order to dethrone Philip, from the year one thousand seven hundred and eleven inclusively, could be no other than these: our design of penetrating into France might have been defeated, and have become fatal to us by a reverse of fortune: our first success might not have obliged the French to submit; and we might have had France to conquer, after we had failed in our first attempt to conquer Spain, and even in order to proceed to a second: the French might have submitted, and the Spaniards

Spaniards not; and whilst the former had been employed to force the latter, according to the scheme of the allies; or whilst, the latter submitting likewise, Philip had evacuated Spain, the high allies might have gone together by the ears about dividing the spoil, and disposing of the crown of Spain. To these issues were things brought by protracting the war; by refusing to make peace, on the principles of the grand alliance at worst, in one thousand seven hundred and six; and by refusing to grant it, even on those of the new plan, in one thousand seven hundred and ten. Such contingent events as I have mentioned stood in prospect before us. The end of the war was removed out of sight; and they, who clamoured rather than argued for the continuation of it, contented themselves to affirm, that France was not enough reduced, and that no peace ought to be made as long as a prince of the house of Bourbon remained on the Spanish throne. When they would think France enough reduced, it was impossible to guess. Whether they intended to join the Imperial and Spanish crowns on the head of Charles, who had declared his irrevocable resolution to continue the war till the conditions insisted upon at Gertruydenberg were obtained: whether

whether they intended to beſtow Spain and the Indies on ſome other prince: and how this great alteration in their own plan ſhould be effected by common conſent: how poſſeſſion ſhould be given to Charles, or to any other prince, not only of Spain but of all the Spaniſh dominions out of Europe, where the attachment to Philip was at leaſt as ſtrong as in Caſtile, and where it would not be ſo eaſy, the diſtance and extent of theſe dominions conſidered, to oblige the Spaniards to ſubmit to another government: Theſe points, and many more equally neceſſary to be determined, and equally difficult to prepare, were neither determined nor prepared; ſo that we were reduced to carry on the war, after the death of the emperor Joseph, without any poſitive ſcheme agreed to, as the ſcheme of the future peace, by the allies. That of the grand alliance we had long before renounced. That of the new plan was become ineligible; and, if it had been eligible, it would have been impracticable, becauſe of the diviſion it would have created among the allies themſelves: ſeveral of whom would not have conſented, notwithſtanding his irrevocable reſolution, that the emperor ſhould be king of Spain. I know not what part the protractors of the war, in the depth of their policy, intended to take. Our nation had contributed, and acted so long under the direction of their councils, for the grandeur of the house of Austria, like one of the hereditary kingdoms usurped by that family, that it is lawful to think their intention might be to unite the Imperial and Spanish crowns. But I rather think they had no very determinate view, beyond that of continuing the war as long as they could. The late lord OXFORD told me, that my lord SOMERS being pressed, I know not on what occasion nor by whom, on the unnecessary and ruinous continuation of the war; instead of giving reasons to shew the necessity of it, contented himself to reply, that he had been bred up in a hatred of France. This was a strange reply for a wise man: and yet I know not whether he could have given a better then, or whether any of his pupils could give a better now.

THE whig party in general acquired great and just popularity, in the reign of our CHARLES the second, by the clamour they raised against the conduct of that prince in foreign affairs. They who succeeded to the name rather than the principles of this party, after the revolution, and who have had the adminiſtration of the government in their hands with very little interruption ever ſince, pretending to act on the ſame principle, have run into an extreme as vicous and as contrary to all the rules of good policy, as that which their predeceſſors exclaimed againſt. The old whigs complained of the inglorious figure we made, whilſt our court was the bubble, and our king the penſioner of France; and inſiſted that the growing ambition and power of Lewis the fourteenth ſhould be oppoſed in time. The modern whigs boaſted, and ſtill boaſt, of the glorious figure we made, whilſt we reduced ourſelves, by their councils, and under their adminiſtrations, to be the bubbles of our penſioners, that is of our allies; and whilſt we meaſured our efforts in war, and the continuation of them, without any regard to the intereſt and abilities of our own country, without a juſt and ſober regard, ſuch an one as contemplates objects in their true light and ſees them in their true magnitude, to the general ſyſtem of power in Europe; and, in ſhort, with a principal regard merely to particular intereſts at home and abroad. I ſay at home and abroad; becauſe it is not leſs true, that they have ſacrificed the wealth of their country

try to the forming and maintaining a party at home, than that they have done so to the forming and maintaining beyond all pretences of neceffity, alliances abroad. Thefe general affertions may be eafily juftified without having recourfe to private anecdotes, as your lordfhip will find when you confider the whole feries of our conduct in the two wars; in that which preceded, and that which fucceeded immediately the beginning of the prefent century, but above all the laft of them. In the adminiftrations that preceded the revolution, trade had flourifhed, and our nation had grown opulent: but the general intereft of Europe had been too much neglected by us; and flavery under the umbrage of prerogative, had been well-nigh eftablifhed among us. In thofe that have followed, taxes upon taxes, and debts upon debts have been perpetually accumulated, till a fmall number of families have grown into immenfe wealth, and national beggary has been brought upon us; under the fpecious pretences of fupporting a common caufe againft France, reducing her exorbitant power, and poifing that of Europe more equally in the public balance: laudable defigns no doubt, as far as they were real, but fuch as, being converted into

mere

mere pretences, have been productive of much evil; some of which we feel and have long felt, and some will extend its consequences to our latest posterity. The reign of prerogative was short: and the evils and the dangers, to which we were exposed by it, ended with it But the reign of false and squandering policy has lasted long, it lasts still, and will finally complete our ruin. Beggary has been the consequence of slavery in some countries: slavery will be probably the consequence of beggary in ours; and if it is so, we know at whose door to lay it. If we had finished the war in one thousand seven hundred and six, we should have reconciled like a wise people, our foreign and our domestic interests as nearly as possible: we should have secured the former sufficiently, and not have sacrificed the latter as entirely as we did by the prosecution of the war afterwards. You will not be able to see without astonishment, how the charge of the war encreased yearly upon us from the beginning of it; nor how immense a sum we paid in the course of it to supply the deficiencies of our confederates. Your astonishment, and indignation too, will increase, when you come to compare the progress that

was

was made from the year one thousand seven hundred and six exclusively, with the expence of more than thirty millions, I do not exaggerate though I write upon memory, that this progress cost us, to the year one thousand seven hundred and eleven inclusively. Upon this view, your lordship will be persuaded that it was high time to take the resolution of making peace, when the queen thought fit to change her ministry, towards the end of the year one thousand seven hundred and ten. It was high time indeed to save our country from absolute insolvency and bankruptcy, by putting an end to a scheme of conduct, which the prejudices of a party, the whimsy of some particular men, the private interest of more, and the ambition and avarice of our allies, who had been invited as it were to a scramble by the preliminaries of one thousand seven hundred and nine, alone maintained. The persons therefore, who came into power at this time, hearkened, and they did well to hearken, to the first overtures that were made them. The disposition of their enemies invited them to do so, but that of their friends, and that of a party at home who had nursed, and been nursed by the war, might have deterred them from it; for the difficulties and dangers, to which

they muſt be expoſed in carrying forward this great work, could eſcape none of them. In a letter to a friend it may be allowed me to ſay, that they did not eſcape me: and that I foreſaw, as contingent but not improbable events, a good part of what has happened to me ſince. Though it was a duty therefore that we owed to our country, to deliver her from the neceſſity of bearing any longer ſo unequal a part in ſo unneceſſary a war, yet was there ſome degree of merit in performing it. I think ſo ſtrongly in this manner, I am ſo incorrigible, my lord, that if I could be placed in the ſame circumſtances again, I would take the ſame reſolution, and act the ſame part. Age and experience might enable me to act with more ability, and greater ſkill; but all I have ſuffered ſince the death of the queen ſhould not hinder me from acting. Notwithſtanding this, I ſhall not be ſurprized if you think that the peace of Utrecht was not anſwerable to the ſucceſs of the war, nor to the efforts made in it. I think ſo myſelf, and have always owned, even when it was making and made, that I thought ſo. Since We had committed a ſucceſsful folly, we ought to have reaped more advantage from it than we did: and, whether we had left PHILIP, or placed another

ther prince on the throne of Spain, we ought to have reduced the power of France, and to have ftrengthened her neighbours, much more than we did. We ought to have reduced her power for generations to come, and not to have contented ourfelves with a momentary reduction of it. France was exhaufted to a great degree of men and money, and her government had no credit: but they, who took this for a fufficient reduction of her power, looked but a little way before them, and reafoned too fuperficially. Several fuch there were however; for as it has been faid, that there is no extravagancy which fome philofopher or other has not maintained, fo your experience, young as you are, muft have fhewn you, that there is no abfurd extreme, into which our party-politicians of Great Britain are not prone to fall, concerning the ftate and conduct of public affairs. But if France was exhaufted: fo were we, and fo were the Dutch. Famine rendered her condition much more miferable than ours, at one time, in appearance and in reality too. But as foon as this accident, that had diftreffed the French and frightened Lewis the fourteenth to the utmoft degree, and the immediate confequences of it were over; it was obvious to obferve, though few made

the

the obfervation, that whilft we were unable to raife in a year, by fome millions at leaft, the expences of the year, the French were willing and able to bear the impofition of the tenth over and above all the other taxes that had been laid upon them. This obfervation had the weight it deferved; and fure it deferved to have fome among thofe who made it, at the time fpoken of, and who did not think that the war was to be continued as long as a parliament could be prevailed on to vote money. But fuppofing it to have deferved none, fuppofing the power of France to have been reduced as low as you pleafe, with refpect to her inward ftate; yet ftill I affirm, that fuch a reduction could not be permanent, and was not therefore fufficient. Whoever knows the nature of her government, the temper of her people, and the natural advantages fhe has in commerce over all the nations that furround her, knows that an arbitrary government, and the temper of her people enable her on particular occafions to throw off a load of debt much more eafily, and with confequences much lefs to be feared, than any of her neighbours can: that although in the general courfe of things, trade be cramped, and induftry vexed by this arbitrary government, yet neither

neither one nor the other is oppreffed; and the temper of the people, and the natural advantages of the country, are fuch, that how great foever her diftrefs be at any point of time, twenty years of tranquility fuffice to re-eftablifh her affairs, and to enrich her again at the expence of all the nations of Europe. If any one doubts of this, let him confider the condition in which this kingdom was left by Lewis the fourteenth; the ftrange pranks the late duke of Orleans played, during his regency and adminiftration, with the whole fyftem of public revenue, and private property; and then let him tell himfelf, that the revenues of France, the tenth taken off, exceed all the expences of her government by many millions of livres already, and will exceed them by many more in another year.

Upon the whole matter, my lord, the low and exhaufted ftate to which France was reduced, by the laft great war, was but a momentary reduction of her power: and whatever real and more lafting reduction the treaty of Utrecht brought about in fome inftances, it was not fufficient. The power of France would not have appeared as great as it did, when England and Holland armed themfelves and armed all Germany againſt her, if ſhe had lain as open to the invaſions of her enemies, as her enemies lay to her's. Her inward ſtrength was great; but the ſtrength of thoſe frontiers which Lewis the fourteenth was almoſt forty years in forming, and which the folly of all his neighbours in their turns ſuffered him to form, made this ſtrength as formidable as it became. The true reduction of the exorbitant power of France, I take no notice of chimerical projects about changing her government, conſiſted therefore in diſarming her frontiers, and fortifying the barriers againſt her, by the ceſſion and demolition of many more places than ſhe yielded up at Utrecht; but not of more than ſhe might have been obliged to ſacrifice to her own immediate relief, and to the future ſecurity of her neighbours. That ſhe was not obliged to make theſe ſacrifices, I affirm was owing ſolely to thoſe who oppoſed the peace: and I am willing to put my whole credit with your lordſhip, and the whole merits of a cauſe that has been ſo much conteſted, on this iſſue. I ſay a cauſe that has been ſo much conteſted; for in truth, I think, it is no longer a doubt any where, except in Britiſh pamphlets, whether the conduct of thoſe who neither declined treating, as was

done

done in one thousand seven hundred and six; nor pretended to treat without a design of concluding, as was done in one thousand seven hundred and nine and ten, but carried the great work of the peace forward to its consummation; or the conduct of those who opposed this work in every step of its progress, saved the power of France from a greater and a sufficient reduction at the treaty of Utrecht. The very ministers, who were employed in this fatal opposition, are obliged to confess this truth. How should they deny it? Those of Vienna may complain that the emperor had not the entire Spanish monarchy, or those of Holland that the States were not made masters directly and indirectly of the whole Low Countries. But neither they, nor any one else that has any sense of shame about him, can deny that the late queen, though she was resolved to retreat because she was resolved to finish the war, yet was to the utmost degree desirous to treat in a perfect union with her allies, and to procure them all the reasonable terms they could expect: and much better than those they reduced themselves to the necessity of accepting, by endeavouring to wrest the negociation out of her hands. The disunion of the allies gave France the advantages she improved. The sole question is, who caused this disunion? and that will be easily decided by every impartial man, who informs himself carefully of the public anecdotes of that time. If the private anecdotes were to be laid open as well as those, and I think it almost time they should, the whole monstrous scene would appear, and shock the eye of every honest man. I do not intend to descend into many particulars at this time: but whenever I, or any other person as well informed as I, shall descend into a full deduction of such particulars, it will become undeniably evident, that the most violent opposition imaginable, carried on by the Germans and the Dutch in league with a party in Britain, began as soon as the first overtures were made to the queen; before she had so much as begun to treat: and was therefore an opposition not to this or that plan of treaty, but in truth to all treaty; and especially to one wherein Great Britain took the lead, or was to have any particular advantage. That the Imperialists meant no treaty, unless a preliminary and impracticable condition of it was to set the crown of Spain on the emperor's head, will appear from this; that prince EUGENE, when he came into England, long after the death of JOSEPH and elevation of CHARLES,

CHARLES, upon an errand moſt unworthy of ſo great a man, treated always on this ſuppoſition: and I remember with how much inward impatience I aſſiſted at conferences held with him concerning quotas for renewing the war in Spain, in the very ſame room, at the cockpit, where the queen's miniſters had been told in plain terms, a little before, by thoſe of other allies, "that their maſters would not con-
"ſent that the Imperial and Spaniſh crowns
"ſhould unite on the ſame head." That the Dutch were not averſe to all treaty, but meant none wherein Great Britain was to have any particular advantage, will appear from this; that their miniſter declared himſelf ready and authorized to ſtop the oppoſition made to the queen's meaſures, by preſenting a memorial, wherein he would declare, "that his maſters entered
"into them, and were reſolved not to con-
"tinue the war for the recovery of Spain,
"provided the queen would conſent that
"they ſhould garriſon Gibraltar and Port
"Mahon jointly with us, and ſhare equally
"the Aſſiento, the South Sea ſhip, and
"whatever ſhould be granted by the Spa-
"niards to the queen and her ſubjects." That the whigs engaged in this league with foreign powers againſt their country, as

well

well as their queen, and with a phrenfy more unaccountable than that which made and maintained the folemn league and covenant formerly, will appear from this; that their attempts were directed not only to wreft the negociations out of the queen's hands, but to oblige their country to carry on the war, on the fame unequal foot that had coft her already about twenty millions more than fhe ought to have contribu ed to it. For they not only continued to abet the emperor, whofe inability to fupply his quota, was confeffed; but the Dutch likewife, after the States, had refufed to ratify the treaty their minifter figned at London towards the end of the year one thoufand feven hundred and eleven, and by which the queen united herfelf more clofely than ever to them; engaging to purfue the war, to conclude the peace, and to guaranty it, when concluded, jointly with them; " pro-
" vided they would keep the engagements
" they had taken with her, and the con-
" ditions of proportionate expence under
" which our nation had entered into the
" war." Upon fuch fchemes as thefe was the oppofition to the treaty of Utrecht carried on: and the means employed, and the means projected to be employed, were worthy of fuch fchemes; open, direct, and
indecent

indecent defiance of legal authority, secret conspiracies against the state, and base machinations against particular men, who had no other crime than that of endeavouring to conclude a war, under the authority of the queen, which a party in the nation endeavoured to prolong, against her authority. Had the good policy of concluding the war being doubtful, it was certainly as lawful for those, who thought it good, to advise it, as it had been for those, who thought it bad, to advise the contrary: and the decision of the sovereign on the throne ought to have terminated the contest. But he who had judged by the appearances of things on one side, at that time, would have been apt to think, that putting an end to the war, or to Magna Charta, was the same thing; that the queen on the throne had no right to govern independently of her successor; nor any of her subjects a right to administer the government under her, tho' called to it by her, except those whom she had thought fit to lay aside. Extravagant as these principles are, no other could justify the conduct held at that time by those who opposed the peace: and as I said just now, that the phrensy of this league was more unaccountable than that of the solemn league and covenant, I might have added,

added, that it was not very many degrees less criminal. Some of those, who charged the queen's ministers, after her death, with imaginary treasons, had been guilty during her life of real treasons: and I can compare the folly and violence of the spirit that prevailed at that time, both before the conclusion of the peace, and, under pretence of danger to the succession after it, to nothing more nearly than to the folly and violence of the spirit that seized the tories soon after the accession of GEORGE the first. The latter indeed, which was provoked by unjust and impolitic persecution, broke out in open rebellion. The former might have done so, if the queen had lived a little longer. But to return.

THE obstinate adherence of the Dutch to this league, in opposition to the queen, rendered the conferences of Utrecht, when they were opened, no better than mock conferences. Had the men who governed that commonwealth been wife and honest enough to unite, at least then, cordially with the queen, and, since they could not hinder a congress, to act in concert with her in it; we should have been still in time to maintain a sufficient union among the allies,

allies, and a sufficient superiority over the French. All the specific demands that the former made, as well as the Dutch themselves, either to incumber the negociation, or to have in reserve according to the artifice usually employed on such occasions, certain points from which to depart in the course of it with advantage, would not have been obtained: but all the essential demands, all in particular that were really necessary to secure the barriers in the Low Countries and of the four circles against France, would have been so. For France must have continued, in this case, rather to sue for peace, than to treat on an equal foot. The first dauphin, son of LEWIS the fourteenth, died several months before this congress began: the second dauphin, his grandson, and the wife and the eldest son of this prince, died soon after it began, of the same unknown distemper, and were buried together in the same grave. Such family misfortunes, following a long series of national misfortunes, made the old king, though he bore them with much seeming magnanimity, desirous to get out of the war at any tolerable rate, that he might not run the risque of leaving a child of five years old, the present king, engaged in it. The queen did all that was morally possible,

possible, except giving up her honour in the negociation, and the interest of her subjects in the conditions of peace, to procure this union with the states general. But all she could do was vain; and the same phrensy, that had hindered the Dutch from improving to their, and to the common advantage the public misfortunes of France, hindered them from improving to the same purposes the private misfortunes of the house of Bourbon. They continued to flatter themselves that they should force the queen out of her measures, by their intrigues with the party in Britain who opposed these measures, and even raise an insurrection against her. But these intrigues, and those of prince EUGENE, were known and disappointed; and monsieur BUYS had the mortification to be reproached with them publicly, when he came to take leave of the lords of the council, by the earl of OXFORD; who entered into many particulars that could not be denied, of the private transactions of this sort, to which BUYS had been a party, in compliance with his instructions, and, as I believe, much against his own sense and inclinations. As the season for taking the field advanced, the league proposed to defeat the success of the congress by the events

events of the campaign. But inftead of defeating the fuccefs of the congrefs, the events of the campaign ferved only to turn this fuccefs in favour of France. At the beginning of the year, the queen and the States, in concert, might have given the law to friend and foe, with great advantage to the former; and with fuch a detriment to the latter, as the caufes of the war rendered juft, the events of it reafonable, and the objects of it neceffary. At the end of the year, the allies were no longer in a ftate of giving, nor the French of receiving the law; and the Dutch had recourfe to the queen's good offices, when they could oppofe and durft infult her no longer. Even then, thefe offices were employed with zeal, and with fome effect for them.

Thus the war ended, much more favourably to France than fhe expected, or they who put an end to it defigned. The queen would have humbled and weakened this power. The allies who oppofed her would have crufhed it, and have raifed another as exorbitant on the ruins of it. Neither one nor the other fucceeded, and they who meant to ruin the French power preserved it, by opposing those who meant to reduce it.

Since I have mentioned the events of the year one thousand seven hundred and twelve, and the decisive turn they gave to the negociations in favour of France, give me leave to say something more on this subject. You will find that I shall do so with much impartiality. The disastrous events of this campaign in the Low Countries, and the consequences of them, have been imputed to the separation of the British troops from the army of the allies. The clamour against this measure was great at that time, and the prejudices which this clamour raised are great still among some men. But as clamour raised these prejudices, other prejudices gave birth to this clamour: and it is no wonder they should do so among persons bent on continuing the war; since I own very freely, that when the first step that led to this separation came to my knowledge, which was not an hour, by the way, before I wrote by the queen's order to the duke of Ormond, in the very words in which the order was advised and given, " that he " should not engage in any siege, nor ha- " zard a battle, till further order," I was surprized and hurt. So much, that if I had had an opportunity of speaking in private to the queen, after I had received monsieur DE TORCY's lettter to me on the subject, and before she went into the council, I should have spoken to her, I think, in the first heat against it. The truth is, however, that the step was justifiable at that point of time in every respect, and therefore that the consequences are to be charged to the account of those who drew them on themselves, not to the account of the queen, nor of the minister who advised her. The step was justifiable to the allies surely, since the queen took no more upon her, no not so much by far, in making it, as many of them had done by suspending, or endangering, or defeating operations in the heat of the war, when they declined to send their troops, or delayed the march of them, or neglected the preparations they were obliged to make, on the most frivolous pretences. Your lordship will find in the course of your enquiries many particular instances of what is here pointed out in general. But I cannot help descending into some view of those that regard the emperor and the States General, who cried the loudest and with the most effect, though they had the least reason, on account of their own conduct, to complain of the queen's. With what face could the emperor, for inſtance, prefume to complain of the orders ſent to the duke of ORMOND? I ſay nothing of his deficiencies, which were ſo great, that he had at this very time little more than one regiment that could be ſaid properly to act againſt France and Spain at his ſole charge; as I affirmed to prince EUGENE before the lords of the council, and demonſtrated upon paper the next day. I ſay nothing of all that preceded the year one thouſand ſeven hundred and ſeven, on which I ſhould have much to ſay. But I deſire your lordſhip only to conſider, what you will find to have paſſed after the famous year one thouſand ſeven hundred and ſix. Was it with the queen's approbation, or againſt her will, that the emperor made the treaty for the evacuation of Lombardy, and let out ſo great a number of French regiments time enough to recruit themſelves at home, to march into Spain, and to deſtroy the Britiſh forces at Almanza? Was it with her approbation, or againſt her will, that, inſtead of employing all his forces and all his endeavours, to make the greateſt deſign of the whole war, the enterprize on Toulon, ſucceed, he detached twelve thouſand men to reduce the kingdom

of

of Naples, that muſt have fallen of courſe? and that an opportunity of ruining the whole maritime force of France, and of ruining or ſubduing her provinces on that ſide, was loſt, merely by this unneceſſary diverſion, and by the conduct of prince EUGENE, which left no room to doubt that he gave occaſion to this fatal diſappointment on purpoſe, and in concert with the court of Vienna?

TURN your eyes, my lord, on the conduct of the States, and you will find reaſon to be aſtoniſhed at the arrogance of the men who governed in them at this time, and who preſumed to exclaim againſt a queen of Great Britain, for doing what their deputies had done more than once in that very country, and in the courſe of that very war. In the year one thouſand ſeven hundred and twelve, at the latter end of a war, when conferences for treating a peace were opened, when the leaſt ſiniſter event in the field would take off from that ſuperiority which the allies had in the congreſs, and when the paſt ſucceſs of the war had already given them as much of this ſuperiority as they wanted to obtain a ſafe, advantageous, honourable, and laſting peace, the queen directed her general to ſuſpend

till

till further order the operations of her troops. In one thousand seven hundred and three, in the beginning of a war, when something was to be risqued or no success to be expected, and when the bad situation of affairs in Germany and Italy required, in a particular manner, that efforts should be made in the Low Countries, and that the war should not languish there whilst it was unsuccessful every where else; the duke of MARLBOROUGH determined to attack the French, but the Dutch deputies would not suffer their troops to go on; defeated his design in the very moment of it's execution, if I remember well, and gave no other reason for their proceeding than that which is a reason against every battle, the possibility of being beaten. The circumstance of proximity to their frontier was urged, I know, and it was said, that their provinces would be exposed to the incursions of the French if they lost the battle. But besides other answers to this vain pretence, it was obvious that they had ventured battles as near home as this would have been fought, and that the way to remove the enemy farther off was by action, not inaction. Upon the whole matter; the Dutch deputies stopped the progress of the confederate army at this time, by exercising an arbitrary and inde-

independent authority over the troops of the States. In one thousand seven hundred and five, when the success of the preceding campaign should have given them an entire confidence in the duke of MARLBOROUGH's conduct, when returning from the Moselle to the Low Countries he began to make himself and the common cause amends, for the disappointment which pique and jealousy in the prince of BADEN, or usual sloth and negligence in the Germans, had occasioned just before, by forcing the French lines; when he was in the full pursuit of this advantage, and when he was marching to attack an enemy half defeated, and more than half dispirited; nay, when he had made his dispositions for attacking, and part of his troops had passed the Dyle—the deputies of the States once more tied up his hands, took from him an opportunity too fair to be lost; for these, I think, were some of the terms of his complaint: and in short the confederacy received an affront at least, where we might have obtained a victory. Let this that has been said serve as a specimen of the independency on the queen, her councils, and her generals, with which these powers acted in the course of the war; who were not ashamed to find fault that the queen, once, and at the latter end of it; presumed to suspend the operation of her troops till farther order. But be it that they forsaw what this farther order would be. They foresaw then, that as soon as Dunkirk should be put into the queen's hands, she would consent to a suspension of arms for two months, and invite them to do the same. Neither this foresight, nor the strong declaration which the bishop of Bristol made by the queen's order at Utrecht, and which shewed them that her resolution was not taken to submit to the league into which they had entered against her, could prevail on them to make a right use of these two months, by endeavouring to renew their union and good understanding with the queen; though I can say with the greatest truth, and they could not doubt of it at the time, that she would have gone more than half way to meet them, and that her ministers would have done their utmost to bring it about. Even then we might have resumed the superiority we began to lose in the congress; for, the queen and the States uniting, the principal allies would have united with them: and, in this case, it would have been so much the interest of France to avoid any chance of seeing the war renewed, that she must, and she would, have made sure of peace,

peace, during the fufpenfion, on much worfe terms for herfelf and for Spain, than fhe made it afterwards. But the prudent and fober States continued to act like froward children, or like men drunk with refentment and paffion; and fuch will the conduct be of the wife governments in every circumftance, where a fpirit of faction and of private intereft prevails, among thofe who are at the head, over reafon of ftate. After laying afide all decency in their behaviour towards the queen, they laid afide all caution for themfelves. They declared " they would carry on the war " without her." Landrecy feemed, in their efteem, of more importance than Dunkirk; and the opportunity of wafting fome French provinces, or of putting the whole event of the war on the decifion of another battle, preferable to the other meafure that lay open to them; that, I mean, of trying in good earneft, and in an honeft concert with the queen, during the fufpenfion of arms, whether fuch terms of peace, as ought to fatisfy them and the other allies might not be impofed on France.

If the confederate army had broke into France, the campaign before this, or in any former campaign; and if the Germans

and the Dutch had exercifed then the fame inhumanity, as the French had exercifed in their provinces in former wars; if they had burnt Verfailles, and even Paris, and if they had difturbed the afhes of the dead princes that repofe at St. Denis, every good man would have felt the horror, that fuch cruelties infpire: no man could have faid that the retaliation was unjuft. But in one thoufand feven hundred and twelve, it was too late, in every refpect, to meditate fuch projects. If the French had been unprepared to defend their frontier, either for want of means, or in a vain confidence that the peace would be made, as our king CHARLES the fecond was unprepared to defend his coaft at the latter end of his firft war with Holland, the allies might have played a fure game in fatisfying their vengeance on the French, as the Dutch did on us in one thoufand fix hundred and fixty feven; and impofing harder terms on them, than thofe they offered, or would have accepted. But this was not the cafe. The French army was, I believe, more numerous than the army of the allies, even before feparation, and certainly in a much better condition than two or three years before, when a deluge of blood was fpilt to diflodge them, for we did no more, at
Mal-

Malplaquet. Would the Germans and the Dutch have found it more eafy to force them at this time, than it was at that? Would not the French have fought with as much obftinacy to fave Paris, as they did to fave Mons: and, with all the regard due to the duke of ORMOND and to prince EUGENE was the abfence of the duke of MARLBOROUGH of no confequence? Turn this affair every way in your thoughts, my lord, and you will find that the Germans and the Dutch had nothing in theirs, but to break, at any rate, and at any rifque, the negociations that were begun, and to reduce Great Britain to the neceffity of continuing what fhe had been too long, a province of the confederacy. A province indeed, and not one of the beft treated: fince the confederates affumed a right of obliging her to keep her pacts with them, and of difpenfing with their obligations to her, of exhaufting her, without rule, or proportion, or meafure, in the fupport of a war, to which fhe alone contributed more than all of them, and in which fhe had no longer an immediate intereft nor even any remote intereft that was not common, or, with refpect to her, very dubious; and, after all this, of complaining that the queen prefumed to hearken to overtures

of

of peace, and to set a negociation on foot, whilst their humour and ambition required that the war should be prolonged for an indefinite time, and for a purpose that was either bad or indeterminate.

The suspension of arms, that began in the Low Countries, was continued, and extended afterwards by the act I signed at Fontainebleau. The fortune of the war turned at the same time: and all those disgraces followed, which obliged the Dutch to treat, and to desire the assistance of the queen, whom they had set at defiance so lately. This assistance they had, as effectually as it could be given in the circumstances, to which they had reduced themselves, and the whole alliance: and the peace of Great Britain, Portugal, Savoy, Prussia, and the States General, was made, without his imperial majesty's concurrence, in the spring of one thousand seven hundred and thirteen; as it might have been made, much more advantageously for them all, in that of one thousand seven hundred and twelve. Less obstinacy on the part of the States, and perhaps more decisive resolutions on the part of the queen, would have wound up all these divided threads in one,

one, and have finished this great work much sooner and better. I say, perhaps more decisive resolutions on the part of the queen; because, although I think that I should have conveyed her orders for signing a treaty of peace with France, before the armies took the field, much more willingly, than I executed them afterwards in signing that of the cessation of arms; yet I do not presume to decide, but shall desire your lordship to do so, on a review of all circumstances, some of which I shall just mention.

The league made for protracting the war having opposed the queen to the utmost of their power, and by means of every sort, from the first appearances of a negociation: the general effect of this violent opposition, on her and her ministers was, to make them proceed by slower and more cautious steps: the particular effect of it was, to oblige them to open the eyes of the nation, and to inflame the people with a desire of peace, by shewing, in the most public and solemn manner, how unequally we were burdened, and how unfairly we were treated by our allies. The first gave an air of diffidence and timidity to their conduct, which encouraged the league, and gave vigour to the oppofition. The fecond irritated the Dutch particularly; for the emperor and the other allies had the modefty at leaft, not to pretend to bear any proportion in the expence of the war; and thus the two powers, whofe union was the moft effential, were the moft at variance, and the queen was obliged to act in a clofer concert with her enemy who defired peace, than fhe would have done if her allies had been lefs obftinately bent to protract the war. During thefe tranfactions, my lord Oxford, who had his correfpondencies apart, and a private thread of negociation always in his hands, entertained hopes that Philip would be brought to abandon Spain in favour of his father-in-law, and to content himfelf with the ftates of that prince, the kingdom of Sicily, and the prefervation of his right of fucceffion to the crown of France. Whether my lord had any particular reafons for entertaining thefe hopes, befides the general reafons founded on the condition of France, on that of the Bourbon family, and on the difpofition of Lewis the fourteenth, I doubt very much. That Lewis, who fought, and had need of feeking peace, almoft at any rate, and who faw that he could not obtain it, even of the queen, unlefs Philip abandoned immediately,

mediately, the crown of Spain, or abandoned immediately, by renunciation and a folemn act of exclufion, all pretenfion to that of France; that Lewis was defirous of the former, I cannot doubt. That Philip would have abandoned Spain with the equivalents that have been mentioned, or either of them, I believe likewife; if the prefent king of France had died, when his father, mother, and eldeft brother did: for they all had the fame diftemper. But Lewis would ufe no violent means to force his grandfon; the queen would not continue the war to force him; Philip was too obftinate, and his wife too ambitious, to quit the crown of Spain, when they had difcovered our weaknefs, and felt their own ftrength in that country, by their fuccefs in the campaign of one thoufand feven hundred and ten: after which my lord Stanhope himfelf was convinced that Spain could not be conquered, nor kept, if it was conquered, without a much greater army, than it was poffible for us to fend thither. In that fituation it was wild to imagine, as the earl of Oxford imagined, or pretended to imagine, that they would quit the crown of Spain, for a remote and uncertain profpect of fucceeding to that of France, and content themfelves to be, in the mean time, princes of very small dominions. PHILIP therefore, after strugling long that he might not be obliged to make his option till the succession of France lay open to him, was obliged to make it, and made it, for Spain. Now this, my lord, was the very crisis of the negociation: and to this point I apply what I said above of the effect of more decisive resolutions on the part of the queen. It was plain, that if she made the campaign in concert with her allies, she could be no longer mistress of the negociations, nor have almost a chance for conducting them to the issue she proposed. Our ill success in the field would have rendered the French less tractable in the congress: our good success there would have rendered the allies so. On this principle, the queen suspended the operations of her troops, and then concluded the cessation.

COMPARE now the appearances and effect of this measure, with the appearances, and effect that another measure would have had. In order to arrive at any peace, it was necessary to do what the queen did, or to do more: and, in order to arrive at a good one, it was necessary to be prepared to carry on the war, as well as to make a shew of it; for she had the hard task upon her,

her, of guarding againſt her allies, and her enemies both. But in that ferment, when few men conſidered any thing coolly, the conduct of her general, after he took the field, though he covered the allies in the ſiege of Queſnoy, correſponded ill, in appearance, with the declarations of carrying on the war vigorouſly that had been made, on ſeveral occaſions, before the campaign opened. It had an air of double dealing; and as ſuch it paſſed among thoſe, who did not combine in their thoughts all the circumſtances of the conjuncture, or who were infatuated with the notional neceſſity of continuing the war. The clamour could not have been greater, if the queen had ſigned her peace ſeparately: and, I think, the appearances might have been explained as favourably in one caſe, as in the other. From the death of the emperor Joseph, it was neither our intereſt, nor the common intereſt, well underſtood, to ſet the crown of Spain on the preſent emperor's head. As ſoon therefore as Philip had made his option, and if ſhe had taken this reſolution early, his option would have been ſooner made, I preſume that the queen might have declared that ſhe would not continue the war an hour longer to procure Spain for his Imperial majeſty; that the engagements, she had taken whilst he was archduke, bound her no more; that, by his accession to the empire, the very nature of them was altered ; that she took effectual measures to prevent, in any future time, an union of the crowns of France and Spain, and, upon the same principle, would not consent, much less fight, to bring about an immediate union of the Imperial and Spanish crowns; that they, who insisted to protract the war, intended this union; that they could intend nothing else, since they ventured to break with her, rather than to treat, and were so eager to put the reasonable satisfaction, that they might have in every other case, without hazard, on the uncertain events of war; that she would not be imposed on any longer in this manner; and that she had ordered her ministers to sign her treaty with France, on the surrender of Dunkirk into her hands; that she pretended not to prescribe to her allies, but that she had insisted, in their behalf, on certain conditions, that France was obliged to grant to those of them, who should sign their treaties at the same time as she did, or who should consent to an immediate cessation of arms, and during the cessation, treat under her mediation. There had been more frankness, and more dignity

dignity in this proceeding, and the effect muſt have been more advantageous. France would have granted more for a ſeparate peace, than for a ceſſation: and the Dutch would have been more influenced by the proſpect of one, than of the other; eſpecially ſince this proceeding would have been very different from theirs at Munſter, and at Nimeghen, where they abandoned their allies, without any other pretence than the particular advantage they found in doing ſo. A ſuſpenſion of the operations of the queen's troops, nay a ceſſation of arms between her and France, was not definitive; and they might, and they did, hope to drag her back under their, and the German yoke. This therefore was not ſufficient to check their obſtinacy, nor to hinder them from making all the unfortunate haſte they did make to get themſelves beaten at Denain. But they would poſſibly have laid aſide their vain hopes, if they had ſeen the queen's miniſters ready to ſign her treaty of peace, and thoſe of ſome principal allies ready to ſign at the ſame time; in which caſe the miſchief, that followed, had been prevented, and better terms of peace had been obtained for the confederacy: a prince of the houſe of Bourbon, who could never be king of France, would have

have sat on the Spanish throne, instead of an emperor; the Spanish scepter would have been weakened in the hands of one, and the Imperial scepter would have been strengthened in those of the other: France would have had no opportunity of recovering from former blows, nor of finishing a long unsuccessful war by two successful campaigns: her ambition, and her power, would have declined with her old king, and under the minority that followed: one of them at least might have been so reduced by the terms of peace, if the defeat of the allies in one thousand seven hundred and twelve, and the loss of so many towns as the French took in that and the following year, had been prevented, that the other would have been no longer formidable, even supposing it to have continued; whereas I suppose that the tranquility of Europe is more due, at this time, to want of ambition, than to want of power, on the part of France. But, to carry the comparison of these two measures to the end, it may be supposed that the Dutch would have taken the same part, on the queen's declaring a separate peace, as they took on her declaring a cessation. The preparations for the campaign in the Low Countries were made; the Dutch like the other confederates

federates, had a just confidence in their own troops, and an unjust contempt for those of the enemy; they were transported from their usual sobriety and caution by the ambitious prospect of large acquisitions, which had been opened artfully to them; the rest of the confederate army was composed of Imperial and German troops: so that the Dutch, the Imperialists, and the other Germans, having an interest to decide which was no longer the interest of the whole confederacy, they might have united against the queen in one case, as they did in the other; and the mischief that followed to them and the common cause, might not have been prevented. This might have been the case, no doubt. They might have flattered themselves that they should be able to break into France, and to force PHILIP, by the distress brought on his grandfather, to resign the crown of Spain to the emperor, even after Great Britain and Portugal, and Savoy too perhaps, were drawn out of the war; for these princes desired as little, as the queen, to see the Spanish crown on the emperor's head. But, even in this case, though the madness would have been greater, the effect would not have been worse. The queen would have been able to serve these confederates

derates as well by being mediator in the negociations, as they left it in her power to do, by being a party in them: and Great Britain would have had the advantage of being delivered so much sooner from a burden, which whimsical and wicked politics had imposed, and continued upon her till it was become intolerable. Of these two measures, at the time when we might have taken either, there were persons who thought the last preferable to the former. But it never came into public debate. Indeed it never could; too much time having been lost in waiting for the option of PHILIP, and the suspension and cessation having been brought before the council rather as a measure taken, than a matter to be debated. If your lordship, or any one else, should judge, that, in such circumstances as those of the confederacy in the beginning of one thousand seven hundred and twelve, the latter measure ought to have been taken, and the gordian knot to have been cut, rather than to suffer a mock treaty to languish on, with so much advantage to the French as the disunion of the allies gave them; in short, if slowness, perplexity, inconsistency, and indecision should be objected, in some instances, to the queen's councils at that time; if it
should

should be said particularly, that she did not observe the precise moment when the conduct of the league formed against her, being exposed to mankind, would have justified any part she should have taken (though she declared, soon after the moment was passed, that this conduct had set her free from all her engagements) and when she ought to have taken that of drawing, by one bold measure, her allies out of the war, or herself out of the confederacy, before she lost her influence on France: if all this should be objected, yet would the proofs brought to support these objections shew, that we were better allies than politicians; that the desire the queen had to treat in concert with her confederates, and the resolution she took not to sign without them, made her bear what no crowned head had ever borne before; and that where she erred, she erred principally by the patience, the compliance, and the condescension she exercised towards them, and towards her own subjects in league with them. Such objections as these may lie to the queen's conduct, in the course of this great affair; as well as objections of human infirmity to that of those persons employed by her in the transactions of it; from which neither those who preceded, nor those who succeeded, have, I presume, been free. But the principles on which they proceeded were honest, the means they used were lawful, and the event they proposed to bring about was just. Whereas the very foundation of all the opposition to the peace was laid in injustice and folly: for what could be more unjust, than the attempt of the Dutch and the Germans, to force the queen to continue a war for their private interest and ambition, the disproportionate expence of which oppressed the commerce of her subjects, and loaded them with debts for ages yet to come? a war, the object of which was so changed, that from the year one thousand seven hundred and eleven, she made it not only without any engagement, but against her own, and the common interest? What could be more foolish; you will think that I soften the term too much, and you will be in the right to think so: what could be more foolish, than the attempt of a party in Britain, to protract a war so ruinous to their country, without any reason that they durst avow, except that of wreaking the resentments of Europe on France, and that of uniting the Imperial and Spanish crowns on an Austrian head? one of which was to purchase revenge at a price too dear; and

the

the other was to expose the liberties of Europe to new dangers, by the conclusion of a war which had been made to assert and secure them.

I have dwelt the longer on the conduct of those who promoted, and of those who opposed, the negociations of the peace made at Utrecht, and on the comparison of the measure pursued by the queen with that which she might have pursued, because the great benefit we ought to reap from the study of history, cannot be reaped unless we accustom ourselves to compare the conduct of different governments, and different parties, in the same conjunctures, and to observe the measures they did pursue, and the measures they might have pursued, with the actual consequences that followed one, and the possible, or probable consequences, that might have followed the other, by this exercise of the mind, the study of history anticipates, as it were, experience, as I have observed in one of the first of these letters, and prepares us for action. If this consideration should not plead a sufficient excuse for my prolixity on this head, I have one more to add that may. A rage of warring possessed a party in our nation till the death of the late queen:

queen: a rage of negociating has poſſeſſed the ſame party of men, ever ſince. You have ſeen the conſequences of one: you ſee actually thoſe of the other. The rage of warring confirmed the beggary of our nation, which began as early as the revolution; but then it gave, in the laſt war, reputation to our arms, and our councils too. For though I think, and muſt always think, that the principle, on which we acted after departing from that laid down in the grand alliance of one thouſand ſeven hundred and one, was wrong; yet muſt we confeſs that it was purſued wiſely, as well as boldly. The rage of negociating has been a chargeable rage likewiſe, at leaſt as chargeable in its proportion. Far from paying our debts, contracted in war, they continue much the ſame, after three and twenty years of peace. The taxes that oppreſs our mercantile intereſt the moſt are ſtill in mortgage; and thoſe that oppreſs the landed intereſt the moſt, inſtead of being laid on extraordinary occaſions, are become the ordinary funds for the current ſervice of every year. This is grievous, and the more ſo to any man, who has the honour of his country, as well as her proſperity at heart, becauſe we have not, in this caſe, the airy conſolation we had in

the

the other. The rage of negociating began twenty years ago, under pretence of confummating the treaty of Utrecht: and, from that time to this, our minifters have been in one perpetual maze. They have made themfelves and us, often, objects of averfion to the powers on the continent; and we are become at laft objects of contempt, even to the Spaniards. What other effect could our abfurd conduct have? What other return has it deferved? We came exhaufted out of long wars; and, inftead of purfuing the meafures neceffary to give us means and opportunity to repair our ftrength and to dminifh our burdens, our minifters have acted, from that time to this, like men who fought pretences to keep the nation in the fame exhaufted condition, and under the fame load of debt. This may have been their view perhaps; and we could not be furprifed if we heard the fame men declare national poverty neceffary to fupport the prefent government, who have fo frequently declared corruption and a ftanding army to be fo. Your good fenfe, my lord, your virtue, and your love of your country, will always determine you to oppofe fuch vile fchemes, and to contribute your utmoft towards the cure of both thefe kinds of rage; the rage of

warring,

warring, without any proportionable interest of our own, for the ambition of others; and the rage of negociating, on every occasion, at any rate, without a sufficient call to it, and without any part of that deciding influence which we ought to have. Our nation inhabits an island, and is one of the principal nations of Europe; but, to maintain this rank, we must take the advantages of this situation, which have been neglected by us for almost half a century; we must always remember that we are not part of the continent, but we must never forget that we are neighbours to it. I will conclude, by applying a rule, that HORACE gives for the conduct of an epic or dramatic poem, to the part Great Britain ought to take in the affairs of the continent, if you allow me to transform Britannia into a male divinity, as the verse requires.

Nec Deus intersit, nisi dignus vindice nodus Inciderit.

If these reflections are just, and I should not have offered them to your lordship, had they not appeared both just and important to my best understanding, you will think that I have not spent your time unprofitably in making them, and exciting you by them to examine the true intereſt of your country relatively to foreign affairs; and to compare it with thoſe principles of conduct, that I am perſuaded, have no other foundation than party-deſigns, prejudices, and habits; the private intereſt of ſome men and the ignorance and raſhneſs of others.

My letter is grown ſo long, that I ſhall ſay nothing to your lordſhip, at this time concerning the ſtudy of modern hiſtory, relatively to the intereſts of your country in domeſtic affairs; and I think there will be no need to do ſo at any other. The Hiſtory of the rebellion by your great grandfather, and his private memorials, which your lordſhip has in manuſcript, will guide you ſurely as far as they go: where they leave you, your lordſhip muſt not expect any hiſtory; for we have more reaſon to make this complaint, "abeſt enim hiſ-"toria literis noſtris," than Tully had to put it into the mouth of Atticus, in his firſt book of laws. But where hiſtory leaves you, it is wanted leaſt: the traditions of this century, and of the latter end of the laſt, are freſh. Many, who were actors in ſome of theſe events, are alive; and many who have converſed with thoſe that were actors in others. The public is in possession of several collections and memorials, and several there are in private hands. You will want no materials to form true notions of transactions so recent. Even pamphlets, wrote on different sides and on different occasions in our party disputes, and histories of no more authority than pamphlets, will help you to come at truth. Read them with suspicion, my lord, for they deserve to be suspected: pay no regard to the epithets given, nor to the judgments passed; neglect all declamation, weigh the reasoning and advert to fact. With such precautions, even BURNET's history may be of some use. In a word, your lordship will want no help of mine to discover, by what progression the whole constitution of our country, and even the character of our nation, has been altered: nor how much a worse use, in a national sense, though a better in the sense of party politicks, the men called Whigs have made of long wars and new systems of revenue, since the revolution; than the men called Tories made, before it, of long peace, and stale prerogative. When you look back three or four generations ago, you will see that the English were a plain, perhaps a rough, but a good-natured hospitable people,

ple, jealous of their liberties, and able as well as ready to defend them, with their tongues, their pens, and their swords. The restoration began to turn hospitality into luxury, pleasure into debauch, and country peers and country commoners into courtiers and men of mode. But whilst our luxury was young, it was little more than elegance: the debauch of that age was enlivened with wit, and varnished over with gallantry. The courtiers and the men of mode knew what the constitution was, respected it, and often asserted it. Arts and sciences flourished, and, if we grew more trivial, we were not become either grossly ignorant, or openly profligate. Since the revolution, our kings have been reduced indeed to a seeming annual dependance on Parliament; but the business of parliament, which was esteemed in general a duty before, has been exercised in general as a trade since. The trade of parliament, and the trade of funds, have grown universal. Men, who stood forward in the world, have attended to little else. The frequency of parliaments, that increased their importance, and should have increased the respect of them, has taken off from their dignity: and the spirit that prevailed, whilst the service in them was duty, has been debased since it became a trade. Few know, and scarce any respect, the British constitution: that of the church has been long since derided; that of the State as long neglected; and both have been left at the mercy of the men in power, whoever those men were. Thus the Church, at least the hierarchy, however sacred in it's origin, or wise in it's institution, is become an useless burden on the State: and the State is become, under ancient and known forms, a new and undefinable monster; composed of a king without monarchical splendour, a senate of nobles without aristocratical independency, and a senate of commons without democratical freedom. In the mean time, my lord, the very idea of wit, and all that can be called taste, has been lost among the great; arts and sciences are scarce alive; luxury has been increased but not refined; corruption has been established, and is avowed. When governments are worn out, thus it is: the decay appears in every instance. Public and private virtue, public and private spirit, science and wit, decline all together.

That you, my lord, may have a long and glorious share in restoring all these, and in drawing our government back to
the

the true principles of it, I wish most heartily. Whatever errors I may have committed in public life, I have always loved my country: whatever faults may be objected to me in private life, I have always loved my friend: whatever usage I have received from my country, it shall never make me break with her: whatever usage I have received from my friends, I never shall break with one of them, while I think him a friend to my country. These are the sentiments of my heart. I know they are those of your lordship's: and a communion of such sentiments is a tye that will engage me to be, as long as I live,

My LORD,

Your most faithful servant.

A PLAN

FOR A

General History of Europe.

LETTER I.

I SHALL take the liberty of writing to you a little oftener than the three or four times a year, which, you tell me, are all you can allow yourself to write to those you like best: and yet I declare to you with great truth, that you never knew me so busy in your life, as I am at present. You must not imagine from hence, that I am writing memoirs of myself. The subject is too slight to descend to posterity, in any other manner, than by that occasional mention which may be made of any little actor in the history of our age. SYLLA, CÆSAR, and others of that rank, were, whilst they lived, at the head of mankind: their story was in some sort the story of the world,

world, and as such, might very properly be transmitted under their names to future generations. But for those who have acted much inferior parts, if they publish the piece, and call it after their own names, they are impertinent; if they publish only their own share in it, they inform mankind by halves, and neither give much instruction, nor create much attention. France abounds with writers of this sort, and, I think, we fall into the other extreme. Let me tell you, on this occasion, what has sometimes come into my thoughts.

There is hardly any century in history which began by opening so great a scene, as the century wherein we live, and shall I suppose, die. Compare it with others, even the most famous, and you will think so. I will sketch the two last, to help your memory.

The loss of that balance which Laurence of Medicis had preserved, during his time, in Italy; the expedition of Charles the eighth to Naples; the intrigues of the duke of Milan, who spun, with all the refinements of art, that net wherein he was taken at last himself; the succesful dexterity of Ferdinand the Catholic,

tholic, who built one pillar of the Auſtrian greatneſs in Spain, in Italy, and in the Indies; as the ſucceſſion of the houſe of Burgundy, joined to the Imperial dignity and the hereditary countries, eſtabliſhed another in the upper and lower Germany: theſe cauſes, and many others, combined to form a very extraordinary conjunᴄture; and, by their conſequences, to render the ſixteenth century fruitful of great events, and of aſtoniſhing revolutions.

THE beginning of the ſeventeenth opened ſtill a greater and more important ſcene. The Spaniſh yoke was well-nigh impoſed on Italy by the famous triumvirate, TOLEDO at Milan, OSSUNA at Naples, and LA CUEVA at Venice. The diſtraᴄtions of France, as well as the ſtate-policy of the queen mother, ſeduced by Rome, and amuſed by Spain; the deſpicable charaᴄter of our JAMES the firſt, the raſhneſs of the eleᴄtor Palatine, the bad intelligence of the princes and ſtates of the league in Germany, the mercenary temper of JOHN GEORGE of Saxony, and the great qualities of MAXIMILIAN of Bavaria, raiſed FERDINAND the ſecond to the Imperial throne; when, the males of the elder branch of the Auſtrian family in Germany being extinguiſhed at the

the death of MATTHIAS, nothing was more, defirable, nor perhaps more practicable, than to throw the empire into another houfe. Germany ran the fame rifque as Italy had done: FERDINAND feemed more likely, even than CHARLES the fifth had been, to become abfolute mafter; and, if France had not furnifhed the greateft minifter, and the North the greateft captain, of that age, in the fame point of time, Vienna and Madrid would have given the law to the weftern world.

As the Auftrian fcale funk, that of Bourbon rofe. The true date of the rife of that power, which has made the kings of France fo confiderable in Europe, goes up as high as CHARLES the feventh, and LEWIS the eleventh. The weaknefs of our HENRY the fixth, the loofe conduct of EDWARD the fourth, and perhaps the overfights of HENRY the feventh, helped very much to knit that monarchy together, as well as to enlarge it. Advantage might have been taken of the divifions which religion occafioned; and fupporting the proteftant party in France would have kept that crown under reftraints, and under inabilities, in fome meafure equal to thofe which were occafioned anciently by the vaft alienations
of

of its demefnes, and by the exorbitant power of its vaffals. But JAMES the firſt was incapable of thinking with fenfe, or acting with fpirit. CHARLES the firſt had an imperfect glympfe of his true intereſt, but his uxorious temper, and the extravagancy of that madman BUCKINGHAM, gave RICHELIEU time to finifh a great part of his project: and the miferies, that followed in England, gave MAZARINE time and opportunity to complete the fyſtem. The laſt great act of this cardinal's adminiſtration was the Pyrenean treaty.

HERE I would begin, by reprefenting the face of Europe fuch as it was at that epocha, the interefts and the conduct of England, France, Spain, Holland. and the empire. A fummary recapitulation fhould follow of all the fteps taken by France, during more than twenty years, to arrive at the great object fhe had propofed to herfelf in making this treaty: the moſt folemn article of which the minifter, who negociated it, defigned fhould be violated; as appears by his letters, wrote from the Ifland of Pheafants, if I miftake not. After this, another draught of Europe fhould have its place according to the relations, which the feveral powers ftood in, one towards

wards another, in one thousand six hundred and eighty eight: and the alterations which the revolution in England made in the politicks of Europe. A summary account should follow of the events of the war that ended in one thousand six hundred and ninety seven, with the different views of king WILLIAM the third, and LEWIS the fourteenth, in making the peace of Ryswic; which matter has been much canvassed, and is little understood. Then the dispositions made by the partition-treaties, and the influences and consequences of these treaties; and a third draught of the state of Europe at the death of CHARLES the second of Spain. All this would make the subject of one or two books, and would be the most proper introduction imaginable to an history of that war with which our century began, and of the peace which followed.

THIS war, foreseen for above half a century, had been, during all that time, the great and constant object of the councils of Europe. The prize to be contended for was the richest that ever had been staked, since those of the Persian and Roman empires. The union of two powers, which separately, and in opposition, had aimed
at

at univerſal monarchy, was apprehended. The confederates therefore engaged in it, to maintain a balance between the two houſes of Auſtria and Bourbon, in order to preſerve their ſecurity, and to aſſert their independance. But with the ſucceſs of the war they changed their views: and, if ambition began it on the ſide of France, ambition continued it on the other. The battles, the ſieges, the ſurpriſing revolutions, which happened in the courſe of this war, are not to be paralleled in any period of the ſame compaſs. The motives, and the meaſures, by which it was protracted, the true reaſons why it ended in a manner, which appeared not proportionable to its ſucceſs; and the new political ſtate into which Europe was thrown by the treaties of Utrecht and Baden, are ſubjects on which few perſons have the neceſſary informations, and yet every one ſpeaks with aſſurance, and even with paſſion. I think I could ſpeak on them with ſome knowledge, and with as much indifference as POLYBIUS does of the negociations of his father LYCORTAS, even in thoſe points where I was myſelf an actor.

I WILL even confeſs to you, that I ſhould not deſpair of performing this part better than

than the former. There is nothing in my opinion so hard to execute, as those political maps, if you will allow me such an expression, and those systems of hints, rather than relations of events, which are necessary to connect and explain them; and which must be so concise, and yet so full; so complicate, and yet so clear. I know nothing of this sort well done by the ancients. SALLUST's introduction, as well as that of THUCYDIDES, might serve almost for any other piece of the Roman or Greek story, as well as for those which these two great authors chose. POLYBIUS does not come up, in his introduction, to this idea neither. Among the moderns, the first book of MACHIAVEL's History of Florence is a noble original of this kind: and perhaps father PAUL's History of Benefices is, in the same kind of composition, inimitable.

THESE are a few of those thoughts, which come into my mind when I consider how incumbent it is on every man, that he should be able to give an account even of his leisure; and in the midst of solitude, be of some use to society.

I KNOW not whether I shall have courage enough to undertake the task I have
chalked

chalked out: I distrust my abilities with reason, and I shall want several informations, not easy, I doubt, for me to obtain. But, in all events, it will not be possible for me to go about it this year; the reasons of which would be long enough to fill another letter, and I doubt that you will think this grown too bulky already.

Adieu.

OF THE

TRUE USE

OF

RETIREMENT and STUDY:

To the Right Honourable
LORD BATHURST.

LETTER II.

SINCE my last to your lordship, this is the first favourable opportunity I have had of keeping the promise I made you. I will avoid prolixity, as much as I can, in the first draught of my thoughts; but I must give you them as they rise in my mind, without staying to marshal them in close order.

As proud as we are of human reason, nothing can be more absurd than the general system of human life, and human knowledge. This faculty of distinguishing true from false, right from wrong, and what is agreeable, from what is repugnant, to nature, either by one act, or by a longer process of intuition, has not been given with so sparing a hand, as many appearances would make us apt to believe. If it was cultivated, therefore, as early, and as carefully as it might be, and if the exercise of it was left generally as free as it ought to be, our common notions and opinions would be more consonant to truth than they are: and, truth being but one, they would be more uniform likewise.

But this rightful mistress of human life and knowledge, whose proper office it is to preside over both, and to direct us in the conduct of one, and the pursuit of the other, becomes degraded in the intellectual œconomy. She is reduced to a mean and servile state, to the vile drudgery of conniving at principles, defending opinions, and confirming habits, that are none of hers. They, who do her most honour, who consult her oftenest, and obey her too very often, are still guilty of limiting her authority according to maxims, and rules, and schemes, that chance, or ignorance, or interest, first devised, and that custom sanctifies: custom, that result of the passions and prejudices of many, and of the designs

Let. 2. RETIREMENT and STUDY, 403

designs of a few: that ape of reason, who usurps her seat, exercises her power, and is obeyed by mankind in her stead. Men find it easy, and government makes it profitable to concur in established systems of speculation and practice: and the whole turn of education prepares them to live upon credit all their lives. Much pains are taken, and time bestowed, to teach us what to think; but little or none of either, to instruct us how to think. The magazine of the memory is stored and stuffed betimes: but the conduct of the understanding is all along neglected, and the free exercise of it is, in effect, forbid in all places, and in terms in some.

THERE is a strange distrust of human reason in every human institution: this distrust is so apparent, that an habitual submission to some authority, or other, is forming in us from our cradles: that principles of reasoning, and matters of fact, are inculcated in our tender minds, before we are able to express that reason, and that, when we are able to exercise it, we are either forbid, or frightened from doing so, even on things that are themselves the proper objects of reason, or that are delivered

vered to us upon an authority whofe fufficiency or infufficiency is fo moft evidently.

On many fubjects, fuch as the general laws of natural religion, and the general rules of fociety and good policy, men of all countries and languages, who cultivate their reafon, judge alike. The fame premifes have led them to the fame conclufions, and fo, following the fame guide, they have trod in the fame path: at leaft, the differences are fmall, eafily reconciled, and fuch as could not of themfelves, contradiftinguifh nation from nation, religion from religion, and fect from fect. How comes it then, that there are other points, on which the moft oppofite opinions are entertained, and fome of thefe with fo much heat, and fury, that the men on one fide of the hedge will die for the affirmative, and the men on the other for the negative? " Toute opinion eft affez forte, " pour fe faire époufer au prix de la vie," fays MONTAGNE, whom I often quote, as I do SENECA, rather for the fmartnefs of expreffion, than the weight or newnefs of matter. Look narrowly into it, and you will find that the points agreed on, and the points difputed, are not proportionable to the
common

common sense and general reason of mankind. Nature and truth are the same every where, and reason shews them every where alike. But the accidental and other causes, which give rise and growth to opinions, both in speculation and practice, are of infinite variety; and where ever these opinions are once confirmed by custom and propagated by education, various, inconsistent, contradictory as they are, they all pretend (and all their pretences are backed by pride, by passion, and by interest) to have reason, or revelation, or both, on their side; though neither reason or revelation can be possibly on the side of more than one, and may be possibly on the side of none.

Thus it happens that the people of Tibet are Tartars and idolaters, that they are Turks and Mahometans at Constantinople, Italians and Papists at Rome; and how much soever education may be less confined, and the means of knowledge more attainable, in France and our own country, yet thus it happens in great measure that Frenchmen and Roman Catholics are bred at Paris, and Englishmen and Protestants at London. For men, indeed, properly speaking, are bred no where: every one thinks

thinks the fyftem, as he fpeaks the language, of his country, at leaft there are few that think, and none that act, in any country according to the dictates of pure unbiaffed reafon; unlefs they may be faid to do fo, when reafon directs them to fpeak and act according to the fyftem of their country, or fect, at the fame time as fhe leads them to think according to that of nature and truth.

Thus the far greateft part of mankind appears reduced to a lower ftate than other animals, in that very refpect, on account of which we claim fo great fuperiority over them; becaufe inftinct, that has its due effect, is preferable to reafon that has not. I fuppofe in this place, with philofophers, and the vulgar, that which I am in no wife ready to affirm, that other animals have no fhare of human reafon: for, let me fay by the way, it is much more likely other animals fhould fhare the human, which is denied, than that man fhould fhare the divine reafon, which is affirmed. But, fuppofing our monopoly of reafon, would not your lordfhip chufe to walk upon four legs, to wear a long tail, and to be called a beaft, with the advantage of being determined by irrefiftible and unerring inftinct to thofe

truths

truths that are neceffary to your well-being; rather than to walk on two legs, to wear no tail, and to be honoured with the title of man, at the expence of deviating from them perpetually? Inftinct acts fpontaneoufly whenever it's action is neceffary, and directs the animal according to the purpofe for which it was implanted in him. Reafon is a nobler and more extenfive faculty; for it extends to the unneceffary as well as neceffary, and to fatisfy our curiofity as well as our wants: but reafon muft be excited, or fhe will conduct us wrong, and carry us farther aftray from her own precincts than we fhould go without her help: in the firft cafe, we have no fufficient guide: and in the fecond, the more we employ our reafon, the more unreafonable we are.

Now if all this be fo, if reafon has fo little, and ignorance, paffion, intereft, and cuftom fo much to do, in forming our opinions and our habits, and in directing the whole conduct of human life; is it not a thing defireable by every thinking man, to have the opportunity, indulged to fo few by the courfe of accidents, the opportunity " fecum effe, et fecum vivere," of living fome years at leaft to ourfelves, and for ourſelves, in a ſtate of freedom, under the laws of reaſon, inſtead of paſſing our whole time in a ſtate of vaſſalage under thoſe of authority and cuſtom? Is it not worth our while to contemplate ourſelves, and others, and all the things of this world, once before we leave them, through the medium of pure, and, if I may ſay ſo, of undefiled reaſon? Is it not worth our while to approve or condemn, on our own authority, what we receive in the beginning of life on the authority of other men, who were not then better able to judge for us, than we are now to judge for ourſelves?

That this may be done, and has been done to ſome degree, by men who remained much more mingled than I deſign to be for the future, in the company and buſineſs of the world, I ſhall not deny: but ſtill it is better done in retreat, and with greater eaſe and pleaſure. Whilſt we remain in the world, we are all fettered down, more or leſs, to one common level, and have neither all the leiſure, nor all the means and advantages to ſoar above it, which we may procure to ourſelves, by breaking theſe fetters, in retreat. To talk of abſtracting ourſelves from matter, laying aſide body, and being reſolved, as it were,

were, into pure intellect, is proud, metaphyfical, unmeaning jargon: but to abſtract ourſelves from the prejudices, and habits, and pleaſures, and buſineſs of the world, is no more than many are, though all are not, capable of doing. They who can do this, may elevate their ſouls in retreat to an higher ſtation, and may take from thence ſuch a view of the world, as the ſecond Scipio took in his dream, from the ſeats of the bleſſed, when the whole earth appeared ſo little to him, that he could ſcarce difcern that ſpeck of dirt, the Roman empire. Such a view as this will encreaſe our knowledge by ſhewing us our ignorance; will diſtinguiſh every degree of probability from the loweſt to the higheſt, and mark the diſtance between that and certainty; will diſpel the intoxicating fumes of philoſophical preſumption, and teach us to eſtabliſh our peace of mind, where alone it can reſt ſecurely, in reſignation: in ſhort, ſuch a view will render life more agreeable, and death leſs terrible. Is not this buſineſs, my lord? Is not this pleaſure too, the higheſt pleaſure? The world can afford us none ſuch; we muſt retire from the world to taſte it with a full guſt; but we ſhall taſte it the better for having been in the world. The ſhare of

ſenſual

sensual pleasures, that a man of my age can promise himself, is hardly worth attention: he should be sated, he will be soon disabled; and very little reflection surely will suffice, to make his habits of this kind lose their power over him, in proportion at least as his power of indulging them diminishes. Besides, your lordship knows that my scheme of retirement excludes none of these pleasures that can be taken with decency and conveniency; and to say the truth, I believe that I allow myself more in speculation, than I shall find I want in practice. As to the habits of business, they can have no hold on one who has been so long tired with it. You may object, that though a man has discarded these habits, and has not even the embers of ambition about him to revive them, yet he cannot renounce all public business as absolutely as I seem to do; because a better principle, a principle of duty, may summon him to the service of his country. I will answer you with great sincerity. No man has higher notions of this duty than I have, I think that scarce any age, or circumstances can discharge us entirely from it; no, not my own. But as we are apt to take the impulse of our own passions, for a call to the performance of this duty; so

when

Let. 2. Retirement and Study. 411

when thefe paffions impel us no longer, the call that puts us upon action muft be real, and loud too. Add to this, that there are different methods, proportioned to different circumftances and fituations, of performing the fame duty. In the midft of retreat, wherever it may be fixed, I may contribute to defend and preferve the Britifh conftitution of government: and you, my lord, may depend upon me, that whenever I can, I will. Should any one afk you, in this cafe, from whom I expect my reward? Anfwer him by declaring to whom I pay this fervice; " Deo immortali, qui me non accipere " modo hæc a majoribus voluit, fed etiam " pofteris prodere."

But, to lead the life I propofe with fatisfaction and profit, renouncing the pleafures and bufinefs of the world, and breaking the habits of both, is not fufficient: the fupine creature whofe underftanding is fuperficially employed, through life, about a few general notions, and is never bent to a clofe and fteady purfuit of truth, may renounce the pleafures and bufinefs of the world, for even in the bufinefs of the world we fee fuch creatures often employed, and may break the habits; nay he may retire

tire and drone away life in folitude, like a monk, or like him over the door of whofe houfe, as if his houfe had been his tomb, fomebody wrote, "Here lies fuch an one." But no fuch man will be able to make the true ufe of retirement. The employment of his mind, that would have been agreeable and eafy if he had accuftomed himfelf to it early, will be unpleafant and impracticable late: fuch men lofe their intellectual powers for the want of exerting them, and, having trifled away youth, are reduced to the neceffity of trifling away age. It fares with the mind juft as it does with the body. He who was born with a texture of brain as ftrong as that of Newton, may become unable to perform the common rules of arithmetic: juft as he who has the fame elafticity in his mufcles, the fame fupplenefs in his joints, and all his nerves and finews as well braced as Jacob Hall, may become a fat unwieldy fluggard. Yet farther, the implicit creature, who has thought it all his life needlefs, or unlawful, to examine the principles or facts that he took originally on truft, will be as little able as the other, to improve his folitude to any good purpofe: unlefs we call it a good purpofe, for that fometimes happens, to confirm and exalt his prejudices, fo that

he

Let. 2. Retirement and Study. 413

he may live and die in one continued delirium. The confirmed prejudices of a thoughtful life are as hard to change as the confirmed habits of an indolent life: and as some must trifle away age because they have trifled away youth, others must labour on in a maze of error, because they have wandered there too long to find their way out.

There is a prejudice in China in favour of little feet, and therefore the feet of girls are swathed and bound up from the cradle, so that the women of that country are unable to walk without tottering and stumbling all their lives. Among the savages of America, there are some who hold flat heads and long ears in great esteem, and therefore press the one, and draw down the others so hard from their infancy, that they destroy irrecoverably the true proportions of nature, and continue all their lives ridiculous to every sight but their own. Just so, the first of these characters cannot make any progress, and the second will not attempt to make any, in an impartial search after real knowledge.

To set about acquiring the habits of meditation and study late in life, is like
getting

getting into a go-cart with a grey beard, and learning to walk when we have loft the ufe of our legs. In general the foundations of an happy old age muſt be laid in youth: and in particular he who has not cultivated his reafon young, will be utterly unable to improve it old "Manent "ingenia fenibus, modo permaneant ſtu-"dium et induſtria."

Not only a love of ſtudy, and a defire of knowledge, muſt have grown up with us, but fuch an induſtrious application likewife, as requires the whole vigour of the mind to be exerted in the purfuit of truth, through long trains of ideas, and all thofe dark receſſes wherein man, not God, has hid it.

This love and this defire I have felt all my life, and I am not quite a ſtranger to this induſtry and application. There has been fomething always ready to whifper in my ear, whilſt I ran the courfe of pleafure and of bufinefs,

"Solve fenefcentem mature fanus equum."

But my Genius, unlike the demon of SOCRATES, whifpered fo foftly, that very often

often I heard him not, in the hurry of thofe paffions by which I was tranfported. Some calmer hours there were: in them I hearkened to him. Reflection had often it's turn, and the love of ftudy and the defire of knowledge have never quite abandoned me. I am not therefore entirely unprepared for the life I will lead, and it is not without reafon that I promife myfelf more fatisfaction in the latter part of it, than I ever knew in the former.

Your lordfhip may think this perhaps a little too fanguine, for one who has loft fo much time already: you may put me in mind, that human life has no fecond fpring, no fecond fummer: you may afk me, what I mean by fowing in autumn, and whether I hope to reap in winter? My anfwer will be, that I think very differently from moft men, of the time we have to pafs, and the bufinefs we have to do in this world. I think we have more of one, and lefs of the other, than is commonly fuppofed. Our want of time, and the fhortnefs of human life, are fome of the principal common-place complaints, which we prefer againft the eftablifhed order of things: they are the grumblings of the vulgar, and the pathetic lamentations of the philo-

philosopher; but they are impertinent and impious in both. The man of business despises the man of pleasure, for squandering his time away; the man of pleasure pities or laughs at the man of business, for the same thing: and yet both concur superciliously and absurdly to find fault with the Supreme Being, for having given them so little time. The philosopher, who misspends it very often as much as the others, joins in the same cry, and authorises this impiety. THEOPHRASTUS thought it extremely hard to die at ninety, and to go out of the world when he had just learned how to live in it. His master ARISTOTLE found fault with nature, for treating man in this respect worse than several other animals: both very unphilosophically! and I love SENECA the better for his quarrel with the Stagirite on this head. We see, in so many instances, a just proportion of things, according to their several relations to one another, that philosophy should lead us to conclude this proportion preserved, even where we cannot discern it; instead of leading us to conclude that it is not preserved where we do not discern it, or where we think that we see the contrary. To conclude otherwise, is shocking presumption. It is to presume that the system
of

of the univerſe would have been more wiſely contrived, if creatures of our low rank among intellectual natures had been called to the councils of the Moſt High: or that the Creator ought to mend his work by the advice of the creature. That life which ſeems to our ſelf-love ſo ſhort, when we compare it with the ideas we frame of eternity, or even with the duration of ſome other beings, will appear ſufficient, upon a leſs partial view, to all the ends of our creation, and of a juſt proportion in the ſucceſſive courſe of generations. The term itſelf is long: we render it ſhort; and the want we complain of flows from our profuſion, not from our poverty. We are all arrant ſpendthrifts: ſome of us diſſipate our eſtates on the trifles, ſome on the ſuperfluities, and then we all complain that we want the neceſſaries of life. The much greateſt part never reclaim, but die bankrupts to God and man. Others reclaim late, and they are apt to imagine, when they make up their accounts and ſee how their fund is diminiſhed, that they have not enough remaining to live upon, becauſe they have not the whole. But they deceive themſelves: they were richer than they thought, and they are not yet poor. If they huſband well the remainder, it will be found

found sufficient for all the neceffaries, and for fome of the fuperfluities, and trifles too perhaps, of life: but then the former order of expence muft be inverted; and the neceffaries of life muft be provided, before they put themfelves to any coft for the trifles or fuperfluities.

Let us leave the men of pleafure and of bufinefs, who are often candid enough to own that they throw away their time, and thereby to confefs that they complain of the Supreme Being for no other reafon than this, that he has not proportioned his bounty to their extravagance: let us confider the fcholar and the philofopher; who, far from owning that he throws any time away, reproves others for doing it: that folemn mortal, who abftains from the pleafures, and declines the bufinefs of the world, that he may dedicate his whole time to the fearch of truth, and the improvement of knowledge. When fuch an one complains of the fhortnefs of human life in general, or of his remaining fhare in particular; might not a man, more reafonable, though lefs folemn, expoftulate thus with him?

" Your complaint is indeed confiftent
" with your practice; but you would not, poffibly,

"possibly, renew your complaint if you "reviewed your practice. Though reading "makes a scholar; yet every scholar is "not a philosopher, nor every philosopher "a wise man. It cost you twenty years to "devour all the volumes on one side of "your library: you came out a great critic "in Latin and Greek, in the oriental "tongues, in history and chronology; but "you was not satisfied; you confessed that "these were the "literæ nihil sanantes;" "and you wanted more time to acquire "other knowledge. You have had this "time: you have passed twenty years "more on the other side of your library, "among philosophers, rabbies, commen- "tators, schoolmen, and whole legions of "modern doctors. You are extremely "well versed in all that has been written "concerning the nature of God, and of "the soul of man; about matter and form, "body and spirit; and space, and eternal "essences, and incorporeal substances; "and the rest of those profound specula- "tions. You are a master of the contro- "versies that have arisen about nature "and grace, about predestination and free- "will, and all the other abstruse questions "that have made so much noise in the "schools, and done so much hurt in the
"world.

" world. You are going on, as faſt as
" the infirmities you have contracted
" will permit, in the ſame courſe of ſtudy;
" but you begin to foreſee that you
" ſhall want time, and you make grievous
" complaints of the ſhortneſs of human
" life. Give me leave now to aſk you,
" how many thouſand years God muſt pro-
" long your life, in order to reconcile you
" to his wiſdom and goodneſs? It is plain,
" at leaſt highly probable, that a life as
" long as that of the moſt aged of the
" patriarchs would be too ſhort to anſwer
" your purpoſes; ſince the reſearches and
" diſputes in which you are engaged, have
" been already for a much longer time the
" objects of learned enquiries, and remain
" ſtill as imperfect and undetermined as
" they were at firſt. But let me aſk you
" again, and deceive neither yourſelf nor
" me; Have you, in the courſe of theſe
" forty years, once examined the firſt prin-
" ciples, and the fundamental facts on
" which all thoſe queſtions depend, with
" an abſolute indifference of judgment,
" and with a ſcrupulous exactneſs? with
" the ſame that you have employed in
" examining the various conſequences
" drawn from them, and the heterodox
" opinions about them? Have you not
" taken

Let 2. RETIREMENT and STUDY. 421

"taken them for granted, in the whole "courfe of your ftudies? Or, if you have "looked now and then on the ftate of the "proofs brought to maintain them, have "you not done it as a mathematician "looks over a demonftration formerly "made, to refrefh his memory, not to fa- "tisfy any doubt? if you have thus exa- "mined, it may appear marvellous to "fome, that you have fpent fo much time "in many parts of thofe ftudies, which "have reduced you to this hectic condi- "tion, of fo much heat and weaknefs. But "if you have not thus examined, it muft "be evident to all, nay to yourfelf on the "leaft cool reflection, that you are ftill, "notwithftanding all your learning, in a "ftate of ignorance. For knowledge can "alone produce knowledge: and without "fuch an examination of axioms and facts, "you can have none about inferences."

IN this manner one might expoftulate very reafonably with many a great fcholar, many a profound philofopher, many a dogmatical cafuift. And it ferves to fet the complaints about want of time, and the fhortnefs of human life, in a very ridiculous but a true light. All men are taught their opinions, at leaft on the moft import-tant subjects, by rote; and are bred to defend them with obstinacy. They may be taught true opinions; but whether true or false, the same zeal for them, and the same attachment to them is every where inspired alike. The Tartar believes as heartily that the soul of Fòe inhabits in his Daïro, as the Christian believes the hypostatic union, or any article in the Athanasian creed. Now this may answer the ends of society in some respects, and do well enough for the vulgar of all ranks: but it is not enough for the man who cultivates his reason who is able to think, and who ought to think, for himself. To such a man, every opinion that he has not himself either framed, or examined strictly, and then adopted, will pass for nothing more than what it really is, the opinion of other men; which may be true or false for aught he knows. And this is a state of uncertainty, in which no such man can remain, with any peace of mind concerning those things that are of greatest importance to us here, and may be so hereafter. He will make them therefore the objects of his first and greatest attention. If he has lost time, he will lose no more; and when he has acquired all the knowledge he is capable of acquiring on these subjects, he will be the

less

less concerned whether he has time to acquire any farther. Should he have passed his life in the pleasures or business of the world; whenever he sets about this work, he will soon have the advantage over the learned philosopher. For he will soon have secured what is necessary to his happiness, and may sit down in the peaceful enjoyment of that knowledge: or proceed with greater advantage and satisfaction to the acquisition of new knowledge; whilst the other continues his search after things that are in their nature, to say the best of them, hypothetical, precarious, and superfluous.

But this is not the only rule, by observing of which we may redeem our time, and have the advantage over those who imagine they have so much in point of knowledge over your lordship or me, for instance, and who despise our ignorance. The rule I mean is this; to be on our guard against the common arts of delusion, spoken of already; which, every one is ready to confess, have been employed to mislead those who differ from him. Let us be diffident of ourselves, but let us be diffident of others too: our own passions may lead us to reason wrong: but the passions

paſſions and intereſts of others may have the ſame effect. It is in every man's power, who ſets about it in good earneſt, to prevent the firſt: and when he has done ſo, he will have a conſcious certainty of it. To prevent the laſt, there is one, and but one ſure method; and that is, to remount, in the ſurvey of our opinions, to the firſt and even remoteſt principles on which they are founded. No reſpect, no habit, no ſeeming certainty whatever, muſt divert us from this: any affectation of diverting us from it, ought to increaſe our ſuſpicion: and the more important our examination is, the more important this method of conducting it becomes. Let us not be frighted from it, either by the ſuppoſed difficulty or length of ſuch an enquiry; for, on the contrary, this is the eaſieſt and the ſhorteſt, as well as the only ſure way of arriving at real knowledge; and of being able to place the opinions we examine in the different claſſes of true, probable, or falſe, according to the truth, probability, or falſhood of the principles from whence they are deduced, If we find theſe principles falſe, and that will be the caſe in many inſtances, we ſtop our enquiries on theſe heads at once; and ſave an immenſe deal of time that we ſhould otherwiſe miſpend.

The

Let. 2. Retirement and Study. 425

The Muſſulman who enters on the examination of all the diſputes that have ariſen between the followers of Omar and Ali and other doctors of his law, muſt acquire a thorough knowledge of the whole Mahometan ſyſtem; and will have as good a right to complain of want of time, and the ſhortneſs of human life, as any Pagan or Chriſtian divine or philoſopher: but without all this time or learning, he might have diſcovered that Mahomet was an impoſtor, and that the Koran is an heap of abſurdities.

In ſhort, my lord, he who retires from the world, with a reſolution of employing his leiſure, in the firſt place to re-examine and ſettle his opinions, is inexcuſable if he does not begin with thoſe that are moſt important to him, and if he does not deal honeſtly by himſelf. To deal honeſtly by himſelf, he muſt obſerve the rule I have inſiſted upon, and not ſuffer the deluſions of the world to follow him into his retreat. Every man's reaſon is every man's oracle: this oracle is beſt conſulted in the ſilence of retirement; and when we have ſo conſulted, whatever the deciſion be, whether in favour of our prejudices or againſt them, we muſt reſt ſatisfied: ſince nothing can be

more

more certain than this, that he who follows that guide in the search of truth, as that was given him to lead him to it, will have a much better plea to make, whenever, or wherever he may be called to account, than he who has resigned himself either deliberately or inadvertently, to any authority upon earth.

When we have done this, concerning God, ourselves, and other men; concerning the relations in which we stand to him and to them; the duties that result from these relations: and the positive will of the Supreme Being, whether revealed to us in a supernatural, or discovered by the right use of our reason in a natural way——we have done the great business of our lives. Our lives are so sufficient for this that they afford us time for more, even when we begin late; especially if we proceed in every other enquiry by the same rule. To discover error in axioms, or in first principles grounded on facts, is like the breaking of a charm. The inchanted castle, the steep rock, the burning lake disappear: and the paths that lead to truth, which we imagined to be so long, so embarrassed, and so difficult, shew as they are, short, open, and easy. When we have secured
the

the neceſſaries, there may be time to amuſe ourſelves with the ſuperfluites, and even with the trifles, of life. "Dulce eſt deſi- "pere," ſaid HORACE: "Vive la baga- "telle!" ſays SWIFT. I oppoſe neither; not the Epicurean, much leſs the Chriſtian philoſopher: but I inſiſt that a principal part of theſe amuſements be the amuſe- ments of ſtudy and reflection, of reading and converſation. You know what con- verſation I mean; for we loſe the true ad- vantage of our nature and conſtitution, if we ſuffer the mind to come, as it were, to a ſtand. When the body, inſtead of ac- quiring new vigour, and taſting new plea- ſures, begins to decline, and is ſated with pleaſures, or grown incapable of taking them, the mind may continue ſtill to im- prove and indulge itſelf in new enjoyments. Every advance in knowledge opens a new ſcene of delight? and the joy that we feel in the actual poſſeſſion of one, will be heightened by that which we expect to find in another: ſo that, before we can exhauſt this fund of ſucceſſive pleaſures, death will come to end our pleaſures and our pains at once. "In his ſtudiis laboribuſque vi- "venti, non intelligitur quando obrepit "ſenectus: ita ſenſim ſine ſenſu ætas ſe- "neſcit,

" nefcit, nec fubito frangitur, fed diuturni-
" tate extinguitur.

THIS, my lord, is the wifeft, and the moft agreeable manner in which a man of fenfe can wind up the thread of life. Happy is he whofe fituation and circumftances give him the opportunity and means of doing it! Though he fhould not have made any great advances in knowledge, and fhould fet about it late, yet the tafk will not be found difficult, unlefs he has gone too far out of his way; and unlefs he continues too long to halt, between the diffipations of the world, and the leifure of a retired life:

—Vivendi recte qui prorogat horam,
Rufticus expectat dum defluat amnis,—

You know the reft. I am fenfible, more fenfible than any enemy I have, of my natural infirmities, and acquired difadvantages: but I have begun, and I will perfift: for he who jogs forward on a battered horfe, in the right way, may get to the end of his journey; which he cannot do, who gallops the fleeteft courfer of Newmarket, out of it.

ADIEU,

ADIEU, my dear lord. Though I have much more to say on this subject, yet I perceive, and I doubt you have long perceived, that I have said too much, at least for a letter, already. The rest shall be reserved for conversation whenever we meet: and then I hope to confirm under your lordship's eye, my speculations by my practice. In the mean time let me refer you to our friend POPE. He says I made a philosopher of him: I am sure he has contributed very much, and I thank him for it, to the making an hermit of me.

REFLECTIONS

UPON

EXILE.

ADVERTISEMENT.

THAT the public may not be imposed upon by any lame and unequal tranflation, of the following treatife, from the French, in which language part of it has been lately printed, and retailed in a monthly Mercury; it is judged proper to add it here, at the end of this volume, from the author's original manufcript, as he himfelf had finifhed it for the prefs.

REFLECTIONS UPON EXILE.*

MDCCXVI.

DISSIPATION of mind, and length of time, are the remedies to which the greatest part of mankind trust in their afflictions. But the first of these works a temporary, the second, a slow, effect: and both are unworthy of a wise man. Are we to fly from ourselves that we may fly from our misfortunes, and fondly to imagine that the disease is cured because we find means to get some moments of respite from pain? Or shall we expect from time, the physician of brutes, a lingering and

---

* Several passages of this little treatise are taken from SENECA: and the whole is wrote with some allusion to his style and manner, " quanquam non " omnino temere fit, quod de sententiis illius que- " ritur Fabius," &c. ERAS. Defen. juJ.

uncertain deliverance? Shall we wait to be happy till we can forget that we are miserable, and owe to the weakness of our faculties a tranquillity which ought to be the effect of their strength? Far otherwise. Let us set all our past and our present afflictions at once before our eyes.* Let us resolve to overcome them, instead of flying from them, or wearing out the sense of them by long and ignominious patience. Instead of palliating remedies, let us use the incision knife and the caustic, search the wound to the bottom, and work an immediate and radical cure.

The recalling of former misfortunes serves to fortify the mind against later. He must blush to sink under the anguish of one wound, who surveys a body seamed over with the scars of many, and who has come victorious out of all the conflicts wherein he received them. Let sighs, and tears, and fainting under the lightest strokes of adverse fortune, be the portion of those unhappy people whose tender minds a long course of felicity has enervated: while such, as have passed through years of calamity,

* Sen. De con. ad Hel.

bear up, with a noble and immoveable conftancy, againft the heavieft. Uninterrupted mifery has this good effect, as it continually torments, it finally hardens.

Such is the language of philofophy: and happy is the man who acquires the right of holding it. But this right is not to be acquired by pathetic difcourfe. Our conduct can alone give it us: and therefore, inftead of prefuming on our ftrength, the fureft method is to confefs our weaknefs, and, without lofs of time, to apply ourfelves to the ftudy of wifdom. This was the advice which the oracle gave to Zeno,[*] and there is no other way of fecuring our tranquillity amidft all the accidents to which human life is expofed. Philofophy has, I know, her Thrasos, as well as War: and among her fons many there have been, who, while they aimed at being more than men, became fomething lefs. The means of preventing this danger are eafy and fure. It is a good rule, to examine well before we addict ourfelves to any fect: but I think it is a better rule, to addict ourfelves to none. Let us hear them all, with a perfect indifferency on which fide the truth

[*] Diog. Laert.

lies: and when we come to determine, let nothing appear fo venerable to us as our own underftandings. Let us gratefully accept the help of every one who has endeavoured to correct the vices, and ftrengthen the minds of men; but let us chufe for ourfelves, and yield univerfal affent to none. Thus, that I may inftance the fect already mentioned, when we have laid afide the wonderful and furprifing fentences, and all the paradoxes of the Portique, we fhall find in that fchool fuch doctrines as our unprejudiced reafon fubmits to with pleafure, as nature dictates, and as experience confirms. Without this precaution, we run the rifque of becoming imaginary kings, and real flaves. With it, we may learn to affert our native freedom, and live independent on fortune.

In order to which great end, it is neceffary that we ftand watchful, as centinels, to difcover the fecret wiles and open attacks of this capricious goddefs, before they reach us.[*] Where fhe falls upon us unexpected, it is hard to refift; but thofe who wait for her, will repel her with eafe. The fudden invafion of an enemy over-

[*] Sen. De con ad Hel.

throws

REFLECTIONS upon EXILE.

throws such as are not on their guard; but they who foresee the war, and prepare themselves for it before it breaks out, stand, without difficulty, the first and the fiercest onset. I learned this important lesson long ago, and never trusted to fortune, even while she seemed to be at peace with me. The riches, the honours, the reputation, and all the advantages which her treacherous indulgence poured upon me, I placed so, that she might snatch them away without giving me any disturbance. I kept a great interval between me and them. She took them, but she could not tear them from me. No man suffers by bad fortune, but he who has been deceived by good. If we grow fond of her gifts, fancy that they belong to us, and are perpetually to remain with us, if we lean upon them, and expect to be considered for them; we shall sink into all the bitterness of grief, as soon as these false and transitory benefits pass away, as soon as our vain and childish minds, unfraught with solid pleasures, become destitute even of those which are imaginary. But, if we do not suffer ourselves to be transported by prosperity, neither shall we be reduced by adversity. Our souls will be of proof against the dangers of both these states:

and, having explored our strength, we shall be sure of it; for in the midst of felicity, we shall have tried how we can bear misfortune.

It is much harder to examine and judge, than to take up opinions on trust; and therefore the far greatest part of the world borrow from others, those which they entertain concerning all the affairs of life and death.* Hence it proceeds that men are so unanimously eager in the pursuit of things, which far from having any inherent real good, are varnished over with a specious and deceitful gloss, and contain nothing answerable to their appearances.† Hence it proceeds, on the other hand, that, in those things which are called evils, there is nothing so hard and terrible as the general cry of the world threatens. The word exile comes indeed harsh to the ear, and strikes us like a melancholy and execrable sound, through a certain persuasion which men have habitually concurred in. Thus the multitude has ordained. But the greatest

* Dum unusquisque mavult credere, quam judicare, nunquam de vita judicatur, semper creditur. Sen. De vita beat.

† Sen. De con. ad Hel.

part

part of their ordinances are abrogated by the wife.

REJECTING therefore the judgment of those who determine according to popular opinions, or the firſt appearances of things, let us examine what exile really is.* It is, then, a change of place; and, leſt you ſhould ſay that I diminiſh the object, and conceal the moſt ſhocking parts of it, I add, that this change of place is frequently accompanied by ſome or all of the following inconveniences: by the loſs of the eſtate which we enjoyed, and the rank which we held; by the loſs of that conſideration and power which we were in poſſeſſion of; by a ſeparation from our family and our friends; by the contempt which we may fall into; by the ignominy with which thoſe who have driven us abroad, will endeavour to ſully the innocence of our characters, and to juſtify the injuſtice of their own conduct.

ALL theſe ſhall be ſpoke to hereafter. In the mean while, let us conſider what evil there is, in change of place, abſtractedly and by itſelf.

* SEN. de cón. ad Hel.

To live deprived of one's country is intolerable.* Is it so? How comes it then to pass, that such numbers of men live out of their countries by choice? Observe how the streets of London and of Paris are crowded. Call over those millions by name, and ask them one by one, of what country they are: how many will you find, who, from different parts of the earth, come to inhabit these great cities, which afford the largest opportunities, and the largest encouragement, to virtue and to vice? Some are drawn by ambition, and some are sent by duty; many resort thither to improve their minds, and many to improve their fortunes; others bring their beauty, and others their eloquence, to market. Remove from hence, and go to the utmost extremities of the East or the West: visit the barbarous nations of Africa, or the inhospitable regions of the North: you will find no climate so bad, no country so savage, as not to have some people who come from abroad, and inhabit there by choice.

Among numberless extravagancies which have passed through the minds of men, we

* Sen. De con. ad Hel.

may juftly reckon for one that notion of a fecret affection, independent of our reafon, and fuperior to our reafon, which we are fuppofed to have for our country; as if there were fome phyfical virtue in every fpot of ground, which neceffarily produced this effect in every one born upon it.

"—Amor patriæ ratione valentior omni.*

As if the heimvei was an univerfal diftemper, infeparable from the conftitution of an human body, and not peculiar to the Swifs, who feem to have been made for their mountains, as their mountains feem to have been made for them.† This notion may have contributed to the fecurity and grandeur of ftates. It has therefore been not unartfully cultivated, and the prejudice of education has been with care put on it's fide. Men have come in this cafe, as in many, from believing that it ought to be fo, to perfuade others, and even to believe themfelves that it is fo. Procopius relates that Abgarus came to Rome, and gained the efteem and friendfhip of Augustus to fuch a degree, that this emperor could not refolve to let him return home:

* Ov. De Ponto, El. iv.
† Card. Benti. Let.

that ABGARUS brought several beasts, which he had taken one day in hunting, alive to AUGUSTUS: that he placed in different parts of the Circus some of the earth which belonged to the places where each of these animals had been caught; that as soon as this was done, and they were turned loose every one of them ran to that corner where his earth lay; that AUGUSTUS, admiring their sentiment of love for their country which nature has graved in the hearts of beasts, and struck by the evidence of the truth, granted the request which ABGARUS immediately pressed upon him, and allowed, though with regret, the tetrarch to return to Edessa. But this tale deserves just as much credit as that which follows in the same place, of the letter of ABGARUS to JESUS CHRIST, of our Saviour's answer, and of the cure of ABGARUS. There is nothing, surely, more groundless than the notion here advanced, nothing more absurd. We love the country in which we are born, because we receive particular benefits from it, and because we have particular obligations to it: which ties we may have to another country, as well as to that we are born in; to our country by election, as well as to our country by birth. In all other respects, a wise man looks on himself

self as a citizen of the world: and, when you afk him where his country lies, points, like Anaxagoras with his finger to the heavens.

There are other perfons, again, who have imagined that as the whole univerfe fuffers a continual rotation, and nature feems to delight in it, or to preferve herfelf by it, fo there is in the minds of men, a natural reftleffnefs, which inclines them to change of place, and to the fhifting their habitations.* This opinion has at leaft an appearance of truth, which the other wants; and is countenanced, as the other is contradicted, by experience. But, whatever the reafons be, which muft have varied infinitely in an infinite number of cafes, and an immenfe fpace of time; true it is in fact, that the families and nations of the world have been in a continual fluctuation, roaming about on the face of the globe, driving and driven out by turns. What a number of colonies has Afia fent into Europe! The Phœnicians planted the coafts of the Mediterranean fea, and pufhed their fettlements even into the ocean. The Etrurians were of Afiatic extraction;

* Sen. De con. ad Hel.

and, to mention no more, the Romans, those lords of the world, acknowledged a Trojan exile for the founder of their empire. How many migrations have there been, in return to these, from Europe into Asia? They would be endless to enumerate; for, besides the Æolic, the Ionic, and others of almost equal fame, the Greeks, during several ages, made continual expeditions, and built cities in several parts of Asia. The Gauls penetrated thither too, and established a kingdom. The European Scythians over-ran these vast provinces, and carried their arms to the confines of Egypt. ALEXANDER subdued all from the Hellespont to India, and built towns, and established colonies, to secure his conquests, and to eternise his name. From both these parts of the world Africa has received inhabitants and masters; and what she has received she has given. The Tyrians built the city, and founded the republic, of Carthage; the Greek has been the language of Ægypt. In the remotest antiquity we hear of BELUS in Chaldæa, and of SESOSTRIS planting his tawny colonies in Colchos: and Spain has been, in these later ages, under the dominion of Moors. If we turn to Runic history, we find our fathers, the Goths, led by WODEN

and

and by Thor, their heroes firſt, and their divinities afterwards, from the Aſiatic Tartary into Europe: and who can aſſure us that this was their firſt migration? They came into Aſia perhaps by the eaſt, from that continent to which their ſons have lately ſailed from Europe by the weſt: and thus in the proceſs of three or four thouſand years, the ſame race of men have puſhed their conqueſts and their habitations round the globe; at leaſt this may be ſuppoſed, as reaſonably as it is ſuppoſed, I think by Grotius, that America was peopled from Scandinavia. The world is a great wilderneſs, wherein mankind have wandered and joſtled one another about from the creation. Some have removed by neceſſity, and others by choice. One nation has been fond of ſeizing what another was tired of poſſeſſing: and it will be difficult to point out the country which is to this day in the hands of it's firſt inhabitants.

Thus fate has ordained that nothing ſhall remain long in the ſame ſtate: and what are all theſe tranſportations of people, but ſo many public exiles? Varro, the moſt learned of the Romans, thought,
ſince

since Nature* is the same wherever we go, that this single circumstance was sufficient to remove all objections to change of place, taken by itself, and stripped of the other inconveniencies which attend exile. M. Brutus thought it enough that those, who go into banishment, cannot be hindered from carrying their Virtue along with them. Now if any one judge that each of these comforts is in itself insufficient, he must however confess that both of them joined together, are able to remove the terrors of exile. For what trifles must all we leave behind us be esteemed, in comparison of the two most precious things which men can enjoy, and which, we are sure, will follow us wherever we turn our steps, the same Nature, and our proper Virtue?† Believe me, the providence of God has established such an order in the world, that of all which belongs to us the least valuable parts can alone fall under the will of others. Whatever is best, is safest; lies out of the reach of human power; can neither be given nor taken away. Such is this great and beautiful work of nature, the world. Such is the mind of man, which contemplates

* Sen. De con. ad Hel. † Ib.

and

and admires the world whereof it makes the nobleſt part. Theſe are inſeparably ours, and as long as we remain in one we ſhall enjoy the other. Let us march therefore intrepidly wherever we are led by the courſe of human accidents. Wherever they lead us, on what coaſt ſoever we are thrown by them, we ſhall not find ourſelves abſolutely ſtrangers. We ſhall meet with men and women, creatures of the ſame figure, endowed with the ſame faculties, and born under the ſame laws of nature. We ſhall ſee the ſame virtues and vices, flowing from the ſame general principles, but varied in a thouſand different and contrary modes, according to that infinite variety of laws and cuſtoms which is eſtabliſhed for the ſame univerſal end, the preſervation of ſociety. We ſhall feel the ſame revolution of ſeaſons, and the ſame ſun and moon* will guide the courſe of our year. The ſame azure vault, beſpangled with ſtars, will be every where

---

* PLUT. Of baniſhment. He compares thoſe who cannot live out of their own country, to the ſimple people who fancied that the moon of Athens was a finer moon than that of Corinth.

——— labentem cœlo quæ ducitis annum.
V IR G. Georg.

spread over our heads. There is no part of the world from whence we may not admire those planets which roll, like ours, in different orbits round the same central sun; from whence we may not discover an object still more stupendous, that army of fixed stars hung up in the immense space of the universe, innumerable suns whose beams enlighten and cherish the unknown worlds which roll around them: and whilst I am ravished by such contemplations as these, whilst my soul is thus raised up to heaven, it imports me little what ground I tread upon.

Brutus,* in the book which he wrote on virtue, related that he had seen Marcellus in exile at Mitylene, living in all the happiness which human nature is capable of and cultivating with as much assiduity as ever, all kinds of laudable knowledge. He added that this spectacle made him think that it was rather he who went into banishment, since he was to return without the other, than the other who remained in it. O Marcellus, far more happy when Brutus approved thy exile, than when the commonwealth approved

* Sen. De con. ad Hel.

thy

thy confulſhip! How great a man muſt thou have been to extort admiration from him who appeared an object of admiration even to his own CATO! the fame BRUTUS reported further, that CÆSAR overſhot Mitylene, becauſe he could not ſtand the ſight of MARCELLUS reduced to a ſtate ſo unworthy of him. His reſtoration was at length obtained by the public interceſſion of the whole ſenate, who were dejected with grief to ſuch a degree, that they ſeemed all upon this occaſion to have the ſame ſentiments with BRUTUS, and to be ſuppliants for themſelves, rather than for MARCELLUS.* This was to return with honour: but ſurely he remained abroad with greater, when BRUTUS could not reſolve to leave him, nor CÆSAR to ſee him; for both of them bore witneſs of his merit. BRUTUS grieved, and CÆSAR bluſhed to go to Rome without him.

Q. METELLUS NUMIDICUS had undergone the ſame fate ſome years before, while the people, who are always the ſureſt in-

---

* MARCELLUS was aſſaſſinated at Athens, in his return home, by CHILO, an old friend and fellow-ſoldier of his. The motive of CHILO is not explained in hiſtory. CÆSAR was ſuſpected, but he ſeems to be juſtified by the opinion of BRUTUS.

ſtruments

struments of their own servitude, were laying under the conduct of MARIUS, the foundations of that tyranny which was perfected by CÆSAR. METELLUS alone, in the midst of an intimidated senate, and outrageous multitude, refused to swear to the pernicious laws of the tribune SATURNINUS. His constancy became his crime, and exile his punishment. A wild and lawless faction prevailing against him, the best men of the city armed in his defence, and were ready to lay down their lives that they might preserve so much virtue to their country. But he, having failed to persuade, thought it not lawful to constrain. He judged in the phrensy of the Roman commonwealth, as PLATO judged in the dotage of the Athenian. METELLUS knew, that if his fellow citizens amended, he should be recalled; and if they did not amend, he thought he could be no where worse than at Rome. He went voluntarily into exile, and wherever he passed he carried the sure symptom of a sickly state, and the certain prognostic of an expiring commonwealth. What temper he continued in abroad will best appear by a fragment of one of his letters which GELLIUS,[*]

[*] Lib. xvii. cap. 2.

in a pedantic compilation of phrases used by the annalist Q. CLAUDIUS, has preserved for the sake of the word frunifcor. "Illi " vero omni jure atque honeftate inter- " dicti: ego neque aqua neque igne careo: " et fumma gloria frunifcor." Happy ME-TELLUS! happy in the confcience of thy own virtue! happy in thy pious fon, and in that excellent friend who refembled thee in merit and in fortune!

RUTILIUS had defended Afia againſt the extortions of the publicans, according to the ſtrict juſtice of which he made profeſ-fion, and to the particular duty of his office. The equeſtrian order were upon this account his enemies, and the Marian faction was fo of courſe, on account of his probity, as well as out of hatred to METEL-LUS. The moſt innnocent man of the city was accufed of corruption. The beſt man was profecuted by the worſt, by API-CIUS; a name dedicated to infamy.* Thofe who had ſtirred up the falfe accufation, fat as judges, and pronounced the unjuſt fen-tence againſt him. He hardly deigned to

* There was another APICIUS, in the reign of TIBERIUS, famous for his gluttony; and a third in the time of TRAJAN.

defend his caufe, but retired into the Eaft, where that Roman virtue, which Rome could not bear, was received with honour.* Shall RUTILIUS now be deemed unhappy, when they who condemned him are, for that action, delivered down as criminals to all future generations? when he quitted his country with greater eafe than he would fuffer his exile to finifh? when he alone durſt refufe the dictator SYLLA, and being recalled home, not only declined to go, but fled farther off?

WHAT do you propofe, it may be faid, by thefe examples, multitudes of which are to be collected from the memorials of former ages? I propofe to fhew that as change of place, fimply confidered, can render no man unhappy, fo the other evils which are objected to exile; either cannot happen to wife and virtuous men; or, if they do happen to them, cannot render them miferable. Stones are hard, and cakes of ice are cold: and all who feel them, feel them alike.† But the good or the bad events, which fortune brings upon us, are felt according to what qualities we, not they, have. They are in themfelves in-

* SEN. L. De prov. cap. 3.
† PLUT. on exile.

different

different and common accidents, and they acquire strength by nothing but our vice or our weakness. Fortune can difpenfe neither felicity nor infelicity unlefs we co-operate with her. Few men, who are unhappy under the lofs of an eftate, would be happy in the poffeffion of it: and thofe, who deferve to enjoy the advantages which exile takes away, will not be unhappy when they are deprived of them.

It grieves me to make an exception to this rule; but TULLY was one fo remarkably, that the example can be neither concealed, nor paffed over. This great man, who had been the faviour of his country, who had feared in the fupport of that caufe, neither the infults of a defperate party, nor the daggers of affaffins, when he came to fuffer for the fame caufe, funk under the weight. He difhonoured that banifhment which indulgent providence meant to be the means of rendering his glory complete. Uncertain where he fhould go, or what he fhould do, fearful as a woman, and froward as a child, he lamented the lofs of his rank, of his riches, and of his fplendid popularity. His eloquence ferved only to paint his ignominy in ftronger colours. He wept over the ruins of his fine houfe which CLODIUS had demolifhed: and his feparation from TERENTIA, whom he repudiated not long afterwards, was perhaps an affliction to him at this time. Every thing becomes intolerable to the man who is once fubdued by grief. * He regrets what he took no pleafure in enjoying, and, overloaded already, he fhrinks at the weight of a feather CIDERO's behaviour, in fhort, was fuch that his friends, as well as his enemies, believed him to have loft his fenfes.† CÆSAR beheld, with a fecret fatisfaction, the man, who had refufed to be his lieutenant, weeping under the rod of CLODIUS. POMPEY hoped to find fome excufe for his own ingratitude in the contempt which the friend, whom he had abandoned, expofed himfelf to. Nay ATTICUS judged him too meanly attached to his former fortune, and reproached him for it. ATTICUS, whofe great talents were ufury and trimming, who placed his principal merit in being rich, and who would have been noted with infamy at Athens, for keeping well with all fides, and venturing on none §: even

* Mitto cætera intolerabilia Etenim fletu impedior. L. iii. Ad Attic. ep. 10.
† Tam fæpe, et tam vehementer objurgas, et animo infirmo eff· dicis. Ib.
§ PLUT. Vit. Solon.

ATTICUS

Atticus blushed for Tully, and the most plausible man alive assumed the style of Cato.

I have dwelt the longer on this instance because, whilst it takes nothing from the truth which has been established, it teaches us another of great importance. Wise men are certainly superior to all the evils of exile. But in a strict sense, he, who has left any one passion in his soul unsubdued, will not deserve that appellation. It is not enough that we have studied all the duties of public and private life, that we are perfectly acquainted with them, and that we live up to them in the eye of the world: a passion that lies dormant in the heart, and has escaped our scrutiny, or which we have observed and indulged as venal, or which we have perhaps encouraged, as a principle to excite and to aid our virtue, may one time or other destroy our tranquillity, and disgrace our whole character. When virtue has steeled the mind on every side, we are invulnerable on every side: but Achilles was wounded in the heel. The least part, overlooked or neglected, may expose us to receive a mortal blow. Reason cannot obtain the absolute dominion of our souls by one victory. Vice has many reserves,

reserves, which muſt be beaten; many ſtrong holds, which muſt be forced; and we may be found of proof in many trials, without being ſo in all. We may reſiſt the ſevereſt, and yield to the weakeſt attacks of fortune. We may have got the better of avarice, the moſt epidemical diſeaſe of the mind, and yet be ſlaves to ambition.* We may have purged our ſouls of the fear of death, and yet ſome other fear may venture to lurk behind. This was the caſe of Cicero. Vanity was his cardinal vice.† It had, I queſtion not, warmed his zeal, quickened his induſtry, animated the love of his country, and ſupported his conſtancy againſt Catiline: but it gave to Clodius an entire victory over him. He was not afraid to

---

* Seneca ſays the contrary of all this, according to the ſtoical ſyſtem, which however he departs from on many occaſions. Si contra unam quamlibet "partem fortunæ ſatis tibi roboris eſt, idem adver- "ſus omnes erit.—Si avaritia dimiſit, vehementiſſi- "ma generis humani peſtis, moram tibi ambitio non "faciet." Si ultimum diem, &c. De con. ad Hel.
Non ſingula vitia ratio, ſed pariter omnia proſternit. In univerſum ſemel vincitur. Ibid.
Nec audacem quidem timoris abſolvimus; ne prodigum quidem avaritia liberamus. De Benef. Liv. iv. c. 27.
Qui autem habet vitium unum, habet omnia. Ib. L. v. c. 15.
† In animo autem gloriæ cupido, qualis fuit Ciceronis, plurimum poteſt. Vel. Pat. L. i.

die

die, and part with eftate, rank, honour, and every thing which he lamented the lofs of: but he was afraid to live deprived of them. " Ut vivus hæc amitterem."[*] He would probably have met death on this occafion with the fame firmnefs with which he faid to POPILIUS LAENUS, his client and his murderer, " Approach, veteran, and, " if at leaft thou canft do this well, cut " off my head." But he could not bear to fee himfelf, and to be feen by others, ftripped of thofe trappings which he was accuftomed to wear. This made him break out into fo many fhameful expreffions. " Poffum oblivifci qui fuerim? " non fentire qui fim? quo caream honore, " qua gloria?" And fpeaking of his brother—" Vitavi ne viderem; ne aut il- " lius luctum fqualoremque afpicerem, aut " me, quem ille florentiffimum reliquerat, " perditum illi afflictumque offerrem." He had thought of death, and prepared his mind for it. There were occafions too where his vanity might be flattered by it. But the fame vanity hindered him in his profperous eftate from fuppofing fuch a reverfe as afterwards happened to him. When it came, it found him unprepared,

[*] Ep. ad Attic. L. iii. ep. 3, 7, 10. et paffim:
† L. iii. ep. 10 ad Attic.

it surprised him, it stunned him; for he was still fond of the pomp and hurry of Rome, " fumum, et opes, strepitumque " Romæ," and unweaned from all those things which habit renders necessary, and which nature has left indifferent.

We have enumerated them above, and it is time to descend into a more particular examination of them. Change of place then may be borne by every man. It is the delight of many. But who can bear the evils which accompany exile? You who ask the question can bear them. Every one who considers them as they are in themselves, instead of looking at them through the false optic which prejudice holds before our eyes. For what? you have lost your estate: reduce your desires, and you will perceive yourself to be as rich as ever, with this considerable advantage to boot, that your cares will be diminished. Our natural and real wants* are confined to nar-

---

* Naturalia desideria finita sunt: ex falsa opinione nascentia ubi definant non habent, nullus enim terminus falso est. SEN. Ep. 16.
Excerp. ex Lib. SEN. falsely so called.
Si ad naturam vives, nunquam eris pauper; si ad opinionem, nunquam dives. Exiguum natura desiderat, opinio immensum. SEN. Ep. 16.

row

row bounds, whilft thofe which fancy and
cuftom create are confined to none. Truth
lies within a little and certain compafs,
but error is immenfe. If we fuffer our defires therefore to wander beyond thefe
bounds, they wander eternally. " Nefcio
" quid curtæ femper abeft rei." We become neceffitous in the midft of plenty,
and our poverty encreafes with our riches.
Reduce your defires, be able to fay with
the apoftle of Greece, to whom Erasmus
was ready to addrefs his prayers, " quam
" multis ipfe non egeo!" banifh out of
your exile all imaginary, and you will
fuffer no real wants. The little ftream
which is left will fuffice to quench the
thirft of nature, and that which cannot
be quenched by it, is not your thirft, but
your diftemper; a diftemper formed by
the vicious habits of your mind, and not
the effect of exile. How great a part of
mankind bear poverty with chearfulnefs,
becaufe they have been bred in it, and are
accuftomed to it?* Shall we not be able
to acquire, by reafon and by reflection,
what the meaneft artifan poffeffes by habit?
Shall thofe who have fo many advantages

* Sen. De con. ad Hel.

over

over him, be flaves to wants and neceffities of which he is ignorant? The rich, whofe wanton appetites neither the produce of one country, nor of one part of the world, can fatisfy, for whom the whole habitable globe is ranfacked, for whom the caravans of the eaft are continually in march, and the remoteft feas are covered with fhips; thefe pampered creatures, fated with fuperfluity, are often glad to inhabit an humble cot, and to make an homely meal. They run for refuge into the arms of frugality. .Madmen that they are, to live always in fear of what they fometimes wifh for, and to fly from that life which they find it luxury to imitate! Let us caft our eyes backwards on thofe great men who lived in the ages of virtue, of fimplicity, of frugality, and let us blufh to think that we enjoy in banifhment more than they were mafters of in the midft of their glory, in the utmoft affluence of their fortune. Let us imagine that we behold a great dictator giving audience to the Samnite ambaffadors, and preparing on the hearth his mean repaft with the fame hand which had fo often fubdued the enemies of the commonwealth, and borne the triumphal laurel to the capitol. Let us remember
that

that Plato had but* three servants, and that Zeno had none.† Socrates, the reformer of his country, was maintained, as Menenius Agrippa, the arbiter of his country was buried, by a contribution.§ While Attilius Regulus beat the Carthaginians in Afric the flight of his ploughman reduced his family to diftrefs at home, and the tillage of his little farm became the public care. Scipio died without leaving enough to marry his daughters, and their portions were paid out of the trea-

* Plato's will, in Diog. Laer. mentions four servants befides Diana, to whom he gave her freedom.

Apuleius makes his eftate confift in a little garden near the academy, two fervants, a patten for facrifices, and as much gold as would ferve to make ear-rings for a child.

† Zeno was owner of a thoufand talents when he came from Cyprus into Greece, and he ufed to lend his money out upon fhips at an high intereft. He kept, in fhort, a kind of infurance office. He loft this eftate perhaps when he faid, "recte fane agit "fortuna, quæ nos ad philofophiam impellit" Afterwards he received many and great prefents from Antigonus. So that his great frugality and fimplicity of life, was the effect of his choice, and not of neceffity. Vid. Dio. Laer.

§ Diog. Laer. Vit. Soc. quotes Aristoxenus for affirming that Socrates ufed to keep a box, and lived upon the money which was put into it: "Pofita igitur arcula colligiffe pecuniam quæ daretur; confumpta autem ea, rurfus pofuiffe."

fury

fury of the state; for sure it was just that the people of Rome should once pay tribute to him, who had established a perpetual tribute on Carthage. After such examples shall we be afraid of poverty? shall we disdain to be adopted into a family which has so many illustrious ancestors? shall we complain of banishment for taking from us what the greatest philosophers, and the greatest heroes of antiquity never enjoyed?

You will find fault perhaps, and attribute to artifice, that I consider singly misfortunes which come altogether on the banished man, and overbear him with their united weight. You could support change of place if it was not accompanied with poverty, or poverty if it was not accompanied with the separation from your family, and your friends, with the loss of your rank, consideration, and power, with contempt and ignominy. Whoever he be who reasons in this manner, let him take the following answer. The least of these circumstances is singly sufficient to render the man miserable who is not prepared for it, who has not divested himself of that passion upon which it is directed to work. But he who has got the mastery of all his passions, who has forsken all these accidents, and
prepared

prepared his mind to endure them all, will be superior to all of them, and to all of them at once as well as singly. He will not bear the loss of his rank, because he can bear the loss of his estate; but he will bear both, because he is prepared for both; because he is free from pride as much as he is from avarice.

You are separated from your family and your friends. Take the list of them, and look it well over. How few of your family, will you find who deserve the name of friends? and how few among these who are really such? Erase the names of such as ought not to stand on the roll, and the voluminous catalogue will soon dwindle into a narrow compass. Regret if you please, your separation from this small remnant. Far be it from me, whilst I declaim against a shameful and vicious weakness of mind, to prescribe the sentiments of a virtuous friendship. Regret your separation from your friends, but regret it like a man who deserves to be theirs. This is strength, not weakness of mind; it is virtue, not vice.

But the least uneasiness under the loss of the rank which we held is ignominious There is no valuable rank among men but

but that which real merit affigns. The princes of the earth may give names, and inftitute ceremonies, and exact the obfervation of them; their imbecility and their wickednefs may prompt them to clothe fools and knaves with robes of honour, and emblems of wifdom and virtue: but no man will be in truth fuperior to another, without fuperior merit; and that rank can no more be taken from us, than the merit which eftablifhes it. The fupreme authority gives a fictitious and arbitrary value to coin, which is therefore not current alike in all times and in all places; but the real value remains invariable, and the provident man, who gets rid as faft as he can of the droffy piece, hoards up the good filver. Thus merit will not procure the fame confideration univerfally. But what then? the title to this confideration is the fame and will be found alike in every circumftance by thofe who are wife and virtuous themfelves. If it is not owned by fuch as are otherwife, nothing is however taken from us; we have no reafon to complain. They confidered us for a rank which we had; for our denomination, not for our intrinfic value. We have that rank, that denomination no longer, and they confider us no longer: they admired

mired in us what we admired not in ourfelves. If they learn to neglect us, let us learn to pity them. Their affiduity was importunate: let us not complain of the eafe which this change procures us; let us rather apprehend the return of that rank and that power, which like a funny day, would bring back thefe little infects, and make them fwarm once more about us. I know how apt we are, under fpecious pretences, to difguife our weakneffes and our vices, and how often we fucceed not only in deceiving the world, but even in deceiving ourfelves. An inclination to do good is infeparable from a virtuous mind, and therefore the man, who cannot bear with patience the lofs of that rank and power which he enjoyed, may be willing to attribute his regrets to the impoffibility which he fuppofes himfelf reduced to of fatisfying this inclination. But let fuch an one know that a wife man contents himfelf with doing as much good as his fituation allows him to do; that there is no fituation wherein we may not do a great deal: and that when we are deprived of greater power to do more good, we efcape at the fame time the temptation of doing fome evil.*

* Sen. de con. ad Hel.

THE inconveniencies, which we have mentioned, carry nothing along with them difficult to be borne by a wife and virtuous man; and thofe which remain to be mentioned, contempt and ignominy, can never fall to his lot. It is impoffible that he who reverences himfelf fhould be defpifed by others; and how can ignominy affect the man who collects all his ftrength within himfelf, who appeals from the judgment of the multitude to another tribunal, and lives independent of mankind, and of the accidents of life? CATO loft the election of prætor, and that of conful; but is any one blind enough to truth to imagine that thefe repulfes reflected any difgrace on him? The dignity of thofe two magiftracies would have been encreafed by his wearing them. They fuffered, not CATO.

You have fulfilled all the duties of a good citizen, you have been true to your truft, conftant in your engagements, and have purfued the intereft of your country without regard to the enemies you created, and the dangers you run. You fevered her intereft, as much as lay in your power, from thofe of her factions, and from thofe of her neighbours and allies too, when they became different. She reaps

reaps the benefit of thefe fervices, and you fuffer for them. You are banifhed, and purfued with ignominy, and thofe whom you hindered from triumphing at her expence, revenge themfelves at yours. The perfons, in oppofition to whom you ferved, or even faved the public, confpire and accomplifh your private ruin. Thefe are your accufers, and the giddy ungrateful crowd your judges. Your name is hung up in the tables of profcription, and art joined to malice, endeavours to make your beft actions pafs for crimes, and to ftain your character. For this purpofe the facred voice of the fenate is made to pronounce a lye, and thofe records, which ought to be the eternal monuments of truth, become the vouchers of impofture and calumny. Such circumftances as thefe you think intolerable, and you would prefer death to fo ignominious an exile. Deceive not yourfelf. The ignominy remains with them who perfecute unjuftly, not with him who fuffers unjuft perfecution. "Recalcitrat undique tutus." Suppofe that in the act which banifhes you, it was declared that you have fome contagious diftemper, that you are crooked, or otherwife deformed. This would render the legiflators

legiflators ridiculous.* The other renders them infamous. But neither one nor the other can affect the man, who in an healthful well proportioned body enjoys a confcience void of all the offences afcribed to him. Inftead of fuch an exile, would you compound, that you might live at home in eafe and plenty, to be the inftrument of blending thefe contrary interefts once more together, and of giving but the third place to that of your country? Would you proftitute her power to the ambition of others, under the pretence of fecuring her from imaginary dangers, and drain her riches into the pockets of the meaneft and vileft of her citizens, under the pretence of paying her debts? If you could fubmit to fo infamous a compofition, you are not the man to whom I addrefs my difcourfe, or with whom I will have any commerce: and if you have virtue enough to difdain it, why fhould you repine at the other alternative? Banifhment from fuch a country, and with fuch circumftances, is like being delivered from prifon. DIOGENES was driven out of the kingdom of Pontus for counterfeiting the coin, and STRATO-

---

* The dialogue between CICERO and PHILISCUS. DION. CAS. L. xxxviii.

NICUS,

nicus thought that forgery might be committed in order to get banished from Scriphos. But you have obtained your liberty by doing your duty.

Banishment, with all its train of evils, is so far from being the cause of contempt, that he who bears up with an undaunted spirit against them, while so many are dejected by them, erects on his very misfortunes a trophy to his honour: for such is the frame and temper of our minds, that nothing strikes us with greater admiration than a man intrepid in the midst of misfortunes. Of all ignominies an ignominious death must be allowed to be the greatest; and yet where is the blasphemer who will presume to defame the death of Socrates[*]? This saint entered the prison with the same countenance with which he reduced thirty tyrants, and he took off ignominy from the place; for how could it be deemed a prison when Socrates was there? Phocion was led to execution in the same city; all those who met the sad procession cast their eyes to the ground, and with throbbing hearts bewailed, not the innocent man, but justice herself, who

[*] Sen. De con. ad Hel.

was in him condemned. Yet there was a wretch found, for monsters are sometimes produced in contradiction to the ordinary rules of nature, who spit in his face as he passed along. PHOCION wiped his cheek, smiled, turned to the magistrate, and said, "Admonish this man not to be so nasty for "the future."

IGNOMINY then can take no hold on Virtue*; for Virtue is in every condition the same, and challenges the same respect. We applaud the world when she prospers; and when she falls into adversity we applaud her. Like the temples of the Gods, she is venerable even in her ruins. After this must it not appear a degree of madness, to defer one moment acquiring the only arms capable of defending us against attacks which at every moment we are exposed to? Our being miserable, or not miserable, when we fall into misfortunes, depends on the manner in which we have enjoyed prosperity. If we have applied ourselves betimes to the study of wisdom, and to the practice of virtue, these evils become indifferent; but if we have neglected to do so, they become necessary. In

* SEN. De con. ad Hel.

one cafe they are evil, in the other they are remedies for greater evils than themfelves. ZENO* rejoiced that a fhipwreck had thrown him on the Athenian coaft: and he owed to the lofs of his fortune the acquifition which he made of virtue of wifdom, of immortality. There are good and bad airs for the mind, as well as for the body. Profperity often irritates our chronical diftempers, and leaves no hopes of finding any fpecfic but in adverfity. In fuch cafes, banifhment is like change of air, and the evils we fuffer are like rough medicines applied to inveterate difeafes. What † ANACHARSIS faid of the vine, may aptly enough be faid of profperity. She bears the three grapes of drunkennefs, of pleafure, and of forrow, and happy it is if the laft can cure the mifchief which the former work. When afflictions fail to have their due effect, the cafe is defperate. They are the laft remedies which indulgent Providence ufes: and if they fail, we muft languifh and die in mifery and contempt. Vain men! how feldom do we know what to wifh or to pray for? When we pray againft misfortunes, and when we fear them moft, we want them moft. It was for this reafon that PYTHAGORAS forbid his

* DIO. LAER.   † SEN.

disciples to ask any thing in particular of GOD. The shortest and the best prayer which we can address to him, who knows our wants, and our ignorance in asking, is this: "Thy will be done."

TULLY says, in some part of his works, that as happiness is the object of all philosophy, so the disputes among philosophers arise from their different notions of the sovereign good. Reconcile them in that point, you reconcile them in the rest. The school of Zeno placed this sovereign good in naked virtue, and wound the principle up to an extreme beyond the pitch of nature and truth. A spirit of opposition to another doctrine, which grew into great vogue while ZENO flourished, might occasion this excess. EPICURUS placed the sovereign good in pleasure. His terms were wilfully, or accidentally mistaken. His scholars might help to prevent his doctrine, but rivalship inflamed the dispute; for in truth there is not so much difference between stoicism reduced to reasonable intelligible terms, and genuine orthodox epicurism, as is imagined. The felicis animi immota tranquillitas, and the voluptas of the latter are near enough a-kin; and I much doubt whether the firmest hero

of

of the Portique would have borne a fit of the ſtone, on the principle of Zeno, with greater magnanimity and patience than Epicurus did, on thoſe of his own philoſophy.* However, Aristotle took a middle way, or explained himſelf better, and placed happineſs in the joint advantages of the mind, the body, and of fortune. They are reaſonably joined; but certain it is, that they muſt not be placed on an equal foot. We can much better bear the privation of the laſt, than of the others; and poverty itſelf, which mankind is ſo afraid of, " per mare pauperiem fu-" giens, per ſaxa, per ignes," is ſurely preferable to madneſs, or the ſtone, though †Chrysippus thought it better to live mad, than not to live! if baniſhment therefore, by taking from us the advantages of fortune cannot take from us the more valuable advantages of the mind and body, when we have them; and if the ſame accident is able to reſtore them to us, when we have

* Compare the repreſentations made ſo frequently of the doctrine of volupty taught by Epicurus, with the account which he himſelf gives in his letter to Menoeceus, of the ſenſe wherein he underſtood this word. Vid. Diog Laer.

† In his third book of Nature, cited by Plutarch, in the treatiſe on the contradictions of the Stoics.

loſt

loſt them, baniſhment is a very ſlight misfortune to thoſe who are already under the dominion of reaſon, and a very great bleſſing to thoſe who are ſtill plunged in vices which ruin the health, both of body and mind. It is to be wiſhed for, in favour of ſuch as theſe, and to be feared by none. If we are in this caſe, let us ſecond the deſigns of Providence in our favour, and make ſome amends for neglecting former opportunities by not letting ſlip the laſt. "Si nolis ſanus, curres hydropicus." We may ſhorten the evils which we might have prevented, and as we get the better of our diſorderly paſſions, and vicious habits, we ſhall feel our anxiety diminiſh in proportion. All the approaches to virtue are comfortable. With how much joy will the man, who improves his misfortunes in this manner, diſcover that thoſe evils, which he attributed to his exile, ſprung from his vanity and folly, and vaniſh with them! He will ſee that, in his former temper of mind, he reſembled the effeminate prince who could drink no* water but that of the river Choaſpes; or the ſimple queen, in one of the tragedies of EURIPIDES, who complained bitterly, that ſhe had not

PLUT. On baniſhment.

lighted

lighted the nuptial torch, and that the river Ifmenus had not furnifhed the water at her fon's wedding. Seeing his former ftate in this ridiculous light, he will labour on with pleafure towards another as contrary as poffible to it; and when he arrives there, he will be convinced by the ftrongeft of all proofs, his own experience, that he was unfortunate, becaufe he was vicious, not becaufe he was banifhed.

If I was not afraid of being thought to refine too much, I would venture to put fome advantages of fortune, which are due to exile, into the fcale againft thofe which we lofe by exile. One there is which has been neglected even by great and wife men. DEMETRIUS PHALEREUS, after his expulfion from Athens, became firft minifter to the king of ÆGYPT; and THEMISTOCLES found fuch a reception at the court of Perfia, that he ufed to fay his fortune had been loft if he had not been ruined. But DEMETRIUS expofed himfelf, by his favour under the firft PTOLMY, to a new difgrace under the fecond: and THEMISTOCLES, who had been the captain of a free people, became the vaffal of the prince he had conquered. How much better is it to take hold of the proper advantage of exile, and to live for ourselves, when we are under no obligation of living for others? SIMILIS, a captain of great reputation under TRAJAN and ADRIAN, having obtained leave to retire, paffed feven years in his retreat, and then dying, ordered this infcription to be put on his tomb: that he had been many years on earth, but that he had lived only feven.* If you are wife, your leifure will be worthily employed, and your retreat will add new luftre to your character. Imitate THUCYDIDES in Thracia, or XENOPHON in his little farm at Scillus. In fuch a retreat you may fit down, like one of the inhabitants of Elis, who judged of the Olympic games, without taking any part in them. Far from the hurry of the world, and almoft an unconcerned fpectator of what paffes in it, having paid in a public life what you owed to the prefent age, pay in a private life what you owe to pofterity. Write, as you live, without paffion; and, build your reputation, as you build your happinefs, on the foundations of truth. If you want the talents, the inclination, or the neceffary materials for fuch a work, fall not however into floth. Endeavour to

* XIPHIL.

copy after the example of Scipio, at Linternum. Be able to say to yourself,

"Innocuas amo delicias doctamque
" quietem."

Rural amusements, and philosophical meditations, will make your hours glide smoothly on; and if the indulgence of Heaven has given you a friend like Lælius, nothing is wanting to make you completely happy.

These are some of those reflections which may serve to fortify the mind under banishment, and under other misfortunes of life, which it is every man's interest to prepare for, because they are common to a'l men*: I say they are common to all men; because they who even escape them are equally exposed to them. The darts of adverse fortune are always levelled at our heads. Some reach us, some graze against us, and fly to wound our neighbours. Let us therefore impose an equal temper on our minds, and pay without murmuring, the tribute which we owe to humanity. The winter brings cold, and

* Sen. Ep. 107.

we muft freeze. The fummer returns with heat, and we muft melt. The inclemency of the air diforders our health, and we muft be fick. Here we are expofed to wild beafts, and there to men more favage than the beafts: and if we efcape the inconveniencies and dangers of the air and the earth, there are perils by water, and perils by fire. This eftablifhed courfe of things it is not in our power to change; but it is in our power to affume fuch a greatnefs of mind as becomes wife and virtuous men; as may enable us to encounter the accidents of life with fortitude, and to conform ourfelves to the order of nature, who governs her great kingdom, the world, by continual mutations. Let us fubmit to this order, let us be perfuaded, that whatever does happen ought to happen, and never be fo foolifh as to expoftulate with nature. The beft refolution we can take is to fuffer what we cannot alter, and to purfue, without repining, the road which Providence who directs every thing, has marked out to us: for it is not enough to follow; and he is but a bad foldier who fighs, and marches on with reluctancy. We muft receive the orders with fpirit and chearfulnefs, and not endeavour to flink

out

out of the poft which is affigned to us in this beautiful difpofition of things, whereof even our fufferings make a neceffary part. Let us addrefs ourfelves to GOD, who governs all, as CLEANTHES did in thofe admirable verfes, which are going to lofe part of their grace and energy in my tranflation of them.

> Parent of nature! Mafter of the World!
> Where'er thy Providence directs, behold
> My fteps with chearful refignation turn.
> Fate leads the willing, drags the backward on.
> Why fhould I grieve, when grieving I muft bear?
> Or take with guilt, what guiltlefs I might fhare.

Thus let us fpeak, and thus let us act: Refignation to the will of GOD is true magnanimity. But the fure mark of a pufillanimous and bafe fpirit, is to ftruggle againft, to cenfure the order of Providence, and, inftead of mending our own conduct, to fet up for correcting that of our maker.

THE END.

Printed in the United States
211907BV00001B/77/A